# The Conservative Movement in Judaism

SUNY series in American Jewish Society in the 1990s
Barry A. Kosmin and Sidney Goldstein, Editors

Sidney Goldstein and Alice Goldstein, *Jews on the Move: Implications for Jewish Identity* (1996).

Moshe Hartman and Harriet Hartman, *Gender Equality and American Jews* (1996).

Bernard Lazerwitz, J. Alan Winter, Arnold Dashefsky, and Ephraim Tabory, *Jewish Choices: American Jewish Denominationalism* (1997).

Daniel J. Elazar and Rela Mintz Geffen, *The Conservative Movement in Judaism: Dilemmas and Opportunities* (2000).

Ariela Keysar, Barry A. Kosmin, and Jeffrey Scheckner, *The Next Generation: Jewish Children and Adolescents* (2000).

Sylvia Barack Fishman, *Jewish Life and American Culture* (2000).

*Jewish Baby Boomers: A Communal Perspective.* Chaim I. Waxman (ed.), (2001).

# The Conservative Movement in Judaism

## Dilemmas and Opportunities

Daniel J. Elazar
and
Rela Mintz Geffen

State University of New York Press

Published by
State University of New York Press, Albany

© 2000 State University of New York

Preparation of this book for publication was made possible through the
Milken Library of Jewish Public Affairs, funded by the Milken Family
Foundation.

For information, address State University of New York Press,
State University Plaza, Albany, N.Y., 12246

Production by Michael Haggett
Marketing by Patrick Durocher

**Library of Congress Cataloging-in-Publication Data**

Elazar, Daniel Judah.
    The Conservative movement in Judaism: dilemmas and
    opportunities/Daniel J. Elazar and Rela Mintz Geffen.
        p. cm.—(SUNY series in American Jewish society in the 1990s)
    Includes bibliographical references and index.
    ISBN 0–7914–4689–1 (acid free)—ISBN 0–7914–4690–5 (pbk. : acid free)
    1. Conservative Judaism—History. 2. Judaism—United States—History.
    3. Judaism—20th century. I. Geffen, Rela M. II. Title. III. Series.

BM197.5 .E43 2000
296.8'342—dc21                                                    99-054414

10  9   8  7  6  5  4  3  2  1

This book is dedicated to the memory of
## Daniel J. Elazar
Scholar, Teacher, Colleague and Friend

ונתתי את לבי לדרוש ולתור בחכמה
על כל אשר נעשה תחת השמים
קהלת א :יג

I set my mind to study and to probe with wisdom
all that happens under the sun.

Ecclesiastes 1: 13

# Contents

# Tables and Figures

# Acknowledgments

The Jerusalem Center for Public Affairs, under whose auspices the study that underlies this book was conducted, is a major independent worldwide Jewish policy studies center. Since 1970, its Center for Jewish Community Studies has been conducting in-depth research on Jewish life throughout the world, including studies of religious movements and institutions and the only comprehensive worldwide study of the structure and functioning of Jewish communities ever completed. This data pool has been used for policy planning in the Conservative Movement and in other Jewish bodies and was available for this study.

The authors bring to this book complementary strengths. Professor Daniel J. Elazar, Founder and President of the Jerusalem Center for Public Affairs, was a political scientist who specialized in the political analysis of Jewish organizational life. As one who grew up within the Conservative Movement in the Midwest and West, he had close connections with many of the Movement's leaders, Rabbi David Aronson, Rabbi Solomon Goldman, and many others, and brought the perspective of the "field" to this book. Having lived in Israel for many years, he had the opportunity to follow and closely examine the development of the Masorti Movement there. Professor Rela Mintz Geffen, a Professor of Sociology at Gratz College, has specialized in studying the American Jewish Community, focusing on the Jewish family, congregational life, and gender roles. She was raised in the shadow of the Jewish Theological Seminary as one of the "family" educated there, and she has maintained her close involvement with the Conservative Movement and its institutions. She brings the perspective of a devoted insider.

The authors would like to thank Zvi Marom and the staff of the Jerusalem Center for Public Affairs for their support, especially Mark Ami-El who helped in many ways to ready the manuscript for publication. Special appreciation is due to the Milken Family Foundation for funds that helped in the preparation of the book for publication. Our editors at SUNY Press, especially the production editor, Michael Haggett, gave generously of their time and were patient with delays caused by special circumstances. The acute comments of anonymous readers helped to hone the final manuscript. While their help was invaluable, the responsibility for any errors is ours.

In the introduction to this volume we note that "In an age when extremism appears to command center stage, the Conservative Movement is as needed as ever to combine seriousness of purpose with intelligent moderation." In a conversation on Saturday night, November 27, 1999 in Jerusalem, we discussed the critical importance of the pursuit of the path of moderation and the difficulties inherent in creating leaders who would themselves be passionate about moderation and be able to inspire others to feel the same. Professor Elazar offered the observation that, to be effective, such leaders must be able to maintain simultaneously a systematic and prismatic worldview.

Without the support of our families this book would not have come to fruition. So, to Harriet, Naomi, Avi, Eitan, Gilad and Ariel, Yonatan and Rutie, and Gideon; and to Uri Zvi, Rebekah Anne and Shoshana Aviva, and Amiel Tuvia, *todah rabah mikerev leyv*.

Daniel J. Elazar and Rela Mintz Geffen
Jerusalem and Philadelphia
22 Kislev 5760
1 December 1999

# Introduction: Conservative Judaism: Past and Future

## THE CONSERVATIVE ACHIEVEMENT

The Conservative Movement is one of the greatest achievements of American Jewry. Its nineteenth-century founders and their heirs built the largest religious movement in the American Jewish community, one that for at least two generations best expressed the synthesis of the Jewish and American ways of life that had developed in the United States in the twentieth century. They did so by taking a set of principles developed by Jewish scholars and intellectuals in Germany and Central Europe in the middle of the nineteenth century, which came to be known as "the historical school" of Judaism, and adapting them to the needs of those American congregations that a generation later wanted to remain traditional without being Orthodox and to adapt to the world around them without becoming Reform.

Some fifty years ago, Marshall Sklare, in his pioneering social study of Conservative Judaism, noted that Conservative Judaism, more than any other American Jewish movement, captured the strengths and weaknesses and ambivalences and hopes of American Jewry.[1] Much has changed since those promising days just after World War II, when Sklare published his first studies. American Jewry entered what has been to date its golden age with a surge of Jewish identification and institutional expansion in the community and well-nigh complete

1

acceptance among the non-Jewish community after several generations of rather intense anti-Semitism. American Jewish scholarship became world class, and Jewish education in the United States was pioneering in its innovativeness. The Conservative Movement was a leader in much of this period of flowering, as Sklare predicted and for the reasons he gave.

Since then, American Jewry has confronted the obverse of easy acceptance into the general community, namely, massive Jewish assimilation into American society and its consequences, including intermarriage, American-style relativism, lower levels of Jewish concern on the part of many who were born Jews, and a shift on their part to the exclusive pursuit of the American dream. The flowering of the postwar generation reached its peak and began to fade as a new generation found items of more importance on its agenda. The "religious revival" (always overestimated as social scientists indicated at the time) gave way to a period of religious neglect, hurting Conservative Judaism even more than other movements, while the ethnicity that replaced religiosity led in other directions.[2]

Nevertheless, the basics have remained constant, with Conservative Judaism still reflecting the ambivalences of American Jewry.[3] Hence the state of the Conservative Movement is a subject that compels the interest of all Jews concerned with the future of Jewish life in the United States and in the twenty-first century generally.

The year 1986 marked the centenary of the founding of the first of the great institutions of the Conservative Movement, the Jewish Theological Seminary of America. The ten students who formed the Seminary's first class numbered over 550 registered in any one semester in all of its programs by 1986. List College, which offers joint undergraduate programs with Columbia University and Barnard College, the Seminary's neighbors on the Morningside Heights section of New York City, and a graduate school that offers M.A., D.H.L., and Ph.D. degrees in a wide range of Jewish academic disciplines, has been added to the Rabbinical School. In addition, a dual degree graduate program in Jewish Communal Service has graduated sixty Columbia M.S.W./J.T.S. M.A. students since its inception. The Seminary's Cantors Institute/ School of Jewish Music grants an M.A. degree in sacred music and prepares cantors for Conservative congregations and scholars in Jewish music.

The Seminary's Rabbinical School alone, over the past 100-plus years, has ordained over 1,200 rabbis. They form the bulk of the Rabbinical Assembly, an international association of Conservative rabbis.

These men, and since 1983, women as well, serve as congregational rabbis, as directors of Hillel Foundations on university campuses, as military and hospital chaplains, as educators of Jewish youth, and as academicians teaching Judaica in universities around the world.

The Seminary's graduate school has the largest population of doctoral students in Judaica in the country. In fact, it may safely be said that until the midpoint of the twentieth century, the Seminary was by far the dominant institution in the United States for the training of Jewish studies scholars. The Seminary's library, housed in its new building, is the foremost Jewish repository of Hebraica and Judaica outside of Israel, with over 260,000 volumes, 10,000 manuscripts and codices, 40,000 Genizah fragments, and thousands of other rare documents and prints.[4]

The congregational arm of Conservative Judaism, the United Synagogue of Conservative Judaism, founded in 1913, now includes well over 800 affiliated congregations. Its network of departments, commissions, and committees provides a wide range of services to congregations on a local, regional, and national basis. The United Synagogue Department of Education, for example, services Jewish congregational schools and the Solomon Schechter Day School movement with its 70-plus affiliated schools, a number that grows every year. The United Synagogue Youth program provides informal social, cultural, and educational programming to over 25,000 American Jewish adolescents.

The Seminary itself has had a major impact on informal and formal Jewish primary and secondary education through its network of Hebrew-speaking Ramah summer camps—seven such in the United States and Canada, with their offshoots in South America, Russia and Israel. In the opinion of many, Ramah is one of American Jewry's major contributions to Jewish education. Over 3,500 children, ages nine through sixteen, attend these camps in any one summer, not to mention the only slightly smaller number of young adults who serve as counselors, teachers, and in other staff capacities and enjoy an educational experience appropriate to their age and interests.

The University of Judaism in Los Angeles, founded a half-century ago, provides advanced and continuing Jewish education under movement auspices in the West. It includes undergraduate and graduate programs, adult education, and, as of 1997, its own full program of rabbinical training. Camp Ramah in California is under its auspices. In 1995, the University of Judaism received an anonymous grant of $22 million to develop its own full-blown Conservative Rabbinical School. This was the proximate cause of the institution declaring its independence from the Jewish Theological Seminary.

The institutional structure of Conservative Judaism also includes the Women's League for Conservative Judaism, an association of women's groups from Conservative congregations, which provides volunteer leadership on a local, regional, and continental basis. A parallel group is the Federation of Jewish Men's Clubs, which provides the same type of volunteer outlet for synagogue-based men's groups. The World Council of Synagogues provides affiliation with Conservative Judaism for congregations as far flung as Argentina, England, Sweden, Hungary, Japan, and of course Israel, where over forty congregations have affiliated themselves with Conservative Judaism through the *Masorti* (Hebrew for traditional) Movement, the name that is becoming standard for Conservative Judaism in Israel and in other parts of the world since the late 1980s.

It is no exaggeration to say that the Conservative Movement has made Judaism meaningful for three generations of Jews at a time when the traditional society from which they or their forebears came could no longer speak to them. By harmonizing the apparently contradictory pulls of tradition and change, the Conservative Movement helped build Jewish religious-cum-social institutions adapted to the American scene. For great numbers of struggling Jewish immigrants and more especially their children, Conservative congregations were the vehicles for maintaining the connection with traditional Judaism.

Equally important, the Jewish Theological Seminary developed an approach to Jewish study that was both historically oriented and pious, modern and critical, yet committed to tradition. Through that approach, the Seminary has educated generations of students as observant Jews who were not afraid to ask questions of Judaism, retaining the tradition through dialogue with it, while at the same time enriching it through their scholarly contributions based on the critical-historical approach.

## CONFRONTING DIFFICULT ISSUES

Conservative Jews can take justifiable pride in all that has been accomplished. Yet with all of its achievements and strength, changing circumstances have brought the Conservative Movement face-to-face with certain vital issues that need careful examination if they are to be confronted and dealt with appropriately.

The problems facing the Conservative Movement at the dawn of the twenty-first century demand systematic and sophisticated attention and analysis by the Movement's key policy makers. This book is designed to stimulate a process of thoughtful, action-oriented planning by rabbinic and lay leaders of the Movement's various institutions. In it, we analyze several of the important problems facing the Movement's key policy makers today. These include:

1. The lack of clarity of ideology, mission, and purpose.
2. The need to cope with potential polarization on doctrinal matters between traditionalists and advocates of further change to accommodate contemporary American standards.
3. Inadequate cooperation among the major institutions of Conservative Judaism.
4. Evidence of decline in affiliation with Conservative congregations, especially relative to the Reform Movement.
5. A shift of loyalty of talented people who are products of the Conservative Movement to other forms of Jewish involvement.
6. The failure to develop a significant body of Conservative Jews seriously committed to *mitzvot* (Torah commandments) or the Jewish way of life espoused by the Movement's standard bearers.
7. The development of the Movement in Israel and in the rest of the diaspora.
8. Weak ties with community federations and other Jewish communal bodies.

These problems are highly interrelated, and solutions to one may well entail solutions to others.

A strong, confident Conservative Movement, following in the spirit of its founders, is vitally necessary to contemporary Jewish life as a middle way. The Reform Movement, although more traditional now than it was at any time in the past century, still rejects the binding status of *halakhah* (Jewish law) in any form and hence is very problematic from the perspective of Jewish tradition. On the other side, the Jewish world confronts a resurgent Orthodoxy that is moving to the right religiously as it gains in strength, thereby requiring its adherents to separate themselves ever further from the contemporary world. A movement that can remain faithful to the *halakhic* (Jewish legal) tradition, while at the same time encouraging its adherents to live in this world, thus becomes more essential than ever.

The Conservative Movement has substantial strength in the form of well-articulated institutions, many strong congregations, intelligent and dedicated leaders, and a large, if declining, group of supporters. On the other hand, the problems confronting the Movement are very real. In some respects, this is because, however desirable the middle way may be, it is the hardest position to occupy emotionally and therefore the hardest for which to develop great enthusiasm.[5] It is the fate of contemporary civilization to have difficulty viewing moderation, with its compromises, as intellectually justified in the face of the apparent logic of extremism. At the same time, moderates are challenged to develop a serious logic of their own and not just to become moderate as the path of least resistance, a phenomenon that has affected the Conservative Movement to no small degree.

A first area of concern in this book is how what was until recently the largest, most dynamic movement within the American Jewish religious community can regain its élan, hold on to its adherents, and continue to grow and attract new ones. To that end, it places special emphasis on the ideological and institutional challenges facing Conservative Judaism, specifically relationships among the major institutions and constituencies of the Movement.

Another area of special concern centers on Israel, where the Movement has yet to capitalize on Israel's potential for enhancing Conservative Judaism in the United States and the rest of the Jewish world. This book explores possibilities for programmatic and educational innovation in this area in some depth.

A third area of concern is the question of enhancing Conservative Jewry's participation in and impact on other spheres of Jewish life. Many leading members of Conservative congregations play prominent roles in all facets of Jewish communal life. Unfortunately, for both the Movement and the larger Jewish community, these leaders generally fail to bring their Conservative Jewish identities to bear upon their activities in the larger Jewish community. Orthodox and Reform Jews maintain much more visible profiles in Federation life with positive institutional and philosophical implications for both movements.

The following chapters identify eight important dimensions of the Conservative Movement and examine each:

*First*, while the book makes no claim to being a historical study of the Movement, it reviews the Movement's *origins* and *history* from its reluctant separation from Orthodoxy to the present struggle over whether to remain a single movement or to become a community of movements from the perspective of the salient elements for our discussion.

*Second*, the book looks at the Movement's *institutions*: the history and changing position of the Jewish Theological Seminary within the Movement; the changing roles of the Rabbinical Assembly, the United Synagogue of Conservative Judaism, the Federation of Mens Clubs, and the Womens League for Conservative Judaism; the congregational heart of the Movement; and the emergence of new institutions in the last several decades, including the Ramah camps, the Solomon Schechter schools, the Jewish Museum, and the *havurot* (fellowships).

*Third*, the book examines the Movement's problems in *articulating an ideology*; the various shifts and stages that have occurred in confronting the ideological problem and the effort to find and establish ideological benchmarks and boundaries.

*Fourth*, and perhaps at the heart of the book, is the discussion of *the style of Conservative Judaism*, beginning with its Sephardic and Litvak founders, its division into an elite and a mass, its tendency to rabbinic predominance, its synagogism, and the emergence of a distinctive Conservative style and pattern of observance.

A *fifth* dimension is *demographics*. We examine the decline in Conservative affiliation or identification in the fourth generation and beyond, the influence of resurgent Orthodoxy and a more traditional Reform Movement, and the changing Jewish family.

A *sixth* dimension examines *leadership* in the Movement, in the individual congregations, and in the Jewish world.

The *seventh* dimension is the *world Conservative/Masorti Movement*, and the *Movement in Israel*.

The *eighth* and final dimension concerns itself with the problem of the *Conservative Movement's links with other Jewish bodies*, basically the missed direction of those links and how that can be changed.


## METHODOLOGY OF THIS STUDY

This study is the product of a wide-ranging exploration of the Conservative Movement and its institutions and achievements in North America, Israel, and elsewhere. The authors have observed dozens of congregations, have sent a mail survey to all of the congregational rabbis patterned on the framework of an earlier study, have interviewed a wide spectrum of Conservative leaders and activists around the world, and have conducted a public opinion survey of attitudes toward Jewish institutions and the Masorti Movement in Israel. We have utilized existing studies, both quantitative and qualitative, especially in connection with religious observance and affiliation. We have drawn upon our own previous studies and a comprehensive study of the American synagogue in transition, which has produced publications on the development of the American synagogue, the changing role of women in religious ritual, synagogue *havurot* and synagogue-Federation relations, and our extensive experience with the Conservative Movement and its congregations and institutions. Finally, we have consulted with a number of individuals who are knowledgeable about the Movement.

In examining each dimension, we have followed the following model:

1. A statement of the problem, its dimensions and background.
2. A review of existing data and literature bearing on the problem.
3. The generation of new data as necessary to understand the problem.
4. An outline of plausible policy alternatives to address that problem.
5. A discussion of the merits and potential dangers associated with each policy option.
6. Ideas for additional information gathering, which would further assist the policy-making process.

The analysis that follows presents the Conservative Movement as we have come to see it—"warts and all," to use Abraham Lincoln's felicitous Oliver Cromwell quotation. Our study tries to be straightforward, at times even blunt in pointing out the problems facing the Movement. Like Lincoln, we believe that only by facing the full reality is it possible to deal with it. It is not our intention to embarrass or to wound people whose devotion and loyalty to Jewish life and to the Conservative Movement goes unquestioned.

## LOOKING TOWARD THE FUTURE

The Movement is presently at a turning point. All of those who were part of its founding or who were educated by the founders have passed away or retired. The new generation taking the lead in the Movement today is a product of the postwar flowering and was influenced by the institutions created in that flowering. Thus a new spirit is abroad within it, and new possibilities offer themselves, giving the Movement important new opportunities. The defection of the most traditional wing to the Union for Traditional Judaism (UTJ), developments affecting the Masorti Movement in Israel, such as the Neeman Commission, and the decision of the University of Judaism to found its own rabbinical school has challenged Seminary and United Synagogue leadership to rethink the structure of the Movement.

In the following pages, we will not only present our understanding of the Movement past and present, but we will try to explain it in the hope that this will make our straightforwardness more palatable as well as more useful. In the last analysis, however, we believe that the Movement, especially its leadership, must face up to its present condition if it is to continue to play the vital role that we believe it must in contemporary Jewish life. In an age when extremism appears to command center stage, the Conservative Movement is as needed as ever to combine seriousness of purpose with intelligent moderation. Therein lies the Movement's future, and it is a promising one. Even as its overall membership is declining, there seems to be emerging a generation of Conservative Jews who take Conservative Judaism seriously. The future of the Movement lies with them, with their ability to take this, their seriousness of purpose, and build a stronger and better articulated Conservative Judaism upon it. There is no reason to believe that whatever the present difficulties, this cannot be done. It is a noble task which, if successful, will well serve the entire Jewish people.

# Part I

# The State of the Movement

# Chapter 1

# *A History of Ambivalence*

Political philosophers and constitutional architects from earliest times have understood that institutions are products of their foundings, and that foundings continue to play a decisive role in the form and behavior of those institutions for generations thereafter. The origins and history of the Conservative Movement reflect its American and Jewish roots and the ambiguities with which it is constantly wrestling, which give it both its strength and its weaknesses.[1]

Conservative Judaism began as (1) a *faction*[2] within an undifferentiated traditional Judaism in the nineteenth century and moved to (2) a brief period when it was simultaneously a faction within an undifferentiated modernizing Judaism (within the Union of American Hebrew Congregations until the Pittsburgh Platform and the notorious *treifa* banquet). (3) It then became a movement designed to articulate a modern version of traditional Judaism without actually breaking with that segment of traditional Judaism to its right, which was on its way to becoming Orthodoxy in the United States. (4) At the beginning of the twentieth century, it achieved articulation as a separate movement within the four ells of *halakhic* Judaism but with a historical approach to understanding *halakhah* and an evolutionary approach to *halakhic* decision making. (5) After World War II, it became a separate *party* (see note 2) within the Jewish religious community in which the organizational interests as a movement/party began to take precedence over earlier ideological positions.

Now Conservative Judaism is faced with the prospect of becoming a *camp* (see note 2) in which there are several parties or institutional frameworks, all coming out of a serious Conservative Jewish perspective and network.

## A RELUCTANT SEPARATION[3]

The coming of the modern epoch in the middle of the seventeenth century and especially its climax in the American and French Revolutions shattered the traditional Jewish communal structure of the autonomous *kehillah* (community) functioning as a state within a state to serve a nation in exile wherever Jews found themselves, with its own constitution and laws, administration and politics, and taxation and foreign relations. Modernity shattered that accepted arrangement, because it shattered the world that tolerated such autonomous communities in its midst. The Jews were first denied autonomy and then to a greater or lesser degree were offered citizenship in the polities in which they found themselves. That citizenship was contingent upon Jewish abjuration of communal autonomy and of its civil dimension and acceptance of unqualified membership in the polities in which they found themselves.

For some Jews, these new possibilities were so enticing that they forsook Judaism altogether, accepting nominal baptism as Christians in a world that they saw was becoming increasingly secular, de facto if not de jure in any case, in which they could be admitted as equal partners without any encumbrances from the past. For those Jews who wished to preserve their Jewish identity in the West, enhanced religious identity of one kind or another was the answer. Three kinds emerged: Reform Judaism elected the way of the Protestant West and tried to turn Judaism into a modern Protestant sect, entirely dropping its political and civil dimensions, rejecting the binding character of *halakhah*, and abjuring the restoration of the people of Israel to the Land of Israel at the end of days or the rebuilding of the Temple and reinstitution of sacrifices. The goal of the new Reform Movement was to transform its members into citizens of the Mosaic faith.

Orthodoxy was another response to modernity. It is a mistake to see Orthodoxy merely as a continuation of the traditional Jewish life of premodern times, since it was a deliberately developed ideology and way of life designed to combat the perils of modernism as much as Reform was. It was based on two new movements of modernity, Hasidism, which developed in Galicia in the latter part of the eighteenth century, parallel to Methodism and other revivalist religious efforts in Europe, and the Lithuanian yeshiva movement, generated at approximately the same time, which emphasized a new learning elite as distinct from the Hassidic emphasis on popular religion.

After the end of the Napoleonic Wars, at the same time that Reform took institutional form, so did Orthodoxy in two manifestations: one, ultra-Orthodox, which took a firm position against any innovation and indeed sought to find ways to stiffen *halakhah* against change or even moderation, and two, modern Orthodoxy, which took a similarly strict stance on what the West considered religious matters but, like Reform, jettisoned the political dimension of Judaism.

Later in that generation a third wave began to emerge, what came to be called the "historical school," which tried to define a middle road. Judaism in full was to be preserved. *Halakhah* was to continue to be binding and all of the messianic hopes kept in place except perhaps the restoration of animal sacrifices, but these were deferred until an unknown future time.

The historical school in Judaism that developed in Europe early in the nineteenth century was an intellectual movement that fostered an evolutionary understanding of the development of Jewish laws and tradition.[4] In the United States, on the other hand, it became a dynamic religious movement, embracing hundreds of thousands of Jews. It is not unfair to claim Isaac Leeser, the first American Jewish religious leader of countrywide influence and a contemporary of the European founders of the historical school, as a precursor of Conservative Judaism. While he was the undisputed leader of traditional Judaism in the mid- nineteenth century United States, his many efforts at institution building had little success. Moreover, he remained within the undifferentiated traditional framework, rejecting the first Union of American Hebrew Congregations, which appeared on the scene during the peak years of his career.

By 1880, there were 200 synagogues in the United States, of which only twelve did not identify with the Reform Movement. Many of these traditional congregations, including Leeser's Mikveh Israel in Philadelphia, were the old Sephardic ones dating from the colonial period, by this time led by rabbis born and trained in Western or Central Europe. Many of these leaders seriously considered the offer of the Reform Movement, to join in a common Union of American Hebrew

Congregations, however, in 1885, the Reform Movement adopted the Pittsburgh Platform in which its rabbis made a decisive break with *halakhah* and traditional Judaism. One year later Rabbis Sabato Morais, H. Pereira Mendes, and Alexander Kohut, joined by a number of prominent non-rabbinical leaders, founded the Jewish Theological Seminary. Its articles of incorporation specified that the Seminary would be dedicated to "the preservation in America of the knowledge of historical Judaism as ordained in the law of Moses, expounded by the prophets and sages of Israel in biblical and talmudic writings."

As Moshe Davis has shown, the first congregations that became the nucleus of the Conservative Movement and, for that matter, the Jewish Theological Seminary itself, were not consciously interested in developing a movement of their own separate from traditional Judaism.[5] Indeed, they were so committed to maintaining Jewish unity that they even went along with the experiment of Reform Judaism to make the Union of American Hebrew Congregations an umbrella organization for American Jewish congregations of all persuasions. Charles Liebman has argued that Davis is wrong about even identifying those early congregations as Conservative, given that they viewed themselves as, at most, a faction within a larger body of traditional Jewish congregations (Orthodoxy as a concept and a movement was essentially absent from the United States, since it was still in the process of being defined in Central Europe).[6] Nevertheless, they can be considered as representing the beginnings of Conservative Judaism because of their deliberate commitment to the historical approach. The first founding of the Jewish Theological Seminary was a reflection of their ambivalence. It was designed to be a seminary to train traditional rabbis who were at home on the American scene and who did not move from that position until the World War I period.[7]

The experiment with a single umbrella synagogue movement failed. The last straw was the famous "*treifa* banquet" in Cincinnati in 1883, where the last attempt to unify all American Jewish congregations failed because the *center* served shell fish to the group, to the horror of the traditional rabbis present.[8] With the breakdown of the Union of American Hebrew Congregations (UAHC) effort, on the one hand, and the arrival of truly committed Orthodox Jews as the result of the mass migration of Jews from Eastern Europe, both occurring at the same time as the founding of the Jewish Theological Seminary (JTS), these pioneering congregations, their rabbis, and nonrabbinical leaders were forced to identify themselves more clearly vis-à-vis both, and the Conservative faction emerged as a movement. They took this step reluctantly. As recently as the 1950s, Louis Finkelstein, the then Chancellor of the JTS, was quoted as saying privately that, "The Conservative Movement is a gimmick to bring Jews back to authentic Judaism."[9]

That statement reflected an accurate view of what the Movement set out to be. It saw itself as totally and thoroughly *halakhic* in the traditional sense. It differed from the then-emergent Orthodoxy, in that it understood *halakhah* as the product of historic evolution and was willing to continue that evolution under conditions of modernity, which the Orthodox feared to do on the grounds that liberal changes by recognized *halakhic* authorities would only hasten the disintegration of the Jewish people.[10] This, indeed, became one of the keystones of the Movement, which will be discussed further.

While the founders of the Movement were principally from Western and Central Europe, and many of them were Sephardim at that, the Movement's success rested upon the fact that the mass immigration of Jews from Eastern Europe began only a few years before the founding of the Seminary. It was these Eastern European Jews who became the backbone of, and in short order captured the leadership of, the new Movement.

At first, the relative handful of traditional Jewish congregations in the United States embraced traditional Jews of all stripes. But hardly more than fifteen years after the founding of the Seminary, those Jews from Eastern Europe who remained Orthodox led a schism whereby the Association of Orthodox Synagogues, founded in 1898, repudiated the authority of the graduates of the Jewish Theological Seminary. They took over and expanded a small *yeshiva* (institution of religious study), now the Rabbi Isaac Elhanan Theological Seminary, the nucleus of Yeshiva University.[11] The JTS was reorganized in 1902 at the initiative of the principal leaders of American Jewry of the time, none of them rabbis, and all, in fact, Reform Jews. They undertook that task because they saw the need for an American yet traditional rabbinical training school to assist in the Americanization of the Eastern European immigrants who would not be Reform and, indeed, who were not wanted by the fancier "uptown" Jews. Scholar-rabbi Solomon (Schneur Zalman) Schechter, the Romanian-born Cambridge lecturer who had uncovered the famous Cairo Geniza, was brought to the States in 1902 as the new head of the reorganized institution.[12] The actual leadership of the Seminary passed to Schechter and to Cyrus Adler, who held a doctorate in Semitics and was active in Congregation Mikveh Israel. Adler was a young member of the "Philadelphia Group," then leaders of American Jewry.[13]

With that act, the Conservative Movement can be said to have been born. Even so, it was not until 1913 that internal conflict over whether to fully organize a separate movement was resolved by the founding of the United Synagogue of America (now the United Synagogue of Conservative Judaism), whose purpose was "the maintenance of Jewish tradition in its historical continuity." The ambivalences that accompanied its founding are reflected in the preamble to its constitution, written by Schechter himself. At that, the new United Synagogue (Schechter brought the name and concept of the United Synagogue with him from England) sought to leave the door open for a broad coalition of non-Reform congregations and was very ambiguous with regard to innovations such as mixed seating for men and women and the use of the organ in the synagogue service.

Schechter, who while broadly traditionalist and strongly committed to Jewish unity was willing to organize separate institutions and build a movement, died prematurely in 1915. He was succeeded by Adler, who had opposed him on the issue of separate institutionalization. Adler was acting president or president of the Seminary from 1915 until his death in 1940. Since he was not a rabbi, leadership in rabbinical matters passed to Professor Louis Ginzberg, one of the faculty members whom Schechter had persuaded to join the JTS faculty after he had come to the United States from his native Lithuania and who became perhaps the leading talmudic scholar in the America of his time.[14]

Adler's successor, Rabbi Louis Finkelstein, also of Litvak descent, continued in the Adlerian tradition and resisted efforts on the part of the majority of the Seminary graduates to more sharply differentiate Conservative Judaism from Orthodoxy. Finkelstein continued in office until 1972. The same year that he became president, Saul Lieberman joined the Jewish Theological Seminary faculty. Upon Ginzberg's death, Professor Lieberman succeeded him as the *Mara d'atra* (authoritative leader) of the Movement, with an even less liberal outlook than his predecessor.

It was not until the accession of Professor Gerson Cohen to the chancellorship in 1972 that the institution came under leadership clearly committed to articulating a separate Conservative approach to Judaism. Despite a severe illness that began early in his tenure, Cohen remained chancellor of the Seminary until 1986, when he was succeeded by Professor Ismar Schorsch. Both Cohen and Schorsch were professional historians. Thus with their accession to the chancellorship the leadership of the JTS passed from the hands of scholars of classical Jewish texts to scholars of how the Jews lived in the past; in essence, from students of continuity to students of change. The results were almost immediately seen in the shift in the balance between continuity and change in the Conservative Movement, in essence, a move from the conservative camp, indicated by its original name, to the liberal side of the ledger. It might be said that until 1972 the movement looked over its shoulder to the right at the Orthodox, whereas after 1972, it looked over its shoulder to the left, to the Reform, even as it tried to stake out a position of its own vis-à-vis both.

In the meantime, the Movement proceeded to grow. Its first great burst of growth came in the 1920s, but an even greater burst came after World War II, with the 1950s being the golden age of Conservative Movement expansion. The Conservative Movement became the largest religious movement among American Jews at that time. As late as 1970, the Movement claimed some 350,000 family members. Using estimates derived from the 1990 National Jewish Population Survey, 36 percent of Jews identified themselves as Conservative of whom approximately half were affiliated with a Conservative synagogue, giving Conservative Judaism 47 percent of the Jews formally affiliated with synagogues in the United States. In contrast, 38 percent identified themselves with Reform Judaism, but only 36 percent of all synagogue members were affiliated with Reform congregations. Orthodoxy, on the other hand, while having only 6 percent of the total who claim identification by movement, had nearly twice that percentage (11 percent) in their share of total synagogue members.

## THE MOVEMENT AS A PARTY

By that time, however, the Movement had long since become a party, what those who were delicate called a "branch" of Judaism and what those who were less delicate and more influenced by the American Protestant environment referred to as a "denomination." There developed a network of institutions, membership in which defined who was a Conservative Jew, and that dominated the development and choosing of leadership for the Movement. Inevitably, that institutional network took on a life of its own in which self-maintenance became an important concern, going beyond larger issues of ideology. In other words, in the normal way of the world, those involved in the Movement had a stake in keeping it and its various institutions and organizations alive and flourishing, even if it was necessary to ignore or downplay earlier ideological commitments to retain members and to otherwise strengthen its various instrumentalities. Often the latter were sacrificed to institutional concerns, except where they were in the custody of senior professors at the Jewish Theological Seminary who did not share that institutional commitment yet, who, because of the nature of the Movement and its leadership (which will be discussed later), retained a dominant influence with its rabbinical leaders.

Accompanying this growth were greater efforts among the congregational rabbis to provide a separate definition of what constituted Conservative Judaism. As early as 1948, the Rabbinical Assembly (incorporated under that name in 1901 to embrace JTS alumni and others seeking Conservative pulpits) rejected any dominant Seminary influence on its Committee on Jewish Law and Standards. Twelve years later, the Law Committee made its first major *halakhic* decision, challenging Orthodox doctrine when in 1960 it permitted the use of electricity on the Sabbath and accepted traveling to the synagogue by motor vehicle for the purpose of attending services.

The work of the Law Committee and its history are deserving of a separate study.[15] What is especially important to note here is that it was a product of efforts of rabbis in the field and, as such, the first effort to reshape the Conservative Movement, which did not come from or through the Seminary. Two figures in particular deserve mention in connection with the Law Committee. Rabbi David Aronson of Beth El Synagogue, Minneapolis, a childhood friend and classmate of Chancellor Finkelstein, shared with the chancellor a strong commitment to *halakhah* but also saw the need for serious change across a number of fronts, particularly in the status of women and in meeting the needs of Conservative congregants in the contemporary world through an active and aggressive *halakhic* process. (In this he differed from the third member of what was then a triumvirate of childhood friends who had become leading Conservative rabbis. Solomon Goldman of Anshe Emet in Chicago increasingly adopted a non-*halakhic* position in his desire for significant change.) Rabbi Aronson was the driving force behind the organization of the Law Committee.

Subsequently, Rabbi Isaac Klein of Buffalo became the Committee's strongest figure because of his high level of scholarship, the fact that he was one of the few *musmahim* (fully ordained rabbis) to come out of the JTS, and because of his willingness to write *teshuvot* (rabbinic responsa). Rabbis Aronson and Klein each produced basic guides to Jewish living for Conservative Jews; the former, *A Jewish Way of Life*, which opened the postwar generation, and the latter, *A Guide to Jewish Religious Practice*.

However, it was only after the departure of Professors Ginzberg, Finkelstein, and Lieberman from the JTS that the Law Committee became fully comfortable with its growing role as religious innovator. Those three giants, as teachers of the vast majority of the Conservative rabbinate, served as a restraining force on the inclinations of so many congregational rabbis to adapt to what they viewed as the realities of American Jewish life. The Law Committee has been most successful in this regard in connection with extending the rights of women to fully participate in religious life, culminating in a JTS decision in 1985 to ordain women as rabbis.[16] In other cases, the committee's permission for change was largely ignored. For example, its 1969 decision to permit individual congregations to observe only one day of full holiday of the pilgrimage festivals, as done in Israel, has rarely been implemented.

Indeed, as part of this adaptation, Conservative synagogues confronted a painful dilemma. On the one hand, they saw themselves as the custodians of tradition; on the other hand, to reach out to the people, their leaders felt that they had to appeal to them on "modern" and "American" terms. Thus in some respects the synagogue, in its effort to retard assimilation, became an agent of assimilation. This is a problem inherent in a centrist, moderate position, whose adherents see themselves as defending tradition by adapting it. Holding the line on essentials while changing the rest leads to continual tension and is very difficult to achieve, especially in a rather populist democratic society where not only being Jewish is voluntary but also how to be Jewish in a competitive marketplace.

Since all Conservative Jews agreed that some assimilation was desirable, the problem was—and is—always how much, where, when, and how to control it. Thus individual congregations adapted and transformed traditional Jewish practices, at times strengthening them by making them more acceptable to moderns, but at other times weakening them. Like most American Jews, their leaders fell into the trap of dropping Hebrew terms in favor of ostensibly "English" ones, such as referring to Sukkot as the Feast of Tabernacles, as though Americans used "tabernacles" in everyday language more than they would have used "Sukkot," had the Hebrew been preserved. But for an immigrant society attempting to acculturate, the Hebrew word reminded them of their foreign origins, while "tabernacles" sounded like elegant English. Or, to take another example, Conservative rabbis seeking better communication with their congregants would refer to them by their English names in ceremonial activities, ceasing to use Hebrew names except in the call-up to the Torah, thereby losing an opportunity to educate.

In Jewish education, the Conservative congregations took over the functions from communal and private afternoon schools. While they raised the standards of the latter, they also lowered the standards and hours of the former to what seemed more "realistic." Their efforts attracted more children to those schools, and by insisting on a minimum number of years of Jewish schooling prior to bar mitzvah or bat mitzvah, they came close to establishing a compulsory standard for Conservative Jews. This they did at the expense of the Hebrew language, other than that of the Siddur, which it was decided was not teachable within the limited time available and was not as important as more substantive subjects relating to the religious tradition. There were serious grounds for such an educational decision, but unfortunately, the movement away from Hebrew language instruction in practice often did not strengthen the substance of religious education but left the focus on "synagogue skills" without rooting them in a proper substantive framework.

In the face of diminishing Jewish observance in the home, traditional home functions were often transferred to the synagogue—the second Passover *Seder*, some Friday night dinners, and the like. While on the one hand, this provided many Jews with experiences no longer available elsewhere, on the other hand, it sent a message that traditional Judaism was something that could be transmitted by the synagogue alone.

It would be a mistake to underestimate the difficulty and pain involved in making these decisions, although all too many rabbinical and lay leaders became militant on behalf of these changes, deliberately seeking to foster "modern" and "American" ways. At the same time, there was the successful development of new customs such as the bat mitzvah ceremony for girls, which attracted American Jewry and spread beyond the confines of the Conservative Movement to influence both Reform and Orthodoxy.

Perhaps the most decisive change was the introduction of the terminology "customs and ceremonies" in place of *dinim* (laws) or *mitzvot* (commandments). In other words, even where traditional practices were fostered, they were justified implicitly, if not explicitly, as being customary, not legally binding, as was commonly understood in all earlier versions of *halakhic* Judaism.

The end results of all of this were mixed. The Conservative Movement did succeed in making the continuity of Jewish tradition a norm for hundreds of thousands of non-Orthodox Jews, and it gave them ways to identify and affiliate Jewishly and to educate their children to do the same. However, the Movement's stated goal, the development of observing *halakhically* committed lay Conservative Jews, was not achieved.

Conservative Judaism spread because it offered second-generation Jews a chance to identify with the traditions of their ancestors, while demanding less in the way of personal religious observance on their part. By paying dues to a Conservative synagogue and supporting a rabbi and other "professionals" who would observe the canons of Conservative Judaism, the congregants endorsed the legitimacy of a modern traditional Judaism, even though they were personally prepared to deviate from it. As long as that generation remained dominant, the Conservative Movement remained powerful.

However, warning signs came fairly early. By 1962, the so-called "religious revival" of the postwar period had come to an end.[17] Synagogue membership, like church membership, stopped growing. After 1965, it even began to decline and continued to decline for nearly a decade before it stabilized.

The changes of the 1960s were particularly hard on the Conservative Movement. In the first place, the expansion of Conservative movement or congregational activities into new spheres was stopped by the rising power of the local Jewish community federations and the Council of Jewish Federations and associated institutions nationally. Second, the crises of the 1960s brought about a youthful rejection of middle-class suburban Judaism, of which the Conservative Movement was the prime example. Delayed marriage and a general reduction in the Jewish birthrate led to a demographic decline that affected all Jewish institutions, especially mass institutions.

By the mid-1970s, it was apparent to academic students of Jewish affairs that the Conservative Movement was facing difficulties, but the Movement itself, deeply involved in its new struggle for separate identity and *halakhic* singularity, continued to ignore the danger signals. It was encouraged in this by the end of the downward trend of the 1960s. By 1975, membership started growing again, although to those who looked carefully, it was apparent that the Reform Movement was growing faster.

By 1985, the elements creating trouble for the Movement had come together to a point where they could no longer be ignored. Not only did the Reform Movement proclaim that year that it was the largest Jewish religious movement in the United States, but fissures appeared within the Conservative Movement itself. The Reconstructionists had left the Movement earlier. A number of the independent *havurot* had left it less dramatically, and now there were threats of secession from the traditional wing as well, in the wake of the women's ordination issue.

## FROM PARTY TO CAMP?

Today the Conservative Movement may be on the threshold of another shift, from party to camp—from a single, all-embracing movement to a community of separate movements that shares a common *masorti* (generally traditional, not necessarily connected with the Conservative Movement) foundation and outlook. What characterized it as a party was the fact that all Conservative Jews who belonged at all were within the same institutional framework. There were tensions, sometimes severe, among the institutions that fit into that framework and that constituted the movement, but essentially all were controlled by a common leadership that was heavily interlocking. Moreover, even given the blurred understanding of what constituted Conservative Judaism, there was a sufficient consensus among the members of the Movement who saw themselves as ideologically as well as institutionally part of the same party.

In the last three decades, this has changed. The Reconstructionist Movement was the first to leave. Mordecai Kaplan developed Reconstructionism in the 1930s, but until the 1960s, it remained a faction within the party rather than anything more separate. This, indeed, was Kaplan's desire, at least until the early 1960s, and it reflects the fact that Kaplan himself, in his 102 years, lived through the entire history of the Movement and its various stages. When he started studying at the Jewish Theological Seminary, the Movement was a faction within what could already be called Orthodoxy. When he graduated, it was just beginning to become a movement. That idea was so new that Kaplan as a young rabbi could still be the founder of Young Israel, which became a major institutional bastion of modern Orthodoxy. His next great invention, the synagogue center, became the key field institution to which the Conservative Movement aspired as the focal point of its development outside of the JTS and, indeed, the key to its success in the major Northeastern metropolitan centers.

By the time the synagogue center was catching on, Kaplan was developing the ideology of Reconstructionism while teaching at the JTS. For the next thirty years or so, that ideology was one of those competing in the struggle to define what constituted the belief system of Conservative Judaism, and it continues to have real echoes to this day.

Kaplan himself did not want to separate Reconstructionism from Conservative Judaism. At most, he sought the establishment of congregations that accepted the Reconstructionist ideology within the framework of the Conservative Movement. Indeed, for at least two decades, he was a restraining influence on his students and younger colleagues who saw Conservative Judaism as too conservative and too unwilling to change and who felt the need to break away.

When Reconstructionism finally did break away in the 1960s, it was either because Kaplan was too old to resist or because he had become more radical ideologically and was less willing to compromise with the right wing of the Conservative Movement and its—to him—slow pace of change. The younger Reconstructionists had no sentimental ties to the Movement and were eager to strike out on their own. At the same time, the Conservative Movement was at the height of its development as a party and was not willing to brook secessionist tendencies or parallel institutions claiming to be in some way Conservative. So when the break came, the Reconstructionists really had to leave.

Even so, for about a decade, it was possible to think of the fledgling Reconstructionist Movement as being akin to Conservative Judaism. It was only in the 1970s, when Reconstructionism took a more radical turn, that it became at first equally akin to Reform and further removed from the tenets of Conservative Judaism through its principled antinomianism. At the end of the 1980s, the Movement formally joined the World Union for Progressive Judaism, the umbrella organization of the Reform camp. Today, most observers agree that the Reconstructionist Movement is at the left of Jewish religious life.[18]

It was precisely at that time that another phenomenon emerged within Conservative ranks—the *havurah* (fellowship) movement.[19] The *havurah* movement was an authentic product of Conservative Judaism, but it was in fact, if not in theory, virtually disowned by its parent. Most of the founders of the *havurot* were products of the Camps Ramah and the various programs of the JTS who had been turned off by what for them was the sterility of the large synagogue, then at the height of its domination of the Conservative Movement. The major Conservative synagogues had come to suffer from an orthodoxy of their own. Neither rabbis nor synagogue lay leaders wanted competition from dissident members within the synagogue walls. In most cases, they preferred to see the younger members go elsewhere and develop their *havurot* outside of the synagogue, where they expressed the kind of Judaism with which they had come to identify as the result of their Ramah and related experiences.

Unlike the Reconstructionist Movement, the *havurah* movement has not broken away from Conservative Judaism, in part because it did not want to become an established movement in its own right and in part because enough connections remained between its members and the mainstream institutions to prevent that. This could be, of course, simply a repeat of the Reconstructionist story, with the *havurah* movement now going through what the Reconstructionists went through from the mid-1930s to the mid-1950s. The difference is that most *havurah* members are more traditional than most Conservative Jews. They are part of the Conservative elite and take seriously the Conservative Jewish understanding of tradition. They are not seeking an alternative understanding of tradition that is less observant in the way that Reconstructionism did, hence there is little incentive for them to leave the Conservative fold. On the other hand, especially now that they have a national body of their own, they are no longer part of the dominant party of Conservative Judaism but may represent a new party that is equally legitimate ideologically but is institutionally more separate. The persistence of some linkage was signified symbolically at the close of the century by the fact that the National Havurah Committee was chaired from 1998 to 2000 by a Conservative pulpit rabbi. This offers the mainstream Conservative Movement a real challenge—to find a strategy for connection or reintegration with one of its most active and dynamic offspring for their mutual benefit.

If the *havurah* movement was the only such phenomenon, the smallness of its size would not make any particular difference for Conservative Judaism as a whole, but it is not. Another group has split from the mainstream. It too is more observant, not less. Indeed, it dropped the word Conservative, which it originally used, from its name to become the Union for Traditional Judaism (UTJ) in 1990 as a result of an effort to merge with the now-defunct Federation of Traditional Orthodox Rabbis (FTOR), a left-wing splinter group of the Rabbinical Council of America (RCA).[20]

The precipitating issue for the founding of the then Union for Traditional Conservative Judaism (UTCJ) was the status of women. Here too the same characteristics were displayed as in the *havurah* movement. The revolt was an affair of the Movement's elite and represented a rightward trend of about 5,000 to 10,000 people who, at the time, had nowhere to go outside of Conservative Judaism. Moreover, for most of the 75 percent who have supported radical changes in the role of women, those changes had been made, in their eyes, within the framework of *halakhah*. Unlike the Reconstructionists, there was no antinomi-

anism present but rather for them what was a more appropriate interpretation of the law had evolved. Thus, in their eyes, their *halakhic* commitment was no less than that of the right wing.[21]

This is not necessarily an unfortunate occurrence. Handled properly, it can become a "plus" for Conservative Judaism, because with three
such groups—and there may be more developing—the Conservative
Movement will become a camp or a community and not simply a party.
The history of Jewish life suggests that this is a natural phenomenon.
Especially in periods of normalcy, Jews have been divided into several
camps, each of which is comprised of several different parties. We need
only mention two examples.

In the last historical epoch, before the destruction of the Second
Commonwealth, the Jews of Eretz Yisrael were divided into Sad-
ducean, Pharisaic, and Essene camps, within which were further divisions. Thus the Pharisees were divided among the House of Hillel and
Shammai, the two major competing parties, plus other smaller ones.
The Essenes constituted the largest party among the sectarians but, as
we now know, since the discovery of the Dead Sea Scrolls, there were
various other sectarian groups as well, each of which constituted a
party in its own right.

In our own times, the Zionist Movement was built upon the same
system. Very early in the history of Zionism, three camps emerged:
labor, civil, and religious. The combination and recombination of parties in the labor camp continued until the emergence of Mapai, Mapam,
and Ahdut Avodah (Labor Unity) in the 1940s, an arrangement that
lasted for nearly a generation, after which there was a subsequent
regrouping into the current Labor, Mapam, and Citizens Rights Movement. The civil camp was originally dominated by the General Zionists, now the Liberals, but it included the Revisionists, now Herut, the
two of which merged in the 1960s to form Gahal. A decade later, they
broadened their base to become the Herut-dominated Likud. Subsequently, it became known as the national camp. The religious camp had
Mizrahi as its anchor, and Agudat Israel, willy-nilly, was linked to it,
even though it was first anti-Zionist and then became non-Zionist.
Today, it is further fragmented, as each of the two main religious parties have splintered.[22]

On the religious front, one of the strengths of contemporary Orthodoxy is that it is a camp comprising a number of parties or movements.
There is no single "Orthodox movement." Rather, Orthodoxy is composed of several different mainstream groups and the moderate ultras
such as Agudat Israel and the ultra-ultras, plus the numerous Hassidic

groups, each with its own *rebbe* (spiritual mentor). The result is that, within Orthodoxy, one can find almost anything that one wants in the way of religious expression, all of which recognize each other, even if sometimes grudgingly, as being within the same camp.

One of the serious problems of the Conservative Movement is that there has been only one way to be an affiliated Conservative Jew: to be a member of a Conservative synagogue (or to be on the faculty or staff of the Jewish Theological Seminary). If one does not fit into that very narrow framework, there has been no way to express oneself within Conservative Judaism. The development of additional avenues of Conservative Jewish expression and affiliation in this sense can only enrich its various movements. Thus, at the end of its first 100 years, the Conservative Movement may be on the threshold of restoring its vigor, not by becoming more monolithic but by becoming a community of movements. This is a prodigious challenge that offers great opportunities for the next century.

Chapter 2

# *Institutions*

The Conservative Movement is understood to have begun with the founding of the Jewish Theological Seminary. Each Movement institution—the Rabbinical Assembly, the United Synagogue, the National Federation of Jewish Men's Clubs, the Women's League for Conservative Judaism, the Educators' and Cantors' Assemblies, and the Jewish Youth Directors Association (JYDA)—was founded separately, as were the Ramah camps and the Solomon Schechter schools. All were offshoots of the JTS. At no point was the Conservative Movement proclaimed. This piecemeal development has led to certain tensions over the years, but it has probably also been at least a modest source of strength.

## THE CHANGING POSITION OF THE SEMINARY

The reasons the Movement developed in this way are tied to its history, especially with its lack of desire to become a separate movement in the early stages. The fact that the JTS was founded first is of great significance. In some respects, the Movement can be seen to have grown up around the school, as Marshall Sklare pointed out many years ago.[1] Since the Movement, after its first years, was given its shape by graduates of Lithuanian yeshivot, it is not an accident that at its heart the JTS long remained a modern functional alternative to a traditional *yeshiva* (institution of religious study).

The traditional *yeshiva* was developed in Lithuania at the end of the eighteenth century to answer the twin challenges of Hassidism and modernity.[2] In a relatively short time, such *yeshivot* became the principal sources of religious teaching and guidance for non-Hassidic Jewry (*misnagdim*) in Eastern Europe. Those who built the present Seminary, coming as they did out of those *yeshivot* but having become modern men, wanted to combine *yeshiva* (religious) and *wissenshaft* studies in their new institution, that is to say, traditional Talmudic learning with the new science of Judaism developed by modern German Jews.[3] Hence, as rigorous as they were in their scholarship, they were ambivalent about the role that the JTS should play as a source of religious teaching and guidance.

Ambivalence led them to avoid taking any deliberate steps to be religious guides. Nevertheless, circumstances and their own rootedness in Jewish tradition, whereby the opinions of the greatest scholars automatically became authoritative, made them such, willy-nilly. Since initially the Seminary was all there was, with newly Conservative congregations gravitating to it as a source of rabbis, its senior faculty, especially the Talmud one, wielded great power over the Movement's *halakhic* decisions. This power was exercised indirectly as they formally refused to be *posekim* (*halakhic* decision makers). Although they succeeded in keeping the Movement within traditional grounds, their own ambivalence limited their effectiveness.

One result was that scholarship and scholars flourished, while congregational rabbis suffered from lack of *halakhic* direction. The Seminary had great success as a modern institution for classical Jewish studies, and it became perhaps the dominant force in Jewish scholarship in America for two generations. In that sense, its faculty was very successful in combining the two traditions of learning, even as its students, the rabbis in the field, became increasingly restive.

Since the passing of the giants of the first two generations after its reorganization by Schechter, the situation has changed. The present senior faculty, in a number of cases as talented scholars as its predecessors, does not have the same stature in the eyes of the rest of the Movement, perhaps because this is not an age of giants anywhere. In part, it is simply because most are former classmates—peers—of the congregational rabbis who constitute their potential *halakhic* constituency.

They are professors of Jewish studies at the Seminary, not putative *posekim*, peers rather than mentors.

On the other hand, most have grown up within Conservative Judaism, so they are much more a part of the Movement and share its spiritual concerns. Indeed, many of them share its party concerns too. They are more likely to consider the institutional needs of the Movement and not only the *halakhah* in the abstract. The vote over the ordination of women reflected the fact that the Talmud department, in the past the bastion of *halakhic* caution, could no longer control decisions on such issues and was itself divided. This marked a potentially decisive change in the control of the JTS. Where Talmudists once reigned supreme, historians are now the group in power. This is hardly surprising in an institution developed out of the historical school, but the decisiveness of the change in the 1970s has had profound effects on the institution and on the Movement.

In short, the Seminary remains an important pillar as the Movement's institution of higher education, but it no longer has the authoritative role it once had. This in itself signals a great shift in the balance of power within the Movement, principally to the Rabbinical Assembly, which has already become evident in recent *halakhic* decisions and will become even more evident over the next generation.

## The Congregational Heart of the Movement

The heart of the Conservative Movement is to be found in its synagogues, just as the brain is to be found in the JTS. The life of the Movement is essentially lived in its synagogues. Indeed, until very recently, it has been difficult to find other places within which to do so and, where such institutions have been developed, the Movement has not accorded them equal status with synagogues.

The critical role of the synagogue is not surprising, since membership in the synagogue remains the most meaningful way for most American Jews to identify with both the Jewish community and Judaism. While we bemoan the fact that no more than half of American Jews are synagogue members at any given time, the studies show that between 75 percent and 85 percent are synagogue members at some time in their lives. Even at 50 percent or less, more Jews join synagogues than contribute to Federation and United Jewish Appeal (UJA) campaigns or engage in any other Jewish activity outside of the home.[4]

It is also true that no membership organization in the community meets more regularly or attracts a larger number of people on a regular basis than do synagogues to their religious services, not to speak of their other activities. Even though the studies show that no more than 15 percent or 20 percent of American Jews attend synagogue at least once a week, even that percentage is far higher than the percentage of Jews engaged in any other collective Jewish activity on a weekly basis.[5] Similar comparisons can be made with regard to any of the other frequency levels measured in the studies. No other institution gives the average Jew a regular, ongoing way of expressing his or her Jewishness.

Thus it is not surprising that the congregation should stand at the vital center of the Movement. Moreover, one of the great successes of Conservative Judaism has been to develop congregations in which Jews can pray, study, celebrate life cycle events, hear speakers on Jewish themes, enjoy Jewish art and music, find friends with similar interests, connect with the Jewish community when they move into a new neighborhood or city, provide for the education of their children, and respond emotionally to the great events that occur in the Jewish and general world.

At the same time, even those who may maintain synagogue membership throughout their lives cannot find all they are seeking in Jewish life, or even in the Conservative Movement, through the contemporary American synagogue. Hence the Jewish community at large has fostered other institutions, from social and fraternal organizations to Jewish community federations, to provide other points of connection to Jewish life as a whole. The Movement needs to do the same with regard to connections with Conservative Judaism, even while continuing to recognize the vital importance of the synagogue.

Conservative Jews, by and large, identify the Movement with synagogue life as led by their rabbis. Though traditionally the home was the primary arena of Jewish observance, today it has become a secondary arena and is so perceived even by those who tout a return to its centrality. Liebman noted two decades ago that the Jewish Theological Seminary was central to the Movement, but with the exception of those currently studying within its walls and to a lesser extent its alumni, the JTS is a remote father figure referred to reverentially in the context of fund-raising campaigns or as a source of scholars in residence for synagogue weekends. The apathy of most congregations vis-à-vis the JTS is a frequent complaint of the Seminary leadership.

At the same time, the United Synagogue has not been able to overcome the extremely strong congregationalism inherent in the American synagogue system to attract even that much interest and loyalty on the part of the average Conservative Jew. Thus, though the JTS is remote, its chancellor automatically is recognized as the head of the Movement. The leaders of the United Synagogue are less well known within it than is the chancellor, whomever he or she may be.

There is much to be said for American-style congregationalism, whereby every synagogue is an independent, self-governing body, and is so viewed under American laws of private association, albeit for public purposes.[6] Moreover, congregationalism of this kind is generally consistent with the Jewish tradition of congregational self-government as it developed in medieval Europe. Yet congregational independence usually means that synagogues, even within the same city, often are isolated from each other, and their members rarely interact; their rabbis meet only occasionally at Board of Rabbis or Rabbinical Assembly meetings, but they do not really know how to function together as part of a cohesive movement. Since rabbis must always be at their own synagogues on *Shabbat* (the Sabbath) and holidays, they rarely have the opportunity to see how others do things. Non-rabbinic leaders also rarely see how other congregations function—the more they are part of the loyal core of a particular synagogue, the less likely they are to have any contact with alternative or common patterns, except when they go to other synagogues to celebrate the rites of passage of family and friends.

There are scattered examples of intercongregational cooperation, such as intercongregational Hebrew high school systems in some localities. Several congregations share youth and adult educational programming around the country, and recently there have been some informal efforts on the part of congregational leaders to work, discuss, and share information in matters pertaining to board-staff relationships and other areas of governance. Occasionally there are joint membership campaigns in a particular locality. Efforts are made periodically to establish regional councils of synagogues, but they tend to remain peripheral to the heart of the Movement. All of these are steps in the right direction, but they are still too few and far between and are perceived as running against the grain of congregationalism.

This isolation has a number of consequences, perhaps the most important of which is the sense that, for most Conservative Jews, there is no Movement, only the individual synagogue. Our research has confirmed that many rabbis and non-rabbinic leaders complain about the weakness of the Movement, while they assure interviewers that their own synagogues are flourishing! Lay and professional leaders feel

unconnected to the Movement, while recognizing their own synagogue community as a vibrant one that exists in splendid isolation.
There are some limited ongoing attempts to remedy this situation, such
as the weekly United Synagogue page that appears in the *Long Island
Jewish World* and descriptions of various programs in the *United Synagogue Review*, however, the malaise over the perceived ephemeral
nature of the Movement still is pervasive.

While synagogues are organized along the congregational model,
as congregations they are of limited range (this is true even of the great
synagogue centers). In other words, each congregation is autonomous,
established by agreement among its members in a manner not funda-
mentally different from that used to establish an old style *kahal* (congregation), but most Jews join congregations because they are seeking
religious service centers, not because they want to be part of a *kahal*.
Thus they pay their dues to keep the facility and its professional personnel available to them, not because they are seeking to become active
in a community. Even those who are active in the synagogue are likely
to view the synagogue as having a few specialized religious-*cum*-social
functions, with the social designed to keep the members in the fold,
rather than for any larger purpose or for any purposes intrinsic to
social goals. Under these circumstances, the forms are the forms of a
congregation, and under American law, the status is that of a congregation, but the reality is the reality of a synagogue in the modern sense, of
limited scope and drawing power with regard to membership interest.

## THE VARIETY OF CONGREGATIONAL MODELS

At one point, the ideal of the Conservative Movement was the
large, multipurpose congregation, originally defined by Mordecai
Kaplan as the synagogue center. Through that large synagogue, a Conservative style of services, program, and organization developed that
was expected to be standard for the whole Movement. This ideal persisted well into the postwar period, and there are those who would like
to see it maintained to this day.

In fact, however, one of the most positive developments that has
taken place in the Movement is the emergence of a variety of congregational types, each offering a different mode of religious expression.
Each of these modes was generated by the congregation itself, and
each congregation retains its own particular combination of modes. Yet
certain phenomena have become sufficiently widespread to be able to

generalize about them. In communities with more than two Conservative congregations, the differing ambiences are well known to veteran
members of the community and are sometimes made known to new-
comers and unaffiliated Jews who are "shopping around" for a synagogue.

Until very recently, synagogue affiliation was most often linked to
the life cycle. The average family affiliated when the children of the
household reached school age and remained through the bar mitzvah
or bat mitzvah. Under such circumstances, the congregation that was
joined often was picked for convenience rather than ideology, with the
key considerations of prestige, lowest dues, closest location for car-
pooling, or least demanding school schedule. Today, however, when
synagogue life is necessarily becoming more adult oriented (85 percent
of all Jews in the United States are over age sixteen), enhancement and
promotion of the different models of synagogue life available within
the Conservative Movement may be crucial for membership retention,
not to speak of growth. The types presented next are, of course, abstrac-
tions in the nature of "ideal types." As such, no synagogue fits the type
exactly, but the model suggests the varying facets of reality.[7]

*The Cathedral*

In most major cities, there is at least one grand synagogue that is
considered the "establishment" congregation. For many years, it was
the model to which other congregations aspired. Services are stylized
and formal. The rabbi and cantor usually wear robes and assume total
control of the *bimah* (podium), often with the aid of a choir and organ.
The service hardly varies from week to week. Preaching is central to
the service. The rabbi is a formal figure, removed from day-to-day contact with children, teenagers, and young marrieds. He or she relates in
a more personal way to the officers and board and "big-givers" and
manages a team of professionals that provides services for other members. The staff usually includes a cantor, an assistant rabbi, an educational director, youth leaders, ritual and executive directors, and support staff. The rabbi is the CEO who may hold weekly staff meetings.
The rabbi may be active in the larger Jewish community. He or she may
be considered one of its leaders and a representative of the Jews to the
non-Jewish world.

The congregation must have at least 1,000 to 1,500 households to
financially support its staff and programs. This congregation may fit
the earlier typography suggested by Wolfe Kelman as the "supermar-
ket," referred to here as the "service station." Most members join to be

able to purchase specific services from professionals as they need them rather than to become integral members of a community. On the other hand, some former "cathedrals" such as Adas Israel in Washington, Adath Jeshurun in Philadelphia, and Valley Beth Sholom in Encino, California, have pioneered programming for singles, day care facilities for middle-class, dual-career families, and even *havurot*. Size and social status then are not necessarily barriers to the creation of community.

## The "Heimish" (Homey) Congregation

This congregation, usually comprised of about 500 to 1,000 households, specializes in bringing as many members as possible into the "family" by involving as large a percentage as possible in some aspect of congregational activity on a regular basis. Services are less formal than at the "cathedral"; the rabbi and cantor do not wear robes; and there is considerable member participation. The cantor introduces melodies that can be sung by all. Children are encouraged to sit with their parents at services, and special Friday evening services are offered for families, with *Shabbat* dinners following. The rabbi and cantor may clap and lead singing from the *bimah* or even step down off it to dialogue with the congregation in place of a formal sermon. The members build their social lives around the congregation. The key rabbinic role is that of pastor. The rabbi may even have tried to reintroduce the notion of *hevrot* (task groups) around life-cycle events to enhance involvement of members. The work of Rabbis Albert Lewis of Haddon Heights and Arnold Goodman when he was at Adath Jeshurun in Minneapolis falls within the parameters of this mode.

## The Bet Midrash (Study Hall)

The forte of this congregation of about 500 families is its adult education programming. Its rabbi is seen as an intellectual leader who lends tone to the whole enterprise. Congregants boast of their rabbi's erudition and seek to be part of the intellectual cadre that surrounds their spiritual leader. His or her sermon and the dialogue that follows highlight the service that may be somewhat abbreviated to leave time for adequate interchange. Study groups are well attended, and the adult education committee is central to the board of directors. Many members of the congregation are experiencing the "empty nest," though some are young professionals seeking a synagogue "different" from the one in which they grew up, one with a focus on rationalism and the development of the mind. "Our building may not be lavish, but we never shirk on a program," a member may comment. Two scholar-in-residence weekend *kallot* (learning assemblies) are held each year, one usually led by a visiting professor from the Seminary and the other by some leading political or literary figure from Israel. This congregation often is a leader in organizing a community-wide adult education consortium among the Conservative synagogues, so three or four distinguished thinkers may be brought to the community each year and so congregants may take six-week classes at a nominal fee from several of the rabbis and other teachers in the community.

### The Geriatric Congregation

Most often found in center-city neighborhoods or areas of second settlement, these synagogues usually have about 80 percent of their members over age sixty-five. In the retirement communities of South Florida, such synagogues are colloquially referred to as "adult congregations." The golden age group and daily activities to enhance the lives of retirees are important. The rabbi must be a consummate pastor and counselor as well as teacher to many groups. There are more female than male members. A special emphasis on Holocaust survivor groups, lodges of fraternal groups and women's groups such as Hadassah that meet at the synagogue is important. The synagogue functions as a community center for these seniors. The men's club and sisterhood meet during the day and on Sunday mornings, and they are vibrant groups. Seniors look to the synagogue as the focus of their social, religious, and cultural life. They also expect the rabbi and other synagogue personnel to give them reassurance that life is not over but is being reinterpreted and filled with new learning and meaning. Foster grandparent, meals on wheels, and various volunteer programs for the well elderly originate here.

### The Traditional Synagogue

In cities with large Jewish populations in the United States there are often one or even two congregations that are known as "right-wing" Conservative or "traditional." Sometimes these congregations are led by an Orthodox rabbi who has not joined the Rabbinical Assembly, and sometimes they are led by Seminary graduates. If they designate themselves in formal listings as "traditional," then they are usually led by *yeshiva* graduates and rarely affiliate with the United Synagogue. Often they have mixed seating, with an option in side aisles for separate seating. If they do belong to the United Synagogue and have as their rabbis JTS graduates, or *yeshiva* graduates who have joined the Rabbinical Assembly, they may be found in neighborhoods of earlier settlement or even in heavily populated neighborhoods where there are two or three other congregations, all more liberal. The rabbi or some members of this *shul* may be members of the Union for

Traditional Judaism. They may advertise themselves as the synagogue for Conservative Jews who do not wish to participate in egalitarian services. Bat mitzvah, if held at all, is on Friday night, and the main arena for participation of women is the sisterhood. There is no organ or mixed choir.

This synagogue provides an important "safety valve" for those who feel comfortable in more traditional services similar to those with which they grew up who wish to remain a part of the Conservative Movement. Though they may sometimes feel uncomfortable when they visit other Conservative synagogues, they can still relate to their home congregation as part of the Conservative Movement, and they know that they have a base of operations from which they can legitimately put forward their vision of Conservative Judaism. Their spiritual leader reinforces this feeling of security in the Movement, especially if he is a Rabbinical Assembly member who shares their understanding of the Movement. One example is Congregation Melrose B'nai Israel in Philadelphia.

### The Havurah Minyan (group of ten Jewish adults over age thirteen, needed to conduct a traditional prayer service)/davening (prayer) Group in Symbiosis with a "Host" Congregation

In many of the larger Jewish communities, there can be found *havurah minyanim*, which *daven* together weekly, twice a month, or whenever the main congregation has a bar mitzvah or bat mitzvah. Usually they meet in libraries, chapels, or classrooms of one or two congenial Conservative synagogues. In some cases, there are several congregations in the same building, though not of equal status. Congregations within congregations, they often charge separate dues, sponsor yearly retreats, hold holiday celebrations, and feature study groups. Their relationship with the rabbi and board of the host congregation is ambivalent at best, yet they form a key group for young, traditional, egalitarian, Conservative families. Often their members are products of Camp Ramah, 1960s activism, and now of Conservative day schools. Most of their children attend day schools. They are affiliated with the *havurah* because they seek meaningful prayer and study for themselves in a setting that will welcome their children. (They sense that day school children sometimes have a hard time feeling part of congregations.)

There is a certain anticlericalism in this group, though they may accept the rabbi of the host congregation as their *Mara d'atra*. Ordained rabbis who are members of the *havurah* are "no different" from any other members. The rabbi of the host congregation may feel that the core of the *davening* group has left him or her, and that this implies a critique of the main service. (The rabbi is often correct.) This view may be shared by the cantor, who criticizes the *nusah* (style of prayer) of the *minyan*, and by the board, which would like them all to pay dues to the congregation and be active participants in the mainstream structure. The service in the *havurah* is invariably more traditional and participatory than the one in the main sanctuary. There is a full Torah reading, the *shaliah tzibbur* (prayer leader) faces the ark, the *davening* is all in Hebrew, and so on. This congregation may consider itself at once more spiritual, more intellectual, and more socially cohesive than the host congregation.

Often in these newly formulated relationships an uneasy peace is preserved between the *minyan* and the host congregation because of advantages to both groups. The host congregation can "claim" the young, learned, upwardly mobile group as a part of it, and the members of the *minyan* enjoy the stability of the congregational ambiance, facilities, and convenience of having a maintenance staff and nice room to *daven* in without the cost of maintaining a building. This group is "within" the congregation, though not "of" it.

In Philadelphia, for example, during the last quarter of the twentieth century there were four symbiotic groups such as this that varied in the closeness of their relationship to "host" Conservative congregations. These are, in order of their integration into the main synagogue: Beth Hillel-Beth El, Germantown Jewish Center, Adath Jeshurun, and Beth Zion-Beth Israel. At Beth Hillel-Beth El, on the fashionable Mainline, most *havurah* members are also members of the synagogue. They even "move" their *havurah* into the main sanctuary when there is no bar mitzvah or bat mitzvah, and they conduct the services there. Several members of the "Library Minyan," as it is known, are on the board of the congregation. At Germantown Jewish Center, an urban synagogue, in a stable, integrated neighborhood, many members of the two *havurah minyanim* are also dues-paying members of the synagogue. Several have been board members, committee chairpeople, or even officers of the congregation, while others who are professors of Jewish studies at local universities volunteer their services to lead adult education groups for the synagogue. Beth Zion-Beth Israel, in Center City, once actually housed the *havurah* that had developed separately from it. Over the years, however, the two have steadily grown apart, separating physically first and now with little overlap in membership as well. Just recently negotiations have begun with the goal of integrating the center city *Havurah Minyan* into a new alternative service at the synagogue. Initiated at the end of the 1970's by its rabbi, the Adath Jeshurun (AJ) Minyan meets weekly and is open to any Jew who is a dues paying member of a congregation, though most regular participants are active members of the greater AJ community.

## The All-Purpose Synagogue

In many communities where the Jewish population is small, there is only one Conservative synagogue or only one synagogue to serve the whole town that is designated Conservative, though it must meet the needs of all of the local Jews. These small congregations are often the center of Jewish educational, religious, and social life. Their ritual stance is centrist, so all Jews will be able to pray and find community within the one available congregation. Because of their comprehensive character and the smallness of the Jewish population, such congregations often foster very close connections among their members, despite having to serve a wide range of viewpoints and interests. If they have an ideological stance, it is to preserve communal unity.

## Some Experimental Modes

There is, in Manhattan, an experiment that may be emulated of a *havurah*-centered congregation. At Anshei Chesed, three or four *minyanim* make up the congregation. There is no "main sanctuary." Actually, the model of several *minyanim* in the same building, often preserved so a number of mourners could have the honor of leading the service, is an old one. Its new forms, as exemplified at Anshei Chesed, may be a forerunner of a new pattern in gentrified urban areas where old synagogue buildings maintained by a *minyan* of elderly men are still found.

Another pattern, that of Rabbi Harold Schulweis at Valley Beth Shalom in Los Angeles, is of a formerly cathedral-like congregation becoming "familized" through the formation of as many as fifty *havurot*, which do not *daven* apart from the main congregation but study and celebrate holidays and life-cycle events together. Yet another mode is that of a specialized singles congregation that meets on specified Friday nights at one Conservative congregation or rotates among several in one area of a city.

This development of distinctive, specialized congregations is perhaps the most positive one that has taken place within the congregational heart of the Movement in the past generation. It provides new options through which Jews with different senses of what they want from a synagogue can affiliate with the Movement.

It may even be desirable to foster various types of congregations within areas of major Jewish concentration. A synagogue planning to move to a new neighborhood or interested in enlarging its membership might choose to stress or enhance its particular ambiance or areas of expertise. Moreover, certain tasks, such as singles programming, adult education, elementary supplementary school education or adult day care, might best be accomplished for a community through the specialization of various synagogues within that community. While all of the Conservative synagogues in the community would stress certain core ideological values, differences in ambiance would meet the real needs of the panoply of those identifying with the Movement, from periphery to core. *Diversity need not diminish allegiance to a common movement as long as common principles are known and stressed in all of the settings, and as long as the movement leadership is representative of all modes.* Presently, neither the unifying ideology nor truly representative leadership forums that involve core members of all of the ideal types of congregations are functioning well. The issue of coherence in the Movement will be addressed in other chapters dealing with ideology and the integration of the various organizational arms of the Movement.

## A NOTE ON YOUTH MOVEMENTS

The Conservative Movement leadership, like any other intelligent body of leaders, soon realized the necessity for attracting the younger generation. Hence it organized its first youth movement, the Young People's League (YPL) in the interwar generation. It was not until after World War II that the Movement created two immensely successful youth groups, the Leaders Training Fellowship (LTF) and United Synagogue Youth (USY).

The first, yet another idea of Mordecai Kaplan's, had its start in the East at the very end of the war and in the Midwest in 1947. It soon became the vehicle for linking Ramah campers during the rest of the year and for encouraging them to maintain a minimum of six hours of Jewish study a week. In the years of its existence, it was a highly successful vehicle for recruitment to the Conservative elite, developing an élan and a sense of camaraderie which has never been equalled in the Movement and which carries over among Ramah/LTF alumni to this day.

LTF groups followed two patterns. In some cities, they were organized on a citywide basis, in others, by congregation. Each pattern had its successes. By and large, the former was more successful, since in the latter case it depended upon the seriousness of the congregational rabbi to determine whether the LTF group would be more than a paper organization and whether the study requirements would really be maintained. Unfortunately, LTF survived for only a generation. Apparently it died as the result of a conflict at Movement headquarters. It has never been replaced, but such an elite core linked with Ramah as a year-round concept should be revived. The Abraham Joshua Heschel Society of United Synagogue Youth might provide a framework to embrace outstanding youth from Ramah, Solomon Schechter Schools, and USY.

USY, on the other hand, emerged out of the congregations. It was founded by Rabbi Kassel Abelson and his wife Shirley at Beth El Synagogue in Minneapolis, also in 1947, and from there spread rapidly throughout the country. USY became the mass youth movement, congregationally rooted and based, but with appropriate regional and national organizations, including summer camps (one year for a full two months, but in most cases for a week or two). It has proved to be a most vital, successful means of recruitment of congregational leadership and to some extent rabbis as well, and it has maintained a more or less stable membership of close to 25,000 for many years. Its Israel Pilgrimage (begun in 1958), USY on wheels cross-country trips, and Israel-Eastern European trips have been consistently successful personal educational vehicles that also cemented social networks that persisted through life for many participants.

Conservative Movement efforts have been less successful with college age youth, but the Movement is not alone in that respect. All mainstream religious movements have had difficulties with that group. Nativ—the USY Year Course in Israel, founded in 1981, succeeded the previous practice of sending leaders to the Institute for Youth Leaders from Abroad.

Unfortunately, there are indications that, since the demise of LTF, the Conservative Movement as a whole has paid less attention to its youth movements in the past two decades than it should have. From the first, there has been an almost steady conflict between some youth movement leaders who want more rigorous standards in *halakhic* matters, Jewish observance, and Jewish study, and some in the adult generation who tend to resist them. In part, this is a normal conflict between idealistic youth and more realistic adults, but in part it is missing an opportunity. As one of the adults involved in USY told us, "We make an error in underestimating our young people's capacity and interest in *halakhah*. And then we cheat them. Too many kids move away from Judaism because we don't give it to them."

With the demise of LTF, USY has moved toward a greater interest in formal text study, but it has not done much about it, although it has published study materials and set higher standards for chapter and regional board members. What it has done is recognized Israel as an opportunity for Jewish learning and tried to increase the numbers of young people traveling and studying there. In the nature of things, however, its programs there have often been less than what the Movement's leadership has anticipated, since the participants come from such varied Jewish backgrounds. The size of USY, like that of other youth movements, has plateaued. However, according to the 1990 National Jewish Population Survey (NJPS), there should be a larger cohort of eligible adolescents in the next decade. This opportunity should be exploited by putting pre-USY (Kadima groups) into all Schechter Day Schools and linking all of the adolescent programs of the movement in a broader framework. Thus older Ramah campers, veterans of Israel trips, USYers, Schechter elementary school alumni, and those in high schools should all be linked in a movement-wide organization.

## New Institutions Emerge

For two generations, the Movement remained fixed on this tripartite structure. Then, in the 1970s, new forces emerged, growing out of the same developments that gave birth to the *havurah* movement. They involved the establishment of synagogue-based *havurot* and the Solomon Schechter day schools. The precursor to these new forces was Camp Ramah.

## The Ramah Camps

One can find a precursor founded in the 1940s that was to be quite significant in shaping all of the new institutions, namely Camp Ramah. The idea for Camp Ramah was, like almost everything else in the Conservative Movement, originally put forward by Mordecai Kaplan, but it did not flourish until a coalition of Conservative educators, rabbis, and lay leaders in the Midwest, particularly Chicago, decided that a

Hebrew-speaking camp was necessary in their region and created one under Conservative auspices. The first Camp Ramah, in Wisconsin, opened its doors in 1947.[8]

Many of the founders of Ramah had been involved in the Jewish camping movement, particularly with the Massad camps in Pennsylvania. These camps catered primarily to children who were from Orthodox or traditional homes and who attended day schools in the New York area such as Ramaz, Yeshiva D'Flatbush, the Hebrew Institute of Long Island, and the Manhattan and Brooklyn Talmudical Academies or Central High School, which were under the aegis of Yeshiva University. The focus of Massad was spoken Hebrew and Zionism.

The efforts of the Midwesterners, although stimulated and encouraged by Professor Moshe Davis and Sylvia Ettenberg of the Teachers Institute, encountered resistance by top leadership at the Seminary, who either did not believe that the initiative should be undertaken, or that it could be viable outside of the New York area or the East, or did not want it undertaken except under their direct control. Additionally, most of the congregational rabbis in the region were not particularly interested in helping in the effort. One of the characteristics of the congregational system is the degree to which each congregation's leadership is almost perforce interested in the affairs of its own congregation above all and considers anything that might compete with those affairs detrimental. Most of the congregational rabbis demonstrated the truth of this in their reluctant acquiescence to the establishment of Camp Ramah and in their general lack of support for the institution. The coalition of lay leaders and educators, supported by a few of the most important local rabbis, did win out, however, and the camp was established successfully.

Camp Ramah in the Poconos, the second camp, also was established by an initiative outside of the Seminary, in this case, Philadelphia leadership under the direction of Rabbi David Goldstein and the *baalei batim* (householders, i.e., lay leaders) of Har Zion, his congregation, one of the great postwar concentrations of talented leadership to emerge from the Conservative Movement. After that, the Seminary was won over and moved energetically to build the Ramah network, taking it as its own. The history of the Ramah camps needs to be written as a case study of the Conservative Movement's strengths and weaknesses, as well as for its own sake.

Perhaps in the way that the Poalei Mizrahi-oriented *kibbutzim* (collective settlements) and the Bnei Akiva institutions in Israel are the quintessential expression of religious Zionism, a strong case can be made that Ramah is the most genuinely Conservative institution in the entire Movement, the only living whole community where an authentically Conservative way of Jewish religious life has been developed, one that lives up to Conservative *halakhic* canons. The best Conservative congregations also have developed an authentic Conservative style, but more in the sociological than in the *halakhic* sense. Ramah's patterns of Jewish observance, its egalitarian/traditional style of worship, and its Jewish educational ideology all reflect what can be done when there is the appropriate combination of space and time, an entirely Jewish turf for a sufficiently extended period.

The success of the Ramah camps in this respect demonstrated that it is possible to have an authentic Conservative Judaism in the way that the founders of the Movement envisaged it, yet that very success led to the alienation of many Ramah alumni from the more shallow sociological Conservative Judaism found in the congregations. This has presented its own problems, but these are the problems of success and should be recognized as such. If anything, the Movement has not properly utilized this success and built upon it.

Ramah also has been the source of most Conservative Jewish creativity since Mordecai Kaplan. Among its spinoffs has been the *havurah* movement, what has become the distinctive Conservative "inquiry" approach to Jewish education, which in turn has been embodied in the Melton program and CAJE (Coalition for the Advancement of Jewish Education). It should be no surprise that it is Ramah alumni who are building the Masorti Movement in Israel and who in doing so are spreading the way of religious worship and practice developed at Ramah. Indeed *"nusah* Ramah" has come to dominate worship in the movement.

Ramah has even provided one of the few significant efforts to reach out to the Jewish handicapped through its Tikva program, which has done especially important work in meeting the Jewish needs of mentally, physically, or psychologically handicapped youngsters since 1970 and is one of the finest examples of American Jewry's efforts in this respect.

It should be noted that in its early days, Camp Ramah in Wisconsin was not a Conservative Movement camp in the narrow sense; rather, it was a Hebrew-speaking camp under the auspices of the Conservative Movement, which attracted young people from all branches of Judaism and all Jewish persuasions. It was only later, in the early 1950s, when control passed to the Seminary, that it was turned into a movement camp, more narrowly defined. This was consonant with the general American Jewish religious picture of the period, which shifted radically as the impact of the sectarian Orthodox grew and as centrist Orthodoxy came into its own. Thus Morasha, the overnight camp under the aegis of Yeshiva University, would supplant and ultimately lead to the demise of the Massad camps.

The end result was a strong network of movement-oriented camps designed most immediately to supplement the education children received in Conservative schools and beyond that narrower perspective to produce Jewishly better educated rabbis. The earlier effort to reach out was curtailed by 1953. By 1956, it was clear that the camps were not even particularly interested in investing in the development of future non-rabbinic leaders for the Movement. The fact that many of those who went through the camps did not become rabbis but did become leaders in Conservative congregations where conditions were right only demonstrates the degree to which the camps could be used to that end. Many more, however, particularly those who did not indicate a desire or could not then become rabbis, were never mobilized as they could have been or have failed to find a place for themselves in the Movement as it is presently organized.

One example that has come to our attention of ex-Ramah campers giving leadership to an American congregation from top to bottom is the Conservative congregation in East Lansing, Michigan. When a group of young faculty members with Ramah backgrounds found themselves at Michigan State University two decades ago, there was no Conservative congregation for them. They became the leaders, because there were no others, and they built an active and a vibrant institution—a model of what a Conservative congregation could be—but with no significant connection to the Movement. Where there were established congregations, the typical congregational leaders—rabbinic and voluntary—often failed to encourage similar people to become active.

In sum, while the contribution of Camp Ramah to the Conservative Movement has been great and extraordinarily positive overall, it has not been nearly as great as it might have been. At the same time, the camps have contributed much to Jewish life overall, helping to raise a generation of Jewish scholars and producing a disproportionate number of *olim* (new immigrants to Israel). But these spin-offs rarely benefited the Conservative Movement, because the Movement had no proper place for many Ramah alumni.

No apology need be made for Ramah's orientation toward the development of a cadre of educated Jews with a *Masorti* way of life who demand more than what is conventionally available in most Conservative congregations—this despite charges of elitism often leveled against the camp. If anything, it is the retreat from this position in the form of lowered standards that we view as problematic, of equal importance with the problem of failing to mobilize the non-rabbinic leadership potential of Ramah alumni in the Movement. (Imagine the strength of a United Synagogue dominated by Ramah alumni!) Ramah's present weaknesses with regard to standards of Hebrew and religious observance and problems of staff recruitment, including the ability to attract Seminary students as staff, are part of the new reality that the Conservative Movement must face.

A program that sponsors rabbinical students at Ramah is an important step in this direction. Originally established in 1991 as the Ohev Shalom Fellowship, it was renamed the Rabbi Alexander Shapiro Fellowship after Rabbi Shapiro, a former Ramah director and rabbi of Ohev Shalom. While in the summer of 1990 just five rabbinical students worked in Ramah camps, in the five years following the inception of these fellowships, 10, 19, 34, 40, and 43 rabbinical students, respectively, have spent the summer. It is having an impact as well on the number of rabbinical students taking concurrent education masters' degrees at JTS.

While the camps have serious problems, they may also open up new opportunities for building another constituency for the Conservative Movement through the Ramah alumni. The nucleus of this constituency may be the Ramah Commissions, which are increasingly populated with Ramah alumni. They could well be the focal point of the proper representation of that constituency within the Conservative Movement.

## THE *HAVUROT*[9]

The *havurot* that emerged at the end of the 1960s were natural outgrowths of the Ramah experience, founded by precisely those people who were serious Conservative Jews but who could not find their place in ordinary Conservative congregations. As independent bodies, organized and maintained by their members, the *havurot* could not be taken over or aborted.

Consequently, at that time, the *havurah* movement, a quintessentially 1960s' anti-establishment trend that remained numerically small but culturally vital, was "lost" to the mainstream Conservative Movement. Today, few recognize that the *havurah* movement was largely the contribution of Conservative Judaism to American Judaism, and many of the *havurah* movement's institutional and ideological leaders feel little attachment to the Conservative Movement as such. Whatever value one may attach to *havurah* Judaism, the institutional defection of some of its most influential pioneers points to some larger problems in the appeal of the Conservative Movement. It was, however, also a product of their anti-establishment and in some cases antinomian tendencies. For others, anti-clerical, this defection was a reflection of the reality that many of the more serious, more educated, and more observant members or potential members of Conservative synagogues found themselves unable to participate comfortably within the mainstream congregations. When they finished university, married, and had children, many formed *havurot* or left to pray as "Conservative Marranos" in Modern Orthodox synagogues.

This trend was brought into the traditional synagogue by rabbis like Harold Schulweis, who, in the late 1970s in Encino California at Valley Beth Shalom, created a *havurah* centered synagogue that was then emulated by his colleagues. More than a few rabbis thought that *havurot* and, more important, the people they attracted, could be captured by being encouraged to develop within the existing synagogue framework so that by 1975, 47 percent of Conservative synagogues claimed to have *havurot*. In some cases, these were merely the old-fashioned study groups by a different name, but in others they represented a new phenomenon. For most rabbis, however, the *havurot* represented competition, drawing off their most "Jewish" congregants. They acquiesced to such *havurot* when they had to, but they did not encourage them.

## THE SOLOMON SCHECHTER SCHOOLS[10]

As the first countrywide network of non-Orthodox day schools, Solomon Schechter schools represent another great achievement of Conservative Jewry. Once again, with some notable exceptions (e.g., Rabbi David Goldstein in Philadelphia), the schools were established principally by coalitions of educators, *baalei batim*, and rabbis (the latter two categories usually those with children of school age), working outside of the formal institutions of the Movement. Most rabbis at best gave lip service to the idea and, in fact, many were unhappy about it because a Solomon Schechter school, willy-nilly, served people from more than one congregation if indeed it required congregational membership at all, and it drew off students from their supplementary schools.

At first, the United Synagogue and to some extent the JTS reacted ambivalently to the Schechter schools. On the one hand, they could not help but view them as important in their efforts to strengthen Jewish life. Yet at the same time, they could not afford to offend their congregations, which were cool to negative toward such schools or were large enough to try to establish their own day schools, at the expense of community-wide Movement efforts. In different regions of the United States, patterns vary. Thus, in Los Angeles, each major Conservative synagogue has its own elementary day school, a development that minimizes conflict, while in cities such as New York, Philadelphia, or Boston, Schechter schools are communal. This had important ramifications for the development of Schechter high schools in the 1990s. There are those who believe that the congregationally based pattern prevented the development of a Conservative high school under the aegis of the University of Judaism in Los Angeles. On the other hand, where leaders of various congregations are used to working cooperatively on Schechter schools, as in northern New Jersey and in Westchester, and Nassau counties in New York, high schools may become the major institutional movement development of the close of the twentieth and beginning of the twenty-first century.

Beyond that, the countrywide bodies wanted to influence the schools, and indeed they have taken credit for fostering the Solomon Schechter network, but neither the United Synagogue nor the Seminary could provide the support needed in personnel or funds, and not much in the way of technical assistance either. As a result, Schechter schools tended to look to the local federations for support and to the market for teachers, both of which undercut the dominance of the organized Movement without necessarily changing the *Masorti* character of the schools. Not surprisingly, many have taken on the characteristics of non-Orthodox community schools with a Conservative name.

In Philadelphia, this has been institutionalized in a particularly detrimental way. While in most of North America, Schechter schools go from *Gan* (kindergarten) through eighth grade—and thus through the age of bar mitzvah and bat mitzvah, an agreement brokered by the Jewish Federation, in return for its support, mandates that the schools end with sixth grade because Akiba, the Jewish community high school, begins with seventh grade, this even though all of the other Schechter and Orthodox schools in the region are K-8. The result is that many children drop out of day school after fifth grade in favor of public middle schools. Moreover, as the community school that "takes over" in seventh grade does not emphasize any religious philosophy, many claim that the support system through bar mitzvah and bat mitzvah and the allegiance to the Masorti Movement are broken. What began as an agreement to bolster the community high school has led to a weakening of that school because of the need to build a whole separate middle school and to the loss of students to the most intensive education offered by the Conservative Movement in the early adolescent years.

Religiously, the schools themselves came to occupy a middle position between the Ramah camps and the *havurot* on one side and the ordinary congregations on the other side. Since they drew from a wide constituency, they could not be as authentically Conservative in an ideological or a *halakhic* sense as the camps or the *havurot*, but neither were they merely sociologically Conservative as in most of the congregations. Their leadership sought more to define a Conservative ideology than a Conservative *halakhah* or sociology, even though they are very important vehicles for the development of all three. This too represents a challenge for the Movement to pick up. Still, some have taken the lead in instructing the teachers about Conservative Judaism, daily prayer is a meaningful reality, and whole communities have been established around the schools.

In time, the Solomon Schechter schools became focal points for institutional involvement on their own. Parents and others concerned with Jewish education became heavily involved with their schools that became, in turn, vehicles for leadership development and avenues for advancement within the community, especially where the tie-ins between the Schechter schools and the Federations were strong. The Schechter school became another constituent agency of the Federation, and strong Schechter school activists could move on into Federation activity.

In some cases, those leaders detoured to take over a congregational presidency, but they found no satisfaction in it so they turned elsewhere, retaining their serious concern with the school as they moved on to other things. Moreover, the parents congregated around the school found in their contacts mutual support for whatever kind of Jewish life they were trying to develop, a support usually lacking in the more amorphous congregations of which they were members, so the schools acquired a social and sociological character as well. Congregational leaders often do not know how to integrate the families with the children in the day school and supplementary school.

This cuts two ways. In one synagogue, all children from the congregation who went to Ramah and had their picture in the synagogue bulletin were labeled "children of the religious school," even though all of them attended Solomon Schechter. In another, in New England, the opposite is the case—the Schechter school meets in the synagogue, and over 200 children from the congregation are enrolled, more than in the synagogue's supplementary school. Here the rabbi worries that the non-day school kids feel inferior!

This whole dilemma is similar to the one faced earlier with integrating Ramah campers into their home synagogues. One day school principal, a former division head at Ramah, says that Ramah is a "subversive institution"—it works! The same is true of Schechter schools. The dilemma is how to structure congregations that can deal with diversity by providing increased opportunities for participation, challenge, and excellence without creating a class system.

In some cases, the parents of children in the Schechter schools found such a high level of mutual interest that they wanted to worship together in the school. This was vigorously attacked by the leadership of existing congregations, which saw it as draining off supporters. It could not view the development of such worship services as the equivalent of groups founding new congregations, since the schools did not fit into the usual congregational mold.

Schechter parents were charged with seeking a "free ride," that is to say, the right to worship without paying synagogue dues. No consideration was given to the fact that they were already paying thousands of dollars in tuition money (it is unlikely that there is a Schechter school in the United States that charges less than $4,000 per student, at least for the first child in a family, far more than the annual dues of any synagogue). This attitude is not only historically wrong (great Conservative congregations such as Beth El in Minneapolis emerged from the Talmud Torah Alumni *minyan* of that city in the 1920s), but it is alienating and self-defeating.

The new institutions are products of elite groups, almost inevitably more traditional than the Conservative Movement's mass membership. This is even true of the Solomon Schechter schools, which are not confined to the leadership group or to the more observant. Hence they appeal to the Movement's cadres or potential cadres, which means that alienating them weakens the whole leadership fabric of the Conservative Movement.

While, as noted, individual rabbis and lay leaders grapple with this issue, it has gone largely undealt with by the Conservative Jewish establishment, which continues to function with the old tripartite structure as though it was all that there was. Indeed, many of the old elites tend to see the emergence of these new institutions as a problem, when in fact they should be seen as offering new opportunities to enrich and deepen Conservative Judaism, to move it from being a tripartite religious structure to a ramified religio-cultural network with connections to the most important spheres of Jewish communal life.

In pursuing this opportunity, the Movement would only be harking back to dimensions of its own ideology when it was emerging as a movement, when its founders saw Conservative Judaism as the avant-garde for the Jewish people as a whole, not simply one party among several. These new institutional developments are manifestations of the dynamism of Conservative Jews; they should be treated by the Movement's establishment as such.

Doing this will require a dramatic reconceptualization of the Movement's institutional structure, but it is a vital, necessary change. It can only be achieved by deliberate, cooperative effort on the part of all segments of the Movement. It should be seen as presenting new opportunities at minimal risk. Were this change to be recognized, accepted, and encouraged, the synagogues would remain the most important local foci for the Movement, but they would no longer have a monopoly on its field organization. They would be supplemented by schools and *havurot* with quasi-independent constituencies of their own, where one could foresee the same kind of interlocking in the local community that one finds in the JTS, the Rabbinical Assembly (RA), and the United Synagogue countrywide. Just as the latter is strengthened for having three components and channels, so too the former would be.

# Chapter 3

# *Ideology and Theology*

Many astute observers of Conservative Judaism—not the least, some of its most prominent lay and rabbinic leaders—sense that there is something amiss with the Movement's ideology or, perhaps more precisely, the extent to which that ideology is understood and the way in which it is being transmitted by rabbis and educators. For example, many Schechter school principals report that their teachers not only fail to transmit an articulated, distinctive philosophy of Conservative Jewish life, but that they would be hard put to define the essence of Conservative Judaism in a clear, concise, and compelling manner. Thus, while most Schechter students can be presumed to have received a quality Jewish and secular education, they may graduate lacking a clear sense of how and why Conservative Judaism offers a preferred way of Jewish living. And if day school students fail to learn the significance of Conservative Judaism, a broad and deep appreciation of Conservative Judaism by Hebrew supplementary school students must be even less common.

The question as to whether or not the Conservative Movement has an ideology, and, if so, what it is, is a perennial one in Conservative circles. In part, this is because the middle-of-the-road position of the Movement has given it a rather eclectic outlook that is not always satisfying, especially for those called upon to defend the Movement's institutional interests who would like to have appropriate ideological reasons for doing so. As part of the Conservative Movement's 100th anniversary efforts at revitalization, a Commission on an Ideology for Conservative Judaism was established, chaired by Professor Robert Gordis. Its task was to clarify the core of beliefs and opinions character-istic of the Conservative community (camp) that distinguishes it from Orthodoxy on the one hand and Reform on the other hand. This Com-mission on Ideology was initially comprised of representatives from the Seminary and the Rabbinical Assembly and was subsequently opened to include lay representatives after the latter protested their exclusion.

The Commission came close to covering the spectrum of ideological positions within the Conservative community, hence it offered consider-able promise for the clarification of the Movement's thinking on a num-ber of important questions. Its members seem to have formed a general consensus on most items of Conservative ideology, including a common approach to *halakhic* interpretation, although not common results.

This chapter will not focus on ideological content per se but on ideological development in the context of the Movement's program and activities. Nevertheless, the results, when published in *Emet Ve-Emunah* ("Truth and Belief"), generally were disappointing.[1] Most Conservative Jews either ignored it or felt that it was full of glittering generalities reflecting the variety of views in the Movement but so har-monized to attain consensus that they were offered few useful guide-lines for action.

Although there have been shifts in Conservative ideology, it would be wrong to suggest that the Movement has been more ideological than it has. In fact, the Movement has been noted within its own ranks as being extremely eclectic and is often criticized for lacking a coherent ideology. No one can deny that eclecticism can be found, especially within Conservative congregations, but it is wrong to assume that this means that there is no ideology. It may reflect a failure of will on the part of the Conservative leadership to enforce whatever rules it makes. Still, the observer can find ideological positions expressed and indeed practiced by those congregations considered the best expressions of Conservative Judaism in each period.

## GOD, TORAH, AND ISRAEL

At some time relatively early on in its history, the leaders of the Conservative Movement sought to articulate Conservative belief through the three dimensions of God, Torah, and Israel. This was and is an appropriate starting point. Virtually all Conservative Jews agree upon the importance of all three elements in the trilogy. The problems begin when these elements have to be translated from slogans into concrete concepts with implications for human behavior.

Of the three, God may be the most problematic. The original founders of the Movement took God for granted. Indeed, both the Sephardim and the Litvaks deemphasized troublesome theological questions, and most of those who found their religious home in the Movement followed the same path, perhaps because the questions were so troubling.

Historically, the Movement's two most eminent theologians were Mordecai M. Kaplan, whose process theology rejected the existence of a personal God, and Abraham Joshua Heschel, whose God was personal in the most mystical sense. These two positions have struggled with one other among those of the Movement's leadership who feel the need to confront theological issues. For most of the rank and file, as in the manner of most Americans, there is perhaps a vague belief in a kind and loving God who does not demand too much, other than that human beings be basically good natured, and who cannot be called upon with any real expectations of response. For a segment of the Movement's elite, there are doubts about the existence of this kind of God.

The Movement's emphasis on Torah and Israel flows in great part from its problems with God. In regard to Torah, the Movement has emphasized the continuing and binding character of Torah as expressed through both tradition and *halakhah*, but with an emphasis on the understanding that the interpretation of Torah changes from generation to generation and has, in certain periods, changed radically. The key to understanding Torah is through the historical-critical method of treating the texts as human or even God inspired and therefore subject to analysis like any other human text. Moreover, such pious but critical analysis is necessary in order to properly understand the texts and draw on them as guides for our own lives. Thus Torah is binding but not immutable in its details—in our terms, a constitution but not a code.

The Seminary reached its greatest excellence in pioneering and developing the historical-critical study of Jewish sacred texts in America, imbuing its students and alumni with a new attitude toward those texts, which is the most visible common denominator among those who have had a serious Jewish education under Conservative auspices. This approach to the sacred texts is the basis for all religious and philosophic speculation in the Conservative Movement. It is an extremely important (if almost overlooked) ingredient of Conservative Judaism, and it cannot be overemphasized in its influence on what makes the Conservative Movement different, even unique, in contemporary Jewish religious life.

Torah also contains a ritual component. For the Conservative Movement, the essence of the Torah's ritual requirements is to be found in the observance of *Shabbat* and *kashrut* (Jewish dietary laws) and the calendar of Jewish holy days and festivals. It is an essentialist model. While Conservative Judaism is committed to the *halakhic* demands of daily prayer and other forms of continuing ritual observance, in fact, its emphasis has been much more limited. Some *mitzvot*, such as the *toharat hamishpaha* (literally "family purity," meaning women's regular use of *mikva*, or ritual bath, and monthly physical separation of husband and wife), have been ignored altogether, neither rejected nor advocated. Other benchmarks include a Conservative understanding of *Shabbat* observance which, since 1951, has included the legitimacy of traveling to synagogue on the Sabbath and of *kashrut* which, by tacit agreement, includes eating otherwise kosher (permitted to be eaten according to Jewish law) foods in restaurants using non-kosher utensils.

It has been difficult enough to bring the average Conservative Jew to observe even the essentialist *mitzvot*. Various studies show that no more than one-third of all of those who consider themselves Conservative Jews really make an effort to observe *Shabbat* (the Sabbath) or *kashrut*, even partially. Perhaps one-quarter regularly attend worship services, and under 10 percent observe *kashrut* outside the home in the Conservative way, as well as inside the home.

Another ideological cornerstone of the Conservative Movement from early in the twentieth century has been its stance on the evolving role of women in public worship and its revisions of gendered references in the liturgy. The earliest manifestations of this stance were the removal of the *mehitzah*, the partition separating women and men during formal prayer, and the participation of mixed gender choirs during services. By 1947, when the Silverman Prayer Book was adopted by the United Synagogue, the reference in the morning benedictions said by Jewish men thanking God for "not making me a woman" (while women thanked God for "making me according to His will") had been changed to the egalitarian "who has made me in the Divine image," to be said by all. As early as 1956, Rabbi Aaron Blumenthal, then chair of the Committee on Law and Standards, wrote a responsum permitting women to be called to the Torah, which allowed the institutionalization of the bat mitzvah. By the late 1950s, many synagogues had introduced late Friday night bat mitzvah ceremonies, and by the mid-1970s, a majority of bat mitzvahs were celebrated on *Shabbat* morning with girls having some Torah honors. While in 1972 just 7 percent of Conservative synagogues granted *aliyot* (Torah honors) to women, by 1976, that figure was 50 percent—truly extraordinary growth by any sociological measure.

The JTS, at first through Kaplan's Teacher's Institute and later through the Seminary College (now List College) and graduate school, opened up the study of classical Jewish texts to women on an advanced level, though as late as 1965 women could not continue on for degrees beyond the B.A. in Talmud, as all graduate rabbinics courses were in the Rabbinical School. In June 1985, the first woman rabbi graduated from the JTS, and the ordination of women as cantors followed soon after. By the end of the century, half of those studying for Ph.D.s in Talmud were women, and the main service for students and faculty was completely egalitarian, even including the names of the matriarchs along with the patriarchs in the opening paragraphs of the *Amidah* prayer (standing silent devotion).

Though a small minority of congregations still struggle with gender issues, by and large, by the close of the 1990s, egalitarianism was the norm in Conservative synagogues. The 1995–1996 study of *Conservative Synagogues and Their Members*, edited by Jack Wertheimer, found a remarkable consensus on gender roles, given the degree of strife over this issue that had characterized the 1970s and 1980s. In fact, describing a major theme of Conservative synagogue life, Wertheimer calls Section 2 of the report "The Triumph of Egalitarianism." After detailing a quarter century of turmoil, he concludes that, "Our surveys indicate that, by the mid-1990s, most of these conflicts have been resolved in favor of women's equality."

Thus though there was some regional variation, in four-fifths of American Conservative synagogues, women were counted in the *minyan*; could lead services; had served as president during the past fifteen years; and bar mitzvah and bat mitzvah celebrants were treated the same way. In Canada, about half of the affiliated synagogues were egalitarian, with 58 percent allowing women to read the Torah and 42 percent counting women in the *minyan*. As it has become normative, gender egalitarianism has lost its association with lenient stands on other matters of Jewish law. The ideology called "traditional-egalitarianism" has become a defining characteristic of fin de siècle Conservative Judaism.

Finally, the Conservative Movement has always taken pride in being committed to *Klal Yisrael* (the whole Community of Israel), which Solomon Schechter referred to as "Catholic Israel," namely, the unity of the entire Jewish people as the basis for testing the legitimacy of any movement within Judaism. At one time, this retarded the growth of Conservative Movement separatism, since Conservative Jewish leaders saw themselves in the vanguard of the emergent American Jewish way of life.[2] To this day, Conservative-sponsored institutions frequently have a serious community dimension (e.g., the Schechter schools), and community institutions adopt the religious practices of Conservative Judaism as the common denominator that will satisfy the vast majority of their constituency. These interlocking arrangements are breaking down as a result of the new Orthodox presence in the community (see below) and the growth in numerical strength of the Reform Movement. The Conservative response has been to seek greater self-definition in separatist terms. This response was stimulated by the antagonism, covert if not overt, between the Conservative congregations and the Jewish community federations and their subsidiary organizations, dating back to the 1950s. In sum, the meaning of the third element in the trilogy is presently unclear.

There are other ideological elements that Conservative Judaism shares with other American Jews, such as strong commitments to: (1) the United States of America and the American way of life; (2) separation of church and state, not only in the American polity but now everywhere, including Israel; and (3) religious pluralism and voluntary individual choice. These basically American elements of Conservative ideology, while not always articulated, have become extremely important to the Movement. Their importance has become particularly manifest as the Movement tries to find a place for itself in Israel, where it is precisely these elements of their ideology that are most foreign to the Israeli scene. Often, the representatives of Conservative Judaism in Israel hold onto them as fervently as their counterparts in the United States. At times, they do so because it is in the best interests of the Movement, but their reasons seem to go beyond even legitimate self-interest to demonstrate how much these principles have become articles of the Conservative Jewish faith, and because they believe that this is part of the unique contribution they can make as American *olim* (immigrants).

## SHIFTS AND STAGES

When the precursors of the Movement were a faction, one could argue that its ideology was adaptation (i.e., remain within the four ells of traditional Judaism, but adapt to the New World). In this respect, it was fully within the Jewish traditional mainstream. As the Movement's institutions took form, the main concern became one of retaining Jews coming from traditional environments who were, by themselves, adapting all too rapidly. Indeed, the goal was to hold them to a framework that would sufficiently conserve tradition in the face of massive adaptation or assimilation. Hence its posture shifted to one of conservatism, as the Movement's name itself suggests, often translated into commitment to changing style to avoid changing substance.

One consequence of this was that the less said about ideology, the better. Stylistic changes, basically in external form or locale of observance, could be introduced without having to formulate more than minimal ideological justification for them. Traditional Jewish religious thought, with its commitment to *halakhah* and *halakhic* procedures, could be maintained as long as major constituencies were not faced with having to acknowledge those traditional positions when they went against their grain. Thus, in ritual matters, it was possible to move the service to a *bimah* in front of the synagogue to recognize the newly dominant roles of rabbi and *hazzan* (cantor) without dealing with the question of how the traditional synagogue organized its internal space; or, to take a more serious issue, to tacitly acknowledge that congregants drove their automobiles to synagogue on Sabbaths and festivals without making any *halakhic* ruling either forbidding or permitting the same. Most of what we know today as Conservative Jewish practice took shape in this period of deliberate ideological haziness.

The one standout exception was Mordecai M. Kaplan, who boldly tackled the central issues of Judaism and modernity head on. Because of his insistence on ideological honesty, he was forced to the periphery of the Conservative Movement, and in the end, he founded his own Reconstructionist Movement, but in fact, Kaplanism became the regnant ideology of Conservative Judaism in everything but overt acknowledgment. To the extent that it developed along the lines enunciated by Kaplan between 1910 and 1935 (roughly), the Conservative Movement had a concrete, broad-based, and even inspiring ideology, focusing on Jewish peoplehood and the unity of Jewish religious expression under changing circumstances. Once the Movement became a party, those grand issues often were set aside or reduced to the level of lip service.

At the very end of this period, three general trends could be perceived in the ideological development of the Conservative Movement. The dominant one—represented by the leaders of the Seminary faculty, such as Professors Finkelstein and Ginzburg—supported the continued avoidance of ideological questions inherent in the gap between Conservative principle and practice. A second trend, represented by rabbis such as Professor Kaplan and Solomon Goldman, advocated far-reaching changes without regard to their *halakhic* validity, arguing that the past should have a vote but not a veto. The third trend, as exemplified by Rabbi David Aronson, advocated radical change through applying *halakhic* methods, thereby preserving the principle that the Conservative Movement remained a *halakhic* movement, and that the *halakhah*, though changed, remained intact. While the first group continued to be dominant through the first postwar generation, by mid-generation, the presence of the third group was being felt, and since the early 1970s, it has become the dominant one.

By the time of the great postwar growth of the Conservative Movement, when congregations were being founded in great numbers, the Movement had come to stand for the right combination of tradition and change for second-generation American Jews, who wanted the warmth of tradition in a modern atmosphere. The Movement itself then shifted its ideology to one of modernization. It became the party, not simply of liberalism, as was the Reform Movement, but the modernization of tradition. Its modernization ranged from the establishment of the principle of desegregation of the sexes in the synagogue to the acceptance of traveling by automobile to the synagogue on Sabbaths and holidays.

During the immediate postwar generation, this modernization remained a cautiously conducted phenomenon. The Talmud faculty at the JTS kept the brakes applied, and the rabbis in the field were of mixed mind, even though many were what were called at the time "Marrano Reconstructionists," in part as a reflection of the contradiction between the rabbis and their congregants. The rabbis were, by and large, committed to traditional observance, but they no longer believed in the traditional rationales for observance. They wanted to continue a rather intense Jewish religious practice but to justify it ideologically in very nontraditional ways. Their congregants, on the other hand, did not want to maintain much in the way of traditional practice but wanted an ideology that supported the claim that nontraditional Judaism required such practice and, most particularly, the belief system that lay behind it.

Both groups wanted modernization for different reasons and in different ways. The rabbis ended up conceding to their congregants more often than not. They preached traditional beliefs and accepted very lax personal practices, often keeping their own ideas to themselves. The fact that they personally maintained a higher level of observance was fine, since that was what their congregants expected from them. The rabbis set the proper tone, even though their congregants did not intend to follow their example.

All that was taught about ideology in Conservative synagogues and schools was that Jewish tradition had always been subject to reinterpretation and change to adapt to conditions in different epochs, and that the Conservative Movement was continuing in that authentic Jewish pattern—as distinct from Orthodoxy, which was frozen, or Reform, which went too far. What that meant more exactly was not clarified.

Meanwhile, in the Movement's intellectual circles, Abraham Joshua Heschel became a powerful influence, rivaling Kaplan. Heschel addressed himself to larger questions of faith and belief in nonrationalistic ways, something needed in the aftermath of the Holocaust, but he did so for all Jews, not specifically for the Conservative Movement. Nor did he address himself to specific issues of Conservative ideology or practice. Indeed, his greatest practical influence was to come in the 1960s, when he played a leading role in the civil rights movement, thereby offering an example of how Judaism should lead to the most vigorous activity on behalf of social justice.

Those who did try to focus on ideological questions did not find a substantial constituency interested in the problems they raised. Indeed, for many Conservative Jews, they were viewed as raising problems that were better left alone. It is only with the passing of the natural constituency of the Conservative Movement, those second- and third-generation Jews who feel most comfortable with Conservative practice and are not much bothered by ideological questions, that it has become necessary to try to define the Movement in ideological terms to make it more attractive for the new generation and at the same time to try to preserve unity in the face of differences of opinion with regard to *halakhic* change.

More recently, there are signs that Conservative ideology has moved from modernizing to "trendy." While this is still far less so than in Reform, which reflects the loss of certain anchors to the right, coupled with the willingness of many, if not most, congregational rabbis to adjust to their congregants' ways, it has led to efforts to keep up with changes in social mores that fail to distinguish between necessary accommodation to external changes and following the latest fads. What distinguishes the Conservative Movement from the Reform

Movement in this regard is that most of its people still seek *halakhic* justification for accepting current trends.

It may be difficult for most of the Conservative Jewish elite to recognize and confront this new reality. Indeed, even those who have accepted the latest fashion are bothered by it. In part, this is because, with the exception of one or two key issues—women's roles being one of them—the shifts in expected observance among the elite have not been that drastic, and indeed, liberalizing trends have almost invariably been followed by more conservative ones, often in paradoxical ways. Thus while the Conservative Movement was moving toward full equality for women, many of the women who were in the forefront of the struggle were themselves on the right wing of Conservative Judaism in matters of observance and other *halakhic* issues. They and their male counterparts developed what are now known as the traditional-egalitarian *havurot* or *minyanim*, because they could not accept the normative suburban congregational service with its concessions to a passive congregation, relatively unfamiliar with Jewish tradition.

Trendiness is a natural hazard in American society, which is so highly committed to "the tradition of the new." It is hard to resist unless one takes a principled, anti-trendy position, and even then it is not easy. Protestant fundamentalists, for example, try to take such a position yet, in fact, they have been subtly reshaped by current trends in American society, almost to the same degree as mainstream Protestants. It is even more difficult for a Jewish movement that seeks to combine tradition and change (i.e., is committed to at least considering the current trends).

American Jews are not only among the first to embrace these trends, but many are leaders in them for reasons that need not concern us here. Moreover, they are good at rationalizing almost anything. That is why Orthodoxy has a greater pull for many people seeking principles in their lives. It, or at least a major segment of the Orthodox camp, can say a flat "no" to change. Not that Orthodoxy is not influenced in some ways, but the flat "no" offers a chance to counteract that influence. Conservative Judaism, in principle, would not want to be in that position. Still, the problem of trendiness must be faced, especially in a movement committed to *halakhah*. In short, the Conservative Movement needs to develop an approach to change that offers consistent guidelines with which to confront a difficult reality.

While explicating and solidifying the core of the Movement, these steps did not satisfy the right wing which, in the fall of 1985, had formed its own group—the Union for Traditional Conservative Judaism (UTCJ). This group took public stands in opposition to decisions of the Committee on Law and Standards of the Rabbinical Assembly and vociferously opposed the ordination of women as rabbis. They eventually established a separate Panel of Halakhic Inquiry, which criticized and rejected the decisions of the Law Committee on the counting of women in the quorum for prayer and the liturgical changes found in *Siddur Sim Shalom*, the prayer book edited by Jules Harlow and published in 1985, which was meant for use in every Conservative synagogue. In 1990, the UTCJ broke completely with the Conservative Movement and later that year changed its name to the Union for Traditional Judaism (UTJ), hoping to encourage moderate Orthodox rabbis to join its ranks.

In 1985 (the same year that the Union for Traditional Conservative Judaism was founded and that the JTS faculty was grappling with the issue of the ordination of women), a Commission on the Philosophy of Conservative Judaism was established by Chancellor Gerson Cohen of the Seminary and Rabbis Alexander Shapiro and Kassel Abelson, immediate past president and president of the Rabbinical Assembly, respectively. Chaired by Rabbi Robert Gordis, it included representatives of the United Synagogue, Women's League for Conservative Judaism, and Federation of Jewish Men's Clubs. Eventually, representatives of the Cantors Assembly and the Jewish Educators Assembly were added as well. In 1988, in conjunction with the Centennial of the JTS, the results of the deliberations of the Commission were published under the title *Emet Ve'Emunah—Statement of Principles of Conservative Judaism*. Rabbi Abelson, with remarkable candor, notes in his foreword to the booklet that:

> For almost a century, it could be argued [this] lack of definition [of Conservative Judaism] was useful since the majority of American Jews wished to be neither Orthodox nor Reform, and therefore joined Conservative organizations. But the situation has radically changed. . . . It is now clear that our avoidance of self-definition has resulted in a lack of self-confidence on the part of Conservative Jews, who are unable to tell others, let alone themselves, what Conservative Judaism stands for. Our goal, then, was to teach members of Conservative congregations to become Conservative Jews. (Foreword: A Personal View)

Eschewing the doctrinaire, the text of the *Statement of Principles* represented a consensus of views within the Movement. Rabbi Gordis notes in his introduction that, "Where more than one position falls within the parameters of Conservative Judaism, that fact is reflected in the *Statement*. Pluralism is a characteristic not only of Judaism as a whole, but of every Jewish school of thought that is nurtured by the spirit of freedom" (p. 14). Nonetheless, he declared that, "All groups within the movement accept the fundamentals of Conservative Judaism which find frequent expression in our *Statement of Principles*" (p. 14).

Gordis, in a clear move toward a platform, then enumerates seven fundamentals. Included in the consensus are: faith in God as the Creator and Governor of the universe; recognition of the *halakhah*, which has never been monolithic or immovable; pluralism as a characteristic of Jewish life and thought through the ages; the rich body of *halakhah* and *aggadah* (literary material) and the later philosophic and mystical literature as a precious resource; viewing all aspects of Jewish law and practice as designed to underscore the centrality of ethics in the life of the Jews; recognition that Israel plays an essential role in our present and future; and, finally, the fact that Jewish law and tradition, properly understood and interpreted, will enrich Jewish life and help mold the world closer to the prophetic vision of the Kingdom of God.

The *Statement* deals with thorny issues such as revelation, messianism, the problem of evil, the covenant and the election of Israel, the status of women, and relations among Jews and between Jews and those of other faiths. A study guide was written for the brief (fifty-page) document, and courses based on it were offered in many synagogues during the last years of the decade of the 1980s. However, the *Statement* has not come into normative usage as a "text," regularly cited in the way that the various platforms of the UAHC have been utilized. Perhaps this is because more than one position is voiced on some critical issues.

More comprehensible lines of demarcation between the movements were drawn for Conservative Jews by the acceptance of the ordination of women as rabbis and cantors, on the one hand, and the rejection of patrilineal descent on the other hand. A decade after the publication of *Emet Ve'Emunah*, it is the confrontation between Conservative and Orthodox Jews in the diaspora and with the Israeli religious establishment, in coalition with the current Israeli government and non-Orthodox Jews, that has highlighted the identity of Conservative Jews. Nevertheless, it was an important decision to convene the commission and to publish the *Statement*. The whole process was a sign of reassessment of elite-mass relationships that was initiated a decade ago and that continues under the aegis of the current chancellor, Rabbi Ismar Schorsch.

## BENCHMARKS AND BOUNDARIES

What this really means, however, is that the Conservative Movement is constantly looking for benchmarks that will give it ideological identity. These are of two kinds: a solid core of beliefs, opinions, and practices around which to rally and clear lines of differentiation at the periphery from Orthodoxy on the one hand, and Reform on the other hand. At the solid core today, there seem to be certain slogans that pass for ideology: the balancing of tradition and change; faithfulness to *halakhah* but willingness to make it evolve in truly new directions; and understanding Jewish tradition historically. It would be good to investigate whether these have any content beyond the slogan level.[3]

Throughout the postwar generation, the two benchmarks were *Shabbat* and *kashrut*, both important but, in the context, problematic. Rabbis would preach on the need to observe both, but they were not in the position to enforce observance. Furthermore, in light of the new vistas of postwar America, neither benchmark had the compelling character that could compete with the vision of the reborn State of Israel.

With regard to the boundaries, Rabbi Kassel Abelson has suggested that, as a result of recent issues in Jewish religious life, the Conservative Movement has taken some clear-cut stands that set it apart from Reform on the one hand and Orthodoxy on the other hand, which have real ideological content and which can be explained to anybody, anywhere. In regard to Reform, the Conservative rejection of patrilineal descent is the crucial dividing line. It is a clear signal that the Conservative Movement is *halakhic* and will not make changes that are not legitimate within the framework of *halakhah*, or at least cannot be justified *halakhically*.[4] In regard to Orthodoxy, the Conservative Movement's full acceptance of equal citizenship for women in every facet of Jewish life clearly sets the two movements apart. This view has been articulated by JTS Chancellor Ismar Schorsch as part of his effort to clarify where Conservative Judaism stands in the spectrum of American Jewish life.

The women's issue also shows that, within *halakhah*, the Conservative Movement is prepared to carry change to its ultimate conclusion. What began as mixed seating culminated in the ordination of women as rabbis and cantors and, as far as some rabbis are concerned, the requirement that women accept the full yoke of the Torah and *mitzvot* just like adult Jewish men.

In addition to the principle of the full equality of Jews, male and female, the Conservative Movement takes clear ideological stances against the performance of mixed marriages (where one of the partners is not Jewish, or not *halakhically* converted to Judaism). Its critical approach to the sacred texts, that is to say, attempting to understand them as historic and not simply as sacred documents through the application of scientific method to their study, is part of its ideology. Making *halakhic* decisions through the Law Committee instead of through individual *posekim* (arbiters of Jewish law) may be on its way to becoming an ideological principle, as is the *mara d'atra* principle that the local rabbi is authoritative when choosing among minority opinions of the Law Committee.

The question of the role of peoplehood as a touchstone in Conservative ideology is quite important, since it reflects another set of ambivalences between ideology and practice. If there was anything that gave the movement a benchmark other than its approach to *halakhah*, it was *Klal Yisrael*. But, once again, the institutional needs of the Movement and the congregations came between an active commitment to *Klal Yisrael* and the reality. On the simplest level, if individual congregations and their leaders could not get together to support the collective institutions of the Conservative Movement, it was hardly likely that they would provide more than verbal support for the collective institutions of the Jewish people in whatever arena, locally, countrywide, or worldwide.

A similar ambivalence developed with regard to Zionism. On the one hand, as the foremost expression of *Klal Yisrael*, Zionism became an article of faith for many of the Movement's founders. In its case, however, localistic limits of congregations came into contradiction with Zionist efforts as well as the institutional interests of the Seminary itself. Seminary leadership early on became committed to a Babylonia and Jerusalem model of Jewish peoplehood, in which the United States would be a center of Jewish life equal to Israel. While this view did not prevent many individual Conservative Jews, including important members of the top leadership, from supporting the Zionist enterprise and the rebuilding of Jewish life in *Eretz Yisrael* (the Land of Israel), it did mean that the very top leadership of the Movement was so much more concerned about building up Jewish life in the United States that it often seemed to denigrate the Zionist enterprise.[5]

Moreover, in the period after World War II, when the Conservative Movement was in the midst of its most rapid growth, it was also most closely identified with the triple melting pot theory developed by Will Herberg, dominant in religious intellectual circles at that time.[6] Judaism and Americanism were seen as so compatible and Jews as integrating so well into American society that the Conservative establishment did not want to rock the boat by suggesting any reservations on the part of Jews. Thus, for a while, in the early 1950s, Chancellor Finkelstein promoted the adoption of a separate Jewish flag of two blue stripes on a white field with the Ten Commandments (deliberately taken from the U.S. Jewish chaplains' insignia) to replace the old Jewish flag, by then the flag of Israel. In this, as in other ways, he was unable to compete with the compelling force of Israel, which so captured the imagination of the Jewish people, and after a few years, the idea was quietly dropped.

In most respects, though, Finkelstein and his people made it clear that America came first in their eyes, a position that continued to be articulated by Finkelstein's successor, Gerson Cohen. This is not to suggest that either man was less than seriously concerned with the fate of the Jewish state, only that their ideological and institutional commitments coalesced to make them the foremost exponents of diasporism in our time, more so than either the Reform or the Orthodox (excluding, of course, those ultra-ultras among the latter who reject the state altogether and most of the diaspora as well). It would be unfair not to recognize the ways in which Israel has become an important part of the Conservative Movement. We will discuss those below, but the old ambivalences are still there.

Recent survey data shows that Conservative Jews stand between Orthodox and Reform in their involvement with Israel, as they do in most other matters. It is important to know, however, that on the most intense measures of involvement, Conservatives are closer to the relatively alienated Reform than to the Orthodox, who are more heavily involved and knowledgeable about matters pertaining to Israel.

The sum total of all of this is that in the postwar generation, the Conservative Movement—the movement most visibly committed to Jewish peoplehood—moved in a different direction than virtually all of American Jewry on the *Klal Yisrael* issue. The Movement did not develop any vehicles through which to comfortably express its commitment, so the commitment declined as part of the ideology, thus increasingly detaching the Conservative Movement from the major trends of contemporary Jewish life.

Perhaps ironically, this was an aspect of Conservative movement ideology that leading members of its congregations took most seriously. They were the backbone of just about every communal organization. In time, this became true even of the Council of Jewish Federations, whose leaders for the first generation were drawn primarily from members of Reform congregations. Members of Conservative congregations also were the least likely to demur from contributing to Jewish causes on narrow ideological grounds.

In one of his first acts as chancellor, Professor Schorsch undertook to define where the Conservative Movement stood in the spectrum of American Jewish life, in what the *New York Times* referred to as "a new Conservative manifesto." The chancellor's concern with this issue at the very beginning of his tenure reflected its importance. Basically, his manifesto was a strong advocacy of the middle road. He concluded his message as follows, "In its struggle for balance, integrity and moderation, Conservative Judaism is most authentically Jewish. Firmly planted in the soil of tradition, Conservative Judaism is capable of withstanding the blandishments and absorbing the wisdom of its surroundings."

# Chapter 4

# *Style*

Social scientists have learned over the years that, along with ideology and institutions, the style of a social movement is at least equally important in determining who will be its adherents. *The American Heritage Dictionary* defines style as "the way in which something is said or done, as distinguished from its substance" and "the combination of distinctive features of . . . expression, execution or performance characterizing a particular person, people, school, or era."[1] In the last analysis, people find their way into situations because of the harmony of the institutional culture with their personal styles.

Much of the style of a movement is determined by its founders and, unless the movement is refounded at a later date, its initial style is hard to change, since like attracts like. Since the Conservative Movement went through two foundings, the first 100 years ago and the second under Solomon Schechter two decades later, both are reflected in the Movement's style.

## SEPHARDIM AND LITVAKS

The first founders of the Conservative Movement included an exceptionally high proportion of Sephardim or German Jews raised in

Sephardic congregations ("the Philadelphia group"), while the founders who built the Movement as we know it today included an exceptionally high proportion of Litvaks (Jews from Lithuania and surrounding regions).[2] Both of these are important elements in the Conservative equation. Given the Sephardic penchant for moderate traditionalism and openness to the larger world, it was hardly an accident that at the time traditional Judaism was splitting into Orthodox and non-Orthodox wings over the question of modernization and adaptation, so many of the Sephardic congregations or at least their leaders opted for modernization and adaptation. In that, they paralleled what was happening in the Old World in the nineteenth century, when the Ashkenazic (Jews from European countries) rabbinate was becoming increasingly inflexible, while the Sephardic rabbinate sought ways to accommodate the rapid social and technological changes of the age. The Sephardic influence in that sense may continue to be felt in establishing the fundamental principle of combining tradition and change, but it was a limited influence that was replaced by that of the Litvaks, a powerful group in general, headed in this case by powerful intellects.

We can recognize several consequences that arose from this Litvak influence. One has already been mentioned, that is, the role of the JTS as a modern *yeshiva*. Another was the adoption of *Nusah Ashkenaz* as the basis for the Conservative *siddur* (prayer book) and the consequent disappearance of *Nusah Sepharad*—which is not Sephardic, but a kabbalistic (mystical)-Hassidic adaptation of the Sephardic *minhag* (custom)—from the non-Orthodox American Jewish community (this at a time when Israel was being settled by the children and grandchildren of Hassidim who brought an equivalent modernized and secularized Hassidic influence to that country). The predisposition to introduce decorum into the services in a rigid way also was present in the Litvaks, whose characteristic austerity could be translated into decorousness under the conditions of American society. It would be interesting to trace the backgrounds of those latter-generation Conservative Jews who introduced spirit and singing into the services to see where their forebears came from in Eastern Europe. In other words, the Conservative Movement developed a penchant for austere intellectualism on the part of its elites that became part of the style of the Movement.

As the Litvaks gained in influence, the role of the Sephardim declined. We are not suggesting that this was a matter of cause and effect. In part, what happened is that the original Sephardic congregations that helped found the Seminary in 1886 decided to remain within the Orthodox fold when the Conservative Movement crystallized as a separate one two decades later, hence their rabbis had to go with them. These Sephardic congregations continued to recruit rabbis from among JTS graduates as late as the 1950s. For example, Louis Gerstein became the principal rabbi at Shearith Israel in New York and Ezekiel Musleah the rabbi of Mikveh Israel in Philadelphia, although the congregations themselves were affiliated with the Orthodox Union.

Another opportunity to reach out to the Sephardim presented itself after World War II, when the leadership of the Sephardic congregations in the United States came to the Jewish Theological Seminary for support in training rabbis and functionaries for their congregations, preferring the Conservative Movement to Orthodoxy, but at that point the Conservative leadership was interested in building a mass movement, not in reaching out to that small segment of American Jewry. Instead, Yeshiva University saw the opportunity and stepped in, winning the support—at times reluctant—of the Sephardic leadership who had nowhere else to go. While the loss to the American Sephardim, who even today represent no more than 3 percent of American Jewry, was not noticeable, this has had great consequences with regard to the Conservative Movement worldwide, since a strong Sephardic dimension in American Conservative Judaism would have made it easier for the Masorti Movement in Israel to reach out to what could have been its natural constituency (which will be discussed later) and may even have helped in Latin America.

Today there are a few Sephardic congregations identified with the Conservative Movement, most of which have Ashkenazic rabbis, but they are on the peripheries of the Movement as a whole. What remains are elements of moderation that may or may not have their roots in the Sephardic origins of the Movement.


## ELITE AND MASS

The distinction between elite and mass, which is perhaps more characteristic of Conservative Judaism than of any of the other branches of Judaism, also fits into the Litvak pattern translated to the American scene. While all of Eastern European Jewry in its last century suffered from the problem of an educated elite dominating a relatively uneducated mass (who nevertheless were very observant, since they lived within a Jewish framework), this was particularly characteristic of Lithuania and environs from whence the Litvaks came. Further to the south, the Hassidic Movement developed in the eighteenth century precisely to counteract that elite-mass division, but it did not penetrate the Litvak world.

In contemporary Orthodoxy, whose small numbers make them in a certain sense a self-contained elite, the elite-mass distinction has virtually disappeared. It continues to exist only in connection with great *talmidei hakhamim* (religious scholars) and *posekim* (religious decision makers). Even so, the ordinary Orthodox Jew shares in the same activities as his *gedolim* (great scholars), only he does them less well or less intensively. In the Reform Movement, on the other hand, the differences between leaders and members are essentially differences of role, not of expectation, of either religious knowledge or religious practice. In the Conservative Movement, the elites were and are expected to be more observant and more knowledgeably Jewish than the masses, so much so that Conservative Judaism is one of the few phenomena in Jewish or American life where the elite-mass distinction is truly important.

The distance between elites and the public in the Conservative Movement was institutionalized in the first decade of the twentieth century. This has had some positive consequences. According to Mordecai Waxman, this concentration

> made it possible for the more traditional elements in individual congregations to exercise a greater control over synagogue patterns than they would be entitled to by their numbers. [(Thus,)] the Conservative movement has, in the past, successfully operated on the assumption that if guidance were forthcoming and properly communicated, it would be accepted.[3]

This view holds that the layperson as the privileged recipient of Torah from his or her teachers or rabbis who should be honored to provide fiscal support for the institutions that will preserve Jewish learning in America has been institutionalized. However, it also has its counterproductive aspects. The United Synagogue and its leadership have suffered from decades of "benign neglect" on the part of the Seminary and its leaders; both lay and professional are rife with alienation. In the short run, the policy of disattention isolated the Seminary from the need to be pragmatic. There could be little pressure from a lay public that did not understand, or a rabbinate that treated the faculty with veneration. Indeed, Waxman contends that the clerical elitism of the Movement has been a basic policy.

The Seminary and the Movement have paid a considerable price for this policy. Because of it, laypeople have often been discouraged and even precluded from dealing with ideology and basic policies. Indeed, few of the best of the voluntary leadership were attracted to become active in the Movement, even if many of them were members of Conservative synagogues. While enhancing the influence of the Seminary and its scholars, this has also contributed to the abandonment of ritual observances by a majority of the laity. Laypeople felt that their rabbis should be public models of piety, while their own private practice could lapse. Thus while the rabbi was expected to strictly observe *kashrut* and *Shabbat*, for instance, even the officers and board members of the congregation did not need to do so. This policy may even have prevented the inculcation of a sense of personal responsibility for fulfilling *mitzvot* to the majority of the laity. Without grounding in Jewish law, without a sense of its relevance or power to give meaning and personality to their everyday lives, the laity have often been content to be a silent majority.

Ironically, those who get involved—to the left, to the right, or in the middle—are sometimes inspired to remove themselves from the establishment Conservative congregations. Thus many of the most successful products of Ramah, the United Synagogue Youth, and the Solomon Schechter Day Schools, rejecting this secondary and passive role in the Movement and its synagogues, have gone on to found *havurot*, the former Union for Traditional Conservative Judaism (UTCJ), and some have left for Reconstructionist synagogues or modern Orthodoxy. In this regard, the founders of the UTCJ and of the *Havurah* Movement were similar. Both stressed personal commitment to *mitzvot*, to regular communal worship, study, and celebration. Both groups argued that the laity must reclaim its power through real rather than delegated participation in religious life, whether through leading worship or visiting the sick.[4]

We have already suggested that one of the characteristics of Conservative Judaism is a standard of observance that is acknowledged by the membership but principally honored in the breach. In effect, only the elite is expected to maintain that level of observance. With regard to Jewish knowledge, both elites and masses anticipate that the latter will not know all that much, while the elites definitely shall. Thus the Movement has been polarized between a small elite core and a large mass membership.

Daniel J. Elazar and Charles Liebman have estimated that there are no more than 40,000 to 50,000 members of that core, that is, people who live up to the standards of Conservative Judaism as defined by its leadership and who see themselves as Conservative Jews. Most of them are *klei kodesh* (religious officiants) or their families—rabbis, educators, cantors, with a small number of congregants—this in a movement that claims 1.25 to 1.5 million adherents. The consequences of this are great. While there is some co-optation of new members of the elite from among the younger members of the mass in every generation, as a few young people raised in ordinary Conservative households choose the rabbinate or other Jewish fields or simply become more observant, the elite families seem to marry among one another as was true among the rabbinical families in the Old World. This adds to their already extraordinary separation from the masses with whom they communicate only in an official capacity. Except when unavoidable because of family ties, social relations between the elite and mass are minimal. Indeed, there is every indication that the elites feel very uncomfortable with the masses in the Movement.

There are signs that a group of more serious Conservative Jews, albeit not as observant or knowledgeable as those in the elite, is developing among those who stay with Conservative Judaism after the third generation. Many are products of the Ramah camps, USY, and Jewish day schools. They may share a common language with the elite, and in due course they may come to serve as a bridge between the two groups, but that still seems to be in the future since a gap remains in connection with both observance and knowledge. Still, they represent a real hope and a challenge for overcoming what is an unfortunate dimension of the contemporary Conservative Movement. As such, they should be targeted for special encouragement.

## RABBINICAL PREEMINENCE

Another consequence of this separatism is that with the possible exception of Hassidism, the Conservative Movement is probably the most rabbinically dominated movement in the clericalist sense to have ever existed in Jewish life.[5] This point should be understood clearly. It is not a suggestion that individual rabbis dominate their congregations in every case. It has already been noted that all too many are at the mercy of congregational boards that do not always have the Jewish knowledge or commitment or the milk of human kindness desirable for proper human relations. Our point has to do with how the rabbis with the highest status in the Movement act and who controls which positions within the Movement's organizational structure.

Even in the days of the worst oligarchical control in Eastern Europe, when an alliance of the leading rabbis and the richest *baalei batim* controlled the communities, clericalism was not the issue. Indeed, only in modern times has the title "rabbi" become professionalized. There was no equivalent distinction for what we refer to today as "rabbis" and "laypeople."

In the Conservative Movement, rabbis whose primary function is not as *posekim* but as some combination of *rebbe* (spiritual mentor) and priest, pastor and counselor,[6] dominate every aspect of the Movement. They make the recruitment of serious non-rabbinic leadership more difficult, because they give lay leaders little room to bloom beyond the congregational boardroom where they may have no choice, and most often exclude non-rabbis from positions of importance in the Movement.

This kind of rabbinical preeminence is quite a new phenomenon in Jewish life, a product of the adoption of Christian models in the process of American modernization. It is a relatively minor issue in Orthodoxy, where the powerful and most respected rabbis are *posekim* who do not partake of the clerical dimension of the modern rabbinic role. In fact, the Mizrahi was actually founded to resist the domination of those rabbis within the Orthodox camp. In any case, there is an interplay between rabbis and non-rabbis. Indeed, since so many Orthodox men spend some time studying in *yeshivot*, the distinction is not entirely clear. In any Orthodox community, there are many *musmahim* (fully ordained rabbis) who do not consider themselves rabbis in the clerical sense.

All of this goes against the grain of Jewish tradition from biblical times onward, which holds that God has granted authority to three separate domains that came to be known in the Mishnah as the *keter torah* (Torah rule), *keter malkhut* (civil rule), and *keter kehunah* (priestly rule).[7] The *keter torah*, entrusted in ancient times first to prophets, then to *sofrim* (scribes), then to sages, and in our time to *posekim* and *dayanim* (judges), is the channel through which God teaches Torah to His people, for the past 2,500 years through the sacred texts of Judaism. The *keter malkhut* is responsible for the civil rule of the Jewish people through which its communal business is conducted. It was dominated at various times by elders, *nesi'im* (magistrates), *negidim* (commissioners), judges, kings, and *parnassim* (officers). The *keter kehunah*, dominated by priests and Levites in the period from the Exodus to the destruction of the Second Temple, then passed into the hands of *hazzanim* (cantors) and, in our time, to congregational rabbis. Its task is to give the people a channel through which to communicate with God through ritual and sacerdotal activities. The complete Jewish community has to have manifestations of all three domains, of which no more than two can be linked with one another in the same personae. The only exceptions to this have been the prophet Samuel, who briefly tried to control all three domains and failed, and the Hassidic *rebbes*, who since the eighteenth century have served small portions of the Jewish people in that capacity. Indeed, even individual synagogue congregations rarely embraced all three domains, except in the smallest Jewish communities where the entire community was part of a single congregation.

While from the days of the Pharisees to our times, the *keter torah* was accorded a predominant role, all three *ketarim* continued to function in one way or another. Modern non-Orthodox Judaism brought with it two changes. The effort to adapt Jewish life to the conditions of emancipation brought with it an emphasis on the synagogue as being distinct from the congregation (a term whose original meaning embraced civil as well as religious dimensions to life) and the attenuation of the nonritual functions of Jewish life. As a result, the modern synagogue has found its appropriate location at the intersection of the *keter torah* and the *keter kehunah*. Thus the way was open for the synagogue to claim a greater role in Jewish life and for the rabbi as the leader of the synagogue to claim a preeminent role. For the Conservative rabbi, the temptation was particularly great.

The rabbis who came into close contact with the people essentially ceased to be called upon as *posekim* and became representatives of the *keter kehunah* because the people demanded that of them. In doing so, they became dominant in their congregations, in the manner of Christian priests and ministers. Conservative rabbis tried to combine both *ketarim* in their role.

Significantly, Orthodoxy has preserved the old pattern. Indeed, with the important exception of the Hassidic *rebbes* and their courts, the more Orthodox and more faithful it is to the tradition. Thus the structure of Agudath Yisrael with its *Moetzet Gedolai Hatorah* (Council of Torah Sages) dominant but sharing power with its political leaders is a good example. Modern Orthodoxy, under the influence of Samson Raphael Hirsch, went in a direction similar to the non-Orthodox movements, but in Israel it has since changed back as a result of Zionism. In this respect, Orthodoxy maintains the distinction between the *keter malkhut* and the *keter torah* as separate domains, even if *keter torah* is accorded a favored position, while *keter kehunah* is confined to minor functionaries. Thus Orthodox Judaism, with its strong emphasis on *keter torah,* hardly pays attention to congregational rabbis. Real authority and power are in the hands of the *posekim.*

The modern Reform rabbinate was founded on the premise that the rabbi should become the representative of the *keter kehunah* rather than the *keter torah,* since *halakhic* decision making was no longer relevant, but priestly and pastoral functions were. Even so, in the American Reform Movement, the non-rabbinical leadership has always been very strong, as witnessed by the strength of the Union of American Hebrew Congregations vis-à-vis the Central Conference of American Rabbis. Basically, the Reform rabbi's "edge" over the lay leaders is in superior or rabbinical knowledge of ritual procedures. As it happens, most Reform rabbis, without being Jewish scholars, know more than their constituents, but only those who make the effort actively utilize that knowledge in their work.

While the Conservative Movement was reluctant to accept the modern definition of the rabbinate put forward by Reform Judaism, in fact, its rabbis have also slid over into the *keter kehunah* in terms of their congregational functions, while at the same time maintaining a self-image as bearers of the *keter torah.* Most Conservative congregational rabbis seek to combine both, while emphasizing the latter. This is reflected in the slow change of the JTS Rabbinical School curriculum.[8]

It can be said that the ideal Conservative rabbi uses the functions of the *keter kehunah* to teach Torah. There is every sign that those who are successful in making this combination are the most satisfied and fulfilled—another sign that this is an appropriate combination under the circumstances. On the other hand, where the functions are confused and where the gap between the realities of performing the functions of the *keter kehunah* (such as orchestrating rites of passage or announcing pages at religious services) and the desire to represent the *keter torah* becomes too great, problems arise.

Initially, this rabbinical preeminence developed because of the wide gap between the elite and the mass in Jewish knowledge and observance. At the same time, it failed to take into account the existence of an important, active, and vital non-rabbinical segment in the elite that always had been present. Indeed, a proper history of the Movement would show that in many cases Conservative congregations were developed first by knowledgeable Jews, who later imported rabbis from the JTS who were more suited to their rather clear-cut ideas of how tradition and change should be combined, to serve their own needs. These people were products of good Jewish education in Europe or of good Talmud Torah education in the United States.

Later, a new generation that had passed through the Ramah camps but did not enter the rabbinate could have filled the same roles, but by that time, Seminary and Conservative Movement policy, pushed by the then chancellor of the Jewish Theological Seminary, was clearly in favor of rabbinical dominance. The result has been to transform what was initially an unavoidable weakness into an institutionalized arrangement, compounding its weakening effects.

This change has had wider importance because as rabbis reconciled themselves to their new role and found that their dominance of the *keter kehunah* was the source of their authority and power, they began to emphasize that domain at the expense of others. Rabbis such as David Aronson, Jacob Agus, Ben Zion Bokser, Theodore Friedman, Solomon Goldman, Robert Gordis, Simon Greenberg, Isaac Klein, and Morris Silverman, all congregational rabbis who did find time to make significant scholarly contributions, were exceptions and, by and large, they did not do so at the expense of their congregational responsibilities. Their congregants' regard for them was not based upon those contributions, except in the case of a few appreciative leaders.

Even if they would have preferred emphasizing the *keter torah*, the lack of a constituency for more than the most elementary expressions of Torah and the attractions of even those who would otherwise not be in their constituency but who needed their services for the *keter kehunah* reinforced this dimension of American Judaism in both the Reform and Conservative movements. However, while the Reform Movement had social action as another dimension in which its rabbis had learned to function and in which their role was well accepted, Conservative rabbis tended to remain within their congregations, resting on claims of the centrality of the synagogue in Jewish life to build up their positions and the position of their institutions. This had the additional result of further isolating the Conservative Movement from the larger Jewish world, since it came at a time of a major power shift away from the synagogue in Jewish life.

As a result of the rise of Zionism and other secularizing trends, our age has witnessed a historic shift in the internal balance of power within the Jewish people, replacing the *keter torah* with the *keter malkhut* as the dominant domain. Jews whose religious beliefs and practices have been much weakened have been stimulated in their Jewish identity (itself a modern concept) as a result of the reestablishment of the State of Israel, and they have found ways to express that identity through those instrumentalities that reflect the *keter malkhut* in our time, all of which are tied closely to Israel in one way or another. This situation has been intensified by the sharpening of the division between Orthodox and non-Orthodox, whereby the former will not recognize the latter in anything that has to do with the domain of *keter torah* but will sit with them in institutions falling within the *keter malkhut*.

In the United States today, the *keter malkhut* belongs to the Jewish community federations, institutions in which rabbis do not play a major, much less a preeminent, role, per se. Conservative congregations and their rabbis must accept this fact and must find their place within a community structure in which fund-raising and overall community planning belong to the federations and also find ways to play an even more significant role within this framework. There are some fine examples in the United States of Conservative congregations and rabbis who play such a role—in Minneapolis, for example—that are worth emulating. Moreover, as local and countrywide demographic surveys continue to demonstrate, the link between synagogue membership and contributions to the Federation is very strong. The federations themselves have started to reach out to synagogue leadership accordingly. At least since the late 1970s, the trend has been to achieve a communal structure resting upon both the synagogues and the federations as its pillars.

There is a modest reflection of the tripartite division within synagogues as well, with the board of directors representing the vestiges of the *keter malkhut*. But the modern synagogue is an institution whose *kehunah* (priesthood) and Torah functions are so pronounced that the rabbi who represents those two domains must, perforce, be preeminent.

In the meantime, in the Jewish world as a whole, the *keter torah* may well be undergoing a reconstitution of its own from its relatively monolithic character prior to the nineteenth century to a more pluralistic one. The Conservative rabbinate is presently struggling for its share in this reconstituted *keter torah*, but it is unclear as to what responsibilities it wishes to accept within that *keter* (crown). Does the Conservative Movement wish to develop its own system of *kashrut* supervision and *shochtim* (ritual slaughterers), its own *mohelim* (circumcision specialists), its own *mikvaot* (ritual baths), even if only for converts?[9] The Movement is already developing its own *posekim*. These are questions that it will have to ask itself and answer over the coming decades. What are the advantages of doing so? What are the risks of greater internal disunion within the Jewish people if that is done?


SYNAGOGISM

This ties in with another element of the style of Conservative Judaism, its strong synagogal focus within a congregational framework. This is not at all unreasonable in the American context, and saying so is not a criticism. The modern synagogue is what it is, and it serves a vital purpose, but it is part of a community, not a community itself.

Nor can the modern congregation replicate the old *kahal*. First, in a voluntary setting in which the Jews are fully integrated into the larger society, they do not need institutions of such comprehensiveness, nor do they seek them. Beyond that, modern specialization being what it is and contemporary Jewish communities being as large as they are, outside of the very smallest communities, no one institution is able to play the role that the old *kahal* did when all Jewish communities were very small. Today, many individual synagogues have more members than major Jewish communities in the past. The very size of the American Jewish community and most of the local communities in which Jews reside requires institutional professional specialization, so congregations cannot be comprehensive in the old ways. That specialization has led to the development of other institutions to serve many of the traditional functions of the Jewish community, capped by the Jewish community federations.

The Conservative Movement must build and reinforce existing ties with the larger community so that it interacts with the cosmopolitan institutions of the community in ways that are mutually reinforcing rather than seeking to compete with or ignore them, two approaches that certainly weaken the Movement.

The synagogue-center was designed to compete with this trend, but it did not work. It could not. In fact, even in those areas where the synagogue-center could have worked, it did not because too few Jews looked to the synagogue to play that kind of central role. This is even more true today, when even Jewish community centers that once thrived because they provided places for sports and exercise are in trouble. Private sports and exercise clubs that have developed to serve the growing market do the job for less and do it more effectively. In that respect, the synagogues do best when they stick to that which they can do best, namely, to provide religious services and education within a sufficiently well developed social environment to attract people whose Jewish religious inclinations are in any case attenuated.

What synagogues do best is serve the localistic and private needs of Jews. They fail when they try to compete in serving cosmopolitan ones. This is why the synagogue leadership, other than perhaps some of the rabbis, tends to be comprised of those who find satisfaction in helping satisfy localistic needs. Even cosmopolitans have such needs, which is why cosmopolitans will become synagogue members, even if not leaders.[10] The synagogue specializes in meeting the needs of the private agenda of Jews.

Because of the strong synagogal-congregational commitment of the Conservative Movement and the importance of the synagogue-center in its earlier ideology, this has been a difficult point for its leaders to accept. For many years, the Movement tried to compete with the other institutions of the community, particularly the Jewish community centers that they saw as arms of the federations. Hence they saw themselves as competitors with the Federation itself. This was intensified by the competition for voluntary leadership, in which the synagogues inevitably came in second. This competition reached its height during the decades of Conservative Movement triumphalism in the first half of the postwar generation, when it looked as though the synagogue could indeed expand into areas that had been outside its purview. But despite the rhetoric, there was no way the synagogues could, either subjectively or objectively, compete with the federations and these other forces.

The competition itself was a phenomenon identified primarily with the Conservative Movement. Because Reform Judaism did not see being Jewish as a matter of a comprehensive way of life but rather as a form of religious expression, Reform congregations did not try to do more than provide religious services, perhaps in the broader sense of religious school as well as worship, but not much beyond that. Postwar trends in the other direction were implantations from outside the Reform Movement, and they have not particularly succeeded.

Orthodoxy, precisely because it sees the Jewish way of life as being comprehensive, does not need to put the whole burden for being Jewish on the *shul*. In fact, a *shul* might be hardly more than a *minyan*, a separate group for prayer that is not responsible for sponsoring any other activities except perhaps traditional study groups, while other institutions do the rest. The Orthodox developed Jewish education outside of the synagogue through separate day schools rather than synagogue schools (though there have been a few notable exceptions, such as the Ramaz School in New York) and have most of their other institutions equally separate. It was and is the ideology of the Conservative Movement that insisted on or strongly favored including schools, social activities, and sports and recreation within its synagogues. Thus, with the exception of overnight camps and, in some cases, day schools, the Movement has generally rejected efforts to develop such institutions outside of the synagogue.

The congregation is a wonderful institution. It is portable and easily established. Even the edifice complex-building fund syndrome that plagues so much of American Jewry has not changed that.[11] The flexibility of the Movement, its ability to respond to internal and external changes in the way that it has, is closely linked to its congregational character. This is true whether we are talking of moving synagogues as neighborhoods change or changing their internal character as populations shift. All told, this is a precious dimension of Jewish life in general and the Conservative Movement specifically.

On the other hand, the kind of synagogism that has become dominant in the Conservative Movement has: reinforced some of its counterproductive trends; heightened the clerical dimension of the rabbinate (this despite their own self-image as teachers); assured that the bulk of the lay leadership would be drawn from among locals rather than cosmopolitans; and at least, until recently, offered the elite no institutions of their own, only positions serving the masses, thereby strengthening the elite-mass distinction.

The Conservative Movement is certainly not going to abandon its synagogue base, nor should it, as that is the great source of its strength. But it is necessary to supplement and broaden that base with other institutions giving the Movement additional opportunities for member identification.

## RELIGIOUS OBSERVANCE

Over the years, there has evolved a Conservative Jewish style of religious observance, honored by the elite and honored mostly in the breach by the mass membership but implicitly recognized for what it is, distinct from both Orthodox and Reform and, more recently, Reconstructionist. Ritual observance patterns form an important element in the shaping of Conservative Jewish identity and distinctiveness that has not always been presented for what it is. It is possible to identify several key elements that coalesce to constitute this style.

First is a commitment in principle to *halakhah*, along with an openness to *halakhic* change, either on an individual congregational basis or through the mediation of the Rabbinical Assembly Law Committee. This is coupled with individual selectivity in responding to *halakhic* demands. This means that while *halakhah* remains the benchmark, *halakhic* observance is not pursued consistently as it is among the Orthodox. For many members, *halakhah* becomes a kind of abstraction, treated concretely only from time to time. Perhaps the best way to describe the distinction is to suggest that for many Conservative Jews, *halakhah* is considered the expression of a constitution—the Torah—emphasizing general principles, rather than as a code emphasizing details of daily life as it is for Orthodoxy. For others it is not even that but more like a set of traditional guidelines that may or may not be considered binding.

A second dimension is the strong emphasis placed on *Shabbat* and *kashrut*, again as concepts rather than as phenomena shaped by a detailed *halakhic* code. Thus the Conservative Movement, in choosing between synagogue attendance on *Shabbat* and traveling on that day, chose the former. For example, Conservative synagogues organize schools on *Shabbat* morning before children's services.

Still, the notion that there has to be some kind of comprehensive *Shabbat*, marked by candle lighting Friday night to *havdalah* (ceremony marking the end of the Sabbath) time Saturday night, is real and indeed is at the core of the Movement's preaching and teaching. However, as in the case of riding, in the Conservative view, technology is designed to serve the *Shabbat* more than it is to limit permissible *Shabbat* activities. The permitted use of electricity, microphones in the synagogues, telephone, television, and radio in the home reflects this. Outside of Israel, there are very few Conservative families who do not use these devices, including the Conservative elite. Indeed, clear *halakhic* grounds have been established by the Movement's *halakhic* decision makers to make them available.

Much the same is true with regard to *kashrut*, which is a basic concept with a few benchmark rules that cannot be violated, such as eating non-kosher meat or seafoods which by their nature or preparation are non-kosher or meat and dairy together, but these rules are softened by the acceptance of eating otherwise kosher foods outside of the home or synagogue on non-kosher dishes where the level of control over preparation is limited. The extent of care exercised in such matters is left to individual discretion.

In general, the Conservative Movement emphasizes observance of the Jewish calendar, especially through collective religious activity, and encourages it, even when it does not particularly emphasize individual or family religious activity. It certainly does not reject such activities; it simply does not emphasize them beyond the core of *Shabbat*, holiday, and *kashrut* observance.

For the elite, home observance is very important, tempered by the reality of the fact that so many of the elite are *klei kodesh*, which means that they have synagogue responsibilities that take them out of the home at precisely the time when they probably wish to be at home, namely, on Sabbaths and holidays. One of the most positive aspects of the Movement in recent years is the way in which home observance has spread beyond the elite. In great part, this is because of the intensive efforts of Conservative synagogues to promote them and to teach children and adults how to perform them.

Evidence of this basic Conservative pattern of religious observance is mounting, especially for those who are members of synagogues, a much broader group than the elite defined earlier. Of the 1990 National Jewish Population Survey respondents, 40 percent said that their denominational preference was Conservative (compared to 42 percent in 1971). Of synagogue members in 1990, 51 percent reported that they were Conservative (compared to 49 percent in 1971). While the percentage preferring the Conservative and Reform denominations in 1990 is almost identical in the total adult population, Conservative (51 percent) is a more common preference than Reform (35 percent) among those who are synagogue members.[12]

The analysis of Boston's 1995 Jewish population survey reflects a similarly stable profile of the proportion of Jews who consider themselves Conservative. They report that "Denominational identification remains high: 79 percent of Boston's Jews identify with one of the four major religious streams. The division among the four branches remains essentially unchanged since 1985." Just one-third (33 percent) of the respondents reported that they consider themselves Conservative in both surveys. The frequency of synagogue attendance was up for Jews in all denominational groups, with 10 percent of Conservative Jews reporting that they attended synagogue once a week or more and another 54 percent saying that they attended once or twice a month or every few months. Denominational identification was also the strongest predictor of observance. In 1995, among Boston's Conservative Jews, 90 percent attended a Passover Seder, 95 percent lit Hanukkah candles, 76 percent fasted on Yom Kippur, 36 percent observed *Shabbat* as special, 32 percent lit *Shabbat* candles, and 19 percent said that they followed the dietary laws.[13]

According to the most recent, definitive set of studies of Conservative synagogues and their members, directed by Jack Wertheimer, there is a significantly higher level of ritual practice among synagogue members, with 24 percent of members versus 6 percent of non-members keeping kosher, 37 percent of members versus 11 percent of non-members lighting *Shabbat* candles, and 90 percent of members versus 60 percent of non-members attending Seder.[14]

This runs counter to an earlier strong tendency in the Conservative Movement to emphasize observance in the synagogue above all. Indeed, one of the characteristics of the Conservative and Reform movements in their formative periods was the tendency to transfer observances from the home to the synagogue. This trend reached its peak in the Conservative Movement in the period between 1920 and 1960. This was the time when even the Pesach Seder was transferred to the synagogue.

The argument on behalf of the transfer was that Jews would not maintain these rituals at home, hence it was necessary to make them available in the synagogue in order to have them observed at all. Since the 1960s, that pattern has been modified or reversed, with a renewed emphasis on Jewish home activities, to the great benefit of Conservative Judaism. Still, there is a residue of the earlier period and, while the message of the Conservative Movement is Judaism in both synagogue and home, with home observance quite important, for the mass of the Conservative membership, synagogue rituals form the core of Jewish religious activity, even to the point of going to the synagogue for a *minyan* during *shiva* (the seven-day mourning period) in many communities.

In no small measure, this reversal has been because the people themselves have wanted it. The anti-institutionalism of the late 1960s led to a reemphasis on small groups and home activity, as in the *Havurah* Movement. It was marked by the emergence of the Pesach Seder (whatever its actual content) as the most widely observed Jewish ritual, surpassing High Holy Day synagogue attendance and even Hanukkah candle lighting. Today, the two most widespread Jewish rituals are home rituals, that is, the Seder and Hanukkah candle lighting.

The significance of this reversal cannot be overestimated. First, the sheer performance of more Jewish acts creates a stronger Jewish home environment and raises the level of Jewish commitment and concern. Beyond that, such observance and the education that goes with it is one of the most effective ways of breaking down the sharp division between the elite and mass. If more and more Conservative Jews maintain the same observances, willy-nilly, the gap between the two groups diminishes. This trend owes much to the Ramah and United Synagogue Youth experience, with products of Ramah camps and USY doing much to foster Jewish observance in their homes, first as children and then as adults with their own families. We have observed in anecdotal ways how this works in different Jewish communities. Home observance of *kashrut*, for example, makes possible greater home-to-home socializing between the two groups. So too with *Shabbat* and festivals. Moreover, the spread of competence reinforces the Jewish self-confidence of individuals and families, thereby leading them willing to try more things Jewish. If this trend continues, the Conservative

Movement may be on the threshold of breaking out of the limits of a small elite to develop substantial cadres of serious Conservative Jews who practice Judaism in a Conservative manner, rather than just attending synagogues where such practice is advocated.

Another dimension of Conservative religious observance was the transformation of the worship service into a programmed production rather than a spontaneous experience. This trend has been characteristic of non-Orthodox movements since their inception over 150 years ago, and it reflects a combination of factors: the desire for decorum, the increasing lack of knowledge and religious skills on the part of the congregation, the enhanced role of the rabbi, and the influence of Christian, particularly Protestant, religious worship. In every case, the thrust was in the same direction—transforming the service into a carefully choreographed production conducted by professionals for an audience rather than encouraging a truly participatory exercise. This has not happened in all congregations, nor at the same pace, nor to the same extent, but the trend was widespread and powerful.

Conservative synagogue architecture reflected this change. For the first time since the invention of the synagogue 2,600 years ago, all activity was concentrated up front. Instead of being located in its traditional place within the middle of the congregation, the *bimah* was moved apart from it. Thus the *bimah* became a stage, one which, in many cases, was elevated far above the congregants so that there was a clear separation between those who sat on the *bimah* and those who did not. This was in sharp contrast to the democratic use of space in the traditional synagogue. In the past, the choice seats along the eastern wall belonged to the civil leaders of the *kahal*—the notables, the *parnassim*, with any rabbis present having appropriately respectable corners in which to pray, think, and study. Now the stage became the focal point of the rabbi and the cantor and perhaps a choir (although that was usually placed elsewhere), with the president included almost as a matter of grace. Approaching the *bimah* involved crossing the division between the mass and elite, rather than having the service conducted from within a participatory community.

The ramifications of this separation cannot be overemphasized. In great part, the success of both *havurot* and Orthodoxy is a reflection of the reaction against this style of worship and the return of the service to the congregation. It is true that many in the Conservative Movement are not interested in returning to the old style. For some, this would place too great of a demand on them, while for others it is simply unfamiliar. One of the reasons the *havurah* movement attracts elites is that many among the masses do not want a synagogue that requires effort on their part; they want a "service station." If there is no space for participatory worship of equals in a Conservative traditional context, then the Movement will be unable to retain the personal commitment of many of its best and brightest who are not *klei kodesh*.

The emphasis on formalism also has come under assault since the late 1960s, and changes in the direction of informality, sometimes helpful and sometimes drastic and trendy, have taken place. Among them have been at least a few examples of new synagogue buildings in which the *bimah* has been restored to the center, including Beth Hillel in Wynnewood, Pennsylvania, perhaps the first; B'nai Israel in Rockville, Maryland; and Har Shalom in Potomac, Maryland. Obviously in less formal settings, such as *havurot*, some of the same intimacy is restored. The changing garb of many rabbis and cantors from formal robes and hats to large wool tallitot on *Shabbat* also has lessened the distance between the *bimah* and the congregation. If these trends become more pronounced, they could signal a reversal of the formalistic norms of congregational worship, no less than the trends toward home observance mark a significant change.

A crucial dimension of the development of Conservative Judaism was the introduction of late Friday night services early in the history of the Movement. Either immediately before World War II or shortly thereafter, the late Friday night service reached its peak in popularity, in many, if not most, congregations, exceeding the *Shabbat* morning service in attracting attendance. The Friday night service of those days tended to be more formal than the services held at more traditional times, since it was constructed as a new artifact, relying partly on the traditional *kabalat Shabbat* (prayers recited at the beginning of the Sabbath on Friday night) prayers and partly on rabbinical and cantorial inventions. In the mid to late 1950s, it also became the service for bat mitzvah observances as distinct from Saturday morning, which was reserved for bar mitzvah ceremonies.

This trend was reversed sometime in the late 1950s as the result of the deliberate efforts of rabbis to encourage more participation on *Shabbat* morning, reinforced by the spread of the five-day work week, which made it easier for many Jews to attend Saturday morning services than heretofore. With the movement toward elimination of ritual distinctions between men and women, bat mitzvah ceremonies also could be celebrated on *Shabbat* morning, further strengthening that service. Slowly, attendance at late Friday night services declined, and elite attendance almost disappeared as the products of the youth movement's Ramah camps, to the extent that they maintained *Shabbat*, preferring *Shabbat* dinner at home to rushing off to services.

Late Friday night services became less formal. Even earlier, they had been redesigned to serve the needs of special groups such as singles, senior citizens, empty nesters, or representatives of other special constituencies such as the men's clubs or sisterhoods to attract attendees. Some of the formalism was then transferred to the *Shabbat* morning service, which in many congregations became less traditional as it began to attract a new generation of less knowledgeable Jews and to lose the older generation, many of whom had grown up at home in Jewish worship. The custom of having *b'nai* and in many cases *b'not mitzvah* learn how to lead services as *ba'alei t'filah* (prayer leaders) and to read the Torah has enhanced the traditional services on Sabbaths and festivals. Since the mid-1970s, adult bat mitzvahs and the lessons of *havurot* also have led to more lay participation in *Shabbat* morning services.

By the late 1950s, a more explicitly Conservative Movement prayer style had developed in the form of *Nusah* Ramah (liturgy of Ramah). Initially developed at the Ramah camps for their services, the *nusah* combined the traditional Ashkenazi prayer service with the modifications earlier inserted for the Conservative Movement as a whole and those specific elements that were deemed to better serve Ramah campers and staff. The service was in Hebrew, it involved much congregational singing and participation, and in time it became egalitarian. It is the *nusach* favored by most *havurot*, and it has been transplanted to Conservative congregations in Israel by Ramah alumni who have settled there.

So many implications have to be drawn from this dimension of style. It may be that, in the last analysis, style is what distinguishes the Movement from its counterparts as much or more than any other dimension. Certainly it is here where the Conservative Movement has to look hardest at its self-definition, and at its difficulties in translating that definition into behavior. At the same time, it is the sphere in which it is hardest to make changes, since formal change is less likely to have an impact. The essence of the Conservative style, of course, is overtly manifested in the Movement's institutions and ideology, which in many cases have taken the form they have as a consequence of that style.

Commenting on the occasion of the fortieth anniversary of the summer camps, on the power of the Ramah experience, which he called "the most important venture ever undertaken by the Seminary,"

Ismar Schorsch emphasized the *nusah* created and transmitted there. He wrote:

> The fervor of communal worship at Ramah altered not only individual lives but also traditional practice. In time, Ramah gave rise to a distinct *nusah*, a recognizable liturgical mode. . . . The ability to generate such a *nusah* is the sign of a praying community. An individual may compose a siddur, but only a community can produce a *nusah*. . . . The diffusion of the Ramah *nusah* is tangible evidence of the impact of Conservative Judaism on popular observance. Whether in Boston or Los Angeles or on French Hill in Jerusalem, the mode of prayer— informality, pervasive participation, fervent and melodious singing, undogmatic study, and varying degrees of egalitarianism betokens the patrimony of Ramah. To be sure the exposure to Ramah often distanced our youngsters from the conservative synagogues to which they returned. . . . The movement as a whole responded sluggishly to the needs of the youngsters who had tasted of the probing and the passion of the Ramah *nusah*. And yet the tension, for all its drawbacks, was fertilizing. (p. 188)[15]

# Chapter 5

# *Demographics*

## CONCENTRIC CIRCLES OF JEWISHNESS[1]

The essentially individualistic character of American society requires that Jews relate to Jewish institutions as individuals. Affiliation in American society is voluntary, in the fullest sense of the word. The patterns of participation in American Jewish life reflect this combination of individualism and voluntarism. In a free society, the Jewish community cannot live within fixed boundaries confining all (or virtually all) of those born Jews and perforce encouraging them to organize to meet their communal needs. Increasingly, American Jews, if they profess any Jewish commitment at all, feel that they are Jews by choice rather than simply by birth. The organic tie continues to undergird the fact of choice, but birth alone is no longer sufficient to keep Jews within the fold. No one is more conscious of this than Jews themselves. As a result, the Jewish community has been transformed into what can be described as a series of uneven concentric circles, radiating outward from a hard core of committed Jews toward areas of vague Jewishness on the fringes (see Figure 5.1).

91

Figures are approximate; see text for full discussion.

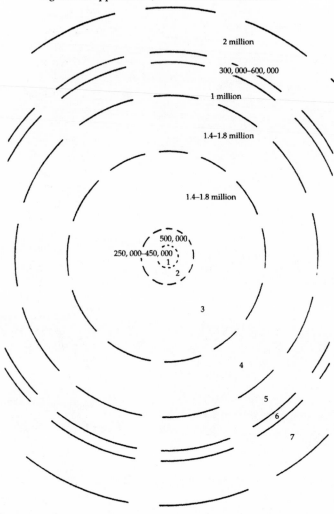

FIGURE 5.1

Key:
1. Integral Jews (living according to a Jewish rhythm)
2. Participants (involved in Jewish life on a regular basis)
3. Affiliated Jews (affiliated with Jewish institutions in some concrete way)
4. Contributors and Consumers (giving money and/or utilizing the services of Jewish institutions from time to time)
5. Peripherals (recognizably Jewish in some way but completely uninvolved in Jewish life)
6. Repudiators (seeking to deny or repudiate their Jewishness)
7. Quasi-Jews (Jewish status unclear as a result of intermarriage or assimilation in some other form)

Source: Community and Polity, D.J. Elazar, Philadelphia, 1995. p. 92

The hard core of the American Jewish community—one might label them Integral Jews—consists of those whose Jewishness is a full-time concern, the central factor of their lives, whether expressed in traditionally religious terms or through some variety of ethnic nationalism or an intensive involvement in Jewish affairs. For them, each day is lived by a substantially Jewish rhythm. They and their families tend to be closely linked to one another through shared Jewish interests and feelings and tend to associate with others of similar concern. Their Jewishness is an intergenerational affair. In short, they live, in one way or another, fully Jewish lives. Perhaps 8 percent of the Jewish population of the United States falls into this category (500,000 to 600,000 Jews).

Surrounding this hard core is a second group—the Participants—consisting of Jews who take part in Jewish life on a regular basis and are considered much more than casually active in Jewish affairs, but to whom living Jewishly is not a full-time matter and whose rhythm of life is essentially that of the larger society. It might be said that, for them, Jewishness is a major avocational interest. They are likely to be officers of Jewish organizations, regular participants in adult Jewish-education programs of various kinds, active fund raisers for Israel, and even regular synagogue attenders. Many members of the "Jewish civil service"—professionals employed by the various Jewish agencies—fall into this category; they spend their days working in a Jewish capacity, but their nonprofessional lives are not integrally Jewish. Ten percent (600,000) is a fair estimate of the percentage of such Jews in the United States today.

Surrounding the participants is a third group—the Affiliated Jews—which consists of those who are affiliated with Jewish institutions or organizations in some concrete way but who are not particularly active in them. This category includes synagogue members whose affiliation does not involve them much beyond the use of synagogue facilities for the Jewish rites of passage or for High Holy Day services, and members of some of the mass-based Jewish organizations, such as Hadassah and B'nai B'rith, or any of the other charitable groups that are identifiably Jewish and whose membership reflects primarily private social interests rather than concern for the public purposes of Jewish life. This is a fairly large category, because it includes all of those who instinctively recognize the need for some kind of associational commitment of Jewish life, even if it is only for the sake of maintaining a proper front before the non-Jewish community. One might estimate that it includes approximately 30 percent (around 1.8 million) of the country's Jewish population.

Beyond that circle is a fourth group—Contributors and Consumers—consisting of Jews who give money to Jewish causes from time to time and periodically utilize the services of Jewish institutions (perhaps even as members) for marriage, burial, bar mitzvah, and the like. In other words, they clearly identify as Jews, but they are minimally associated with the Jewish community as such. Perhaps 25 percent (1.5 million) of all American Jews fall into this category. Many of these people are of college age or are immediately past college, single, never married, or senior citizens, many of whom have such limited incomes that they cannot develop more formal or lasting Jewish attachments in a context that makes financial expenditure a binding factor in the associational process.

Beyond the circle of Contributors and Consumers is a fifth group of Jews that is recognizably Jewish in some way but completely uninvolved in Jewish life. We might call these members Peripherals. While they may be married to Jewish partners and their children are unquestionably of Jewish descent, they have no desire even to utilize Jewish institutions for the rites of passage and have insufficient interest even in Jewish causes such as Israel to contribute money. Perhaps 15 percent of all American Jews fall into this category.

A sixth category—Repudiators—consists of Jews who markedly deny their Jewishness, some of whom have converted to Christianity.[2] Few of those who care are hostile, and few who do not care feel the need to react hostilely to their Jewish origins. There are probably 10 percent in this category today.

Finally, there is an unknown number of what we may call Quasi-Jews, those who are neither inside of the Jewish community nor entirely out of it. They are people who have intermarried, but they have not lost their own personal Jewish label, they are the products of mixed marriages whose Jewish descent and/or affiliation are not clear, or are they Jews who have otherwise assimilated to a point where their Jewish birth is incidental in every respect. We have no firm knowledge of how many such people there are in the country.

The boundaries between these categories as well as their membership are quite fluid (as Figure 5.1 indicates by separating the categories with broken, rather than solid, lines). There is considerable movement in and out of all of the seven categories, though of course there is more movement along the edges of each than across separated circles. Thus Jews in group two (Participants), if they move at all, are more likely to move into the hard core or out into more casual membership than to drop out altogether, while the Peripherals may move into the Quasi-

Jews category with some ease or under other circumstances will be easily brought into the category of Contributors and Consumers.

What this means is that the community is built on a fluid, if not an eroding, base, with a high degree of self-selection involved in determining who is likely to affiliate or is even potentially active in Jewish life. No more than one-fourth of the Jewish population fall into the potentially active category, and by no means do all of them define their Jewish concerns as public ones. For many—especially those in the hard core (Hassidic Jews, for example)—the concerns of the overall Jewish community are not their concerns. While they are interested in leading private lives that are intensely Jewish, they do not seek to channel their Jewishness into the general realm of the Jewish community.

In times of crisis, there will be a general movement of the circles. Thus the Six-Day and Yom Kippur wars probably increased the extent and intensity of Jewish identification in all of the circles, including Repudiators, but only relative to the prior stance of the individuals involved. The Participants may have become totally preoccupied with Jewish affairs during the period of the crisis, and the Peripherals may have become Contributors for the moment, but it is unlikely that Peripherals became Participants (of course, we are speaking here about aggregates, not isolated cases).

There is evidence that significant shifts are taking place in the relationship of the several circles to each another. On the one hand, persons in the inner circles are closing ranks and becoming more intensively Jewish, while those in the outer circles are drifting further away from Jewish life. It is quite likely that a great gap is developing somewhere between circles two and three, a gap paralleled by an even greater division between circles four and five.

Immediately after the Six-Day War, it was widely suggested that many Jews had "come out of the woodwork" in response to the threat to Israel's survival. Subsequent research indicated that even those Jews whose responses were unexpected were, for the most part, already within the third or fourth circles. That is, they were likely to be synagogue members, though very passive ones, or small contributors to the annual Israel fund-raising drives. The war transformed their passive or low-level participation into active and perhaps high-level giving, but (with relatively few exceptions) did not affect people who had never been involved before.

The evidence from the Yom Kippur War indicates that, despite all of the visible excitement of large segments of the American Jewish community, the spreading apart of the circles increased. It has been estimated that perhaps as many as one-third of American Jewry were not caught up by the October 1973 crisis. Those whose concern for Israel had been sharpened in the period between 1967 and 1973 became more concerned than ever before. On the other hand, those who had shown no concern evinced a greater degree of disinterest: the years had taken them further away from Jewish concerns, even at the survival level. This means that American Jewry stands to lose a significant share of its total population, a development that in turn will not only shift the bases of Jewish religious life in the United States, but even erode them. At the same time, there seems to be almost no question that, within the inner circles, the intensity of Jewish feeling has increased. During the 1980s, the debates between Charles Silberman and other "optimists" picked up on the increasing commitment and activity of the inner circles, while the "pessimists" focused on what was happening to the outer circles. The findings of the 1990 National Jewish Population Survey substantially quieted the optimists and brought about a shift in the rhetoric from a debate over advances and declines to one over the best strategies to enhance continuity.

In a free and an open society, the drift away from Jewish life is not surprising. Indeed, the way in which it occurs—so casually and without deliberate intent, so unlinked to ideology, and certainly not to any ideology of assimilationism—is both a reflection on the character of American society and the reason the model of concentric circles is the most appropriate for understanding the social structure of American Jewry. Moreover, the American Jewish model is spreading to other Jewish communities in the diaspora, as they too find themselves in increasingly open societies that welcome the talents of Jews without holding their Jewishness against them.

The result is a community that is far different from one that exists within boundaries, the kind characterized by the State of Israel and, in the past, by the Jewish ghettos. It has become common knowledge that many of the Jews in Israel are no more knowledgeable or serious about their Judaism than those in the United States. Nevertheless, their Jewishness is unquestionably a functional element in their lives, one to which they must constantly respond. That is because they live in a Jewish state and in a Jewish society that is also a civil society, where duly constituted Jewish authorities exercise power, even coercive power, to require actions on the part of citizens directed toward serving what virtually all would agree to be Jewish purposes, if only the elemental one of Jewish survival. Even the most "assimilated" Jew in Israel must serve in the Israeli Army, if he or she is eligible by age and fitness, and thus to take on a task of immediate service to the Jewish people. Every wage earner in Israel, citizen or not, must pay taxes, some of which go to support institutions with clearly Jewish religious purposes. This is all characteristic of a bounded society.

For Conservative Jews, as for other American Jews, what characterizes this society composed of concentric circles is precisely the fact that there are no boundaries; what holds people within it is the pull of its central core, particularly as its outer edges become increasingly blurred. Perhaps the most appropriate image for this is a magnet, able to attract iron particles that come within its magnetic field. This is the condition of American Jewry and, increasingly, of all diaspora Jewry: a magnet at the core pulls those who contain within them the iron filings of Judaism closer to the center, more or less according to the degree of their iron (i.e., Jewish) content.

The question remains: What constitutes the magnet at the core? Prior to emancipation, it was clearly the Jewish system of law, practice, and belief. Since emancipation, the issue has become less clear (which is why the magnetic attraction has weakened). But whatever the magnet happens to be, it has to do with something that is authentically and totally Jewish. In this respect, the American Jewish community, no matter how well acculturated to the American environment, relies upon that which is continually and unremittingly Jewish, regardless of time or place.

Jewish life in an unbounded society has two major implications for the Conservative Movement and the *masorti* Judaism it espouses. First, it means that the Movement is in competition with all other forms of Jewish affiliation and identity. It can expect pulls from various directions, religiously, from Orthodox, Reform, and Reconstructionism.

Second, within the Movement, the Conservative Jewish leadership must struggle to bring its members closer to the inner circles and keep them from drifting into the outer ones. As a movement claiming to represent authentic Judaism, it must have a sufficiently high percentage of its members in the inner core if it is to make that claim meaningful for itself and for others. Yet, as a mass movement, it must reach as far out into the other circles as possible without sacrificing its principles, an extremely difficult task.

Recent demographic studies indicate that the present trends are not encouraging in either direction. Findings of the 1990 Council of Jewish Federations National Jewish Population Survey clearly show a decline in identification with the Conservative Movement from generation to generation. There is a general drift to the left from Movement to Movement, and the percentages of Conservatives have been in decline. This is best illustrated in Tables 19–22, pages 170 and 171, in Sidney Goldstein's "Profile of American Jewry: Insights from the 1990 National Jewish Population Survey" in the 1992 *American Jewish Year Book*. Goldstein shows the current denomination of adult respondents that considers itself Jewish by religion by age groups. For those age sixty-five and over, about 12 percent of adult respondents consider themselves Orthodox, 49 percent Conservative, 31 percent Reform, 8 percent "Just Jewish," and less than 1 percent each for Reconstructionist or "something else." Among those ages forty-five to sixty-four, 5 percent said they were Orthodox, 42 percent Conservative, 43 percent Reform, 7 percent "Just Jewish," 3 percent Reconstructionist, and less than .5 percent "something else." For those aged twenty-five to forty-four, the percentage of Orthodox was steady at 5 percent, the percentage of Conservative had dropped to 33 percent, while those calling themselves Reform included just over half (51 percent) of this group, "Just Jewish" was steady at 7 percent, and Reconstructionist was about the same, at 2 percent. Among the eighteen to twenty-four-year-olds, there appeared to be a reversal of this trend, with 10 percent calling themselves Orthodox, 43 percent Conservative, 35 percent Reform, 10 percent "Just Jewish," and 1 percent Reconstructionist. It is difficult to know if this finding is an artifact of the special nature of the sample from that age group or a genuine cohort change.

In addition to the general decline of the percentage calling themselves Conservative or Jews who consider themselves Jews by religion, there is another interesting trend. Table 22 in the aforementioned Goldstein article shows the current denomination of respondents born Jews by the denomination in which Jews were raised. In 1990, about 89 percent of those denoting themselves Orthodox had been raised in Orthodox homes, with the remaining 5 percent current Orthodox having been raised in Conservative, another 5 percent in "Just Jewish," and 1 percent in non-Jewish homes. About 60 percent of current Conservative respondents had been raised in Conservative homes. An additional 32 percent reported that they had been raised in Orthodox, 4 percent in Reform, 2 percent in "Just Jewish," and 2 percent in non-Jewish homes. Fifty-nine percent of current Reform respondents had been raised in Reform, 26 percent in Conservative, 12 percent in Orthodox, 3 percent in "Just Jewish," and 1 percent in non-Jewish homes. Clearly, the overall trend is to the left, though among the currently Orthodox 11 percent, the currently Conservative about 5 percent, and the currently Reform about 4 percent had moved to the right.

This must be an area of extremely serious concern to the Conservative Movement, particularly since what we are witnessing is a shift away from what the Movement has come to expect. Sometime in the 1920s, the Conservative Movement became the tide of the future for American Jews. In the interwar generation, this was still only partly demonstrable and a matter of faith to a generation of young leaders who took over at that time, some of whom still play important roles in the Movement. After World War II, the promised tide became a reality. The Conservative Movement became the mass religious movement of the American Jewish community. In the 1950s, as Jews, responding to the "religious revival" of the time, rushed to the suburbs and to synagogue membership, the Conservative Movement benefited more than any other. We all know the story, and it need not be repeated here. Since then, things have changed in two ways.

## DECLINE IN THE FOURTH GENERATION

The tide stopped flowing in the early 1960s (1962 seems to have been the turning point). For the next few years, membership in the Movement remained stable and then, beginning in the late 1960s, as America went through its lifestyle revolution, membership in Conservative congregations began to drop. Synagogue membership as a whole stabilized around 1975, but in the Conservative Movement, the drop continued.

The 1970 CJF National Jewish Population study showed that 40 percent of American Jews identified as Conservative.[3] Conservative Judaism was overwhelmingly the most popular preference of second-generation American Jews, and that popularity continued into the third generation. However, in the fourth generation, some children of Conservative Jews either dropped away altogether or turned to Reform congregations. However, as the American Jewish community becomes more entrenched and dominated by fourth-generation and now even fifth-generation American Jews, the Conservative Movement seems to have stabilized, and may even have begun to increase somewhat.

It should be noted that there is a difference between identification and affiliation, with approximately 25 percent more Jews identifying with one or another branch of Judaism than are actually affiliated with synagogues at any given time. Thus, in 1990, the CJF National Jewish Population Survey showed 47 percent of all Jews affiliated with synagogues, while between 70 percent and 80 percent identified themselves

TABLE 5.2
Current Denomination by Denomination Raised* of Adult Respondents
(in percentages)

| Denomination Raised | Current Denomination | | | | | | All Denominations |
|---|---|---|---|---|---|---|---|
| | Orthodox | Conservative | Reform | Reconstructionist | Just Jewish | Other | |
| **Distribution by Denomination-Raised** | | | | | | | |
| Orthodox | 88.9 | 32.5 | 11.8 | 15.6 | 14.4 | 2.7 | 23.4 |
| Conservative | 3.0 | 58.0 | 24.2 | 45.4 | 17.4 | 16.7 | 33.9 |
| Reform | 0.7 | 3.9 | 55.5 | 17.5 | 13.2 | 22.8 | 26.2 |
| Just Jewish | 3.4 | 1.6 | 3.3 | 16.1 | 48.7 | 7.6 | 7.7 |
| Other | 2.5 | 2.5 | 2.2 | 5.4 | 4.2 | 40.6 | 6.0 |
| Non-Jewish | 1.5 | 1.5 | 3.0 | — | 2.1 | 9.7 | 2.8 |
| Total Percent | 100.0 | 100.0 | 100.0 | 100.0 | 100.0 | 100.0 | 100.0 |
| **Distribution by Current Denomination** | | | | | | | Total Percent |
| Orthodox | 23.2 | 49.4 | 19.3 | 0.9 | 6.1 | 1.0 | 100.0 |
| Conservative | 0.5 | 60.9 | 27.3 | 1.9 | 5.1 | 4.4 | 100.0 |
| Reform | 0.2 | 5.3 | 80.9 | 0.9 | 5.0 | 7.7 | 100.0 |
| Just Jewish | 2.8 | 7.4 | 16.0 | 0.9 | 63.9 | 8.9 | 100.0 |
| Other | 2.5 | 15.1 | 13.8 | 1.3 | 6.9 | 60.3 | 100.0 |
| Non-Jewish | 3.3 | 18.4 | 41.0 | — | 7.1 | 30.2 | 100.0 |
| Total | 6.1 | 35.7 | 38.2 | 1.4 | 9.8 | 8.8 | 100.0 |

* Excludes those of unknown denomination raised

Source: Sidney Goldstein and Alice Goldstein, Conservative Jewry in the United States: A Sociodemographic Profile (New York: Jewish Theological Seminary of America, 1998), p. 143.

religiously. The discrepancy has to do with the fact that people will or will not be dues-paying members of a congregation at different periods in their lives. Over 80 percent of those with school-age children are affiliated, but younger and older Jews tend not to actually join synagogues. This does not change the basic demographic picture, but recognition of this fact prevents us from being unduly pessimistic about Jewish religious identification in general.[4]

Since 1979, surveys of Jewish population in the major metropolitan areas reported the following far lower figures: New York (36 percent); Los Angeles (33 percent); Chicago (35 percent); Miami (35 percent); and Philadelphia (always a "Conservative town," 41 percent). Table 5.3 presents the relative percentages of identification with the three religious groups in 1970 and more recent local demographic studies. The shift from Conservative to Reform is clearly visible.

Some evidence of decline can be adduced from comparisons of different age cohorts. In Philadelphia, in 1984, Conservative identification rates slipped from 57 percent among those over seventy years of age, to 47 percent among those ages fifty to sixty-nine, to one-third of those ages thirty to forty-nine. In the 1991 New York area study (a region that embraces almost one-third of American Jews, from Westchester to the five boroughs to all of Long Island), the shift was comparable: 46 percent of those ages sixty-five to seventy-four; 38 percent to 40 percent of those ages forty-five to sixty-four; and 28 percent to 30 percent of those under age forty-five. In Philadelphia, the primary beneficiary of these shifts was the Reform Movement; in New York, both Orthodoxy and Reform seem to have gained at the expense of Conservative Jewish identification. However, the changes in the following decade were less dramatic. In the period 1996–1997, 38 percent of Philadelphia Jews self-defined as Conservative and just 28 percent as Reform. In Boston, in 1995, the rate of Conservative self-definition was 33 percent, 5 percent lower than it had been in 1985, while 31 percent self-identified as Reform, the same as 1985.

The implications of these trends for the future are not very clear. Of course, a "straight line" projection would suggest the ultimate disappearance of the Conservative Movement, but "straight line" projections are invariably misleading. Indeed, the 1990 NJPS showed something of a reversal of the former trend. What is required is a projection based upon an understanding of the dynamics of religious affiliation over time; this suggests a more complex picture. There may already be some evidence of a slowing down of decline. In a 1986 resurvey of Queens, Nassau, and Suffolk counties, the number of those Jews in the

TABLE 5.3
Religious Identification of Jews in Community Studies, 1985–1991
(by percent)

| City (Year) | Orthodox | Conservative | Reform | Reconstructionist | Just Jewish/Other |
|---|---|---|---|---|---|
| Boston (1985) | 6 | 38 | 41 | 2 | 13 |
| Rhode Island (1987) | 7 | 47 | 32 | 0.4 | 13 |
| New York (1991) | 14 | 34 | 37 | 2 | 13 |
| South Broward (1990) | 6 | 39 | 28 | — | 27 |
| Columbus (1990) | 13 | 33 | 47 | 3 | 4 |
| Dallas (1987) | 4 | 34 | 49 | — | 13 |
| San Francisco (1987) | 3 | 20 | 43 | 1 | 33 |
| Seattle (1990) | 8 | 20 | 37 | — | 35 |

Source: Sidney Goldstein and Alice Goldstein, Conservative Jewry in the United States: A Sociodemographic Profile (New York: Jewish Theological Seminary of America, 1998), p. 151.

three counties identifying as Conservative declined from 42 percent to 39 percent in the five years since the previous survey, mostly a result of the passing of the older generation. Nevertheless, in the thirty-five to forty-nine-year-old age group, Conservative identification held at 41 percent. A comparison of the data from the 1990 CJF National Jewish Population Study on current denomination to that in which individuals were raised shows that, on balance, the proportion of Conservatives has hardly changed, remaining close to one-third. On the other hand, the percentage of Orthodox declined from 23 percent to only 6 percent, and the proportion of Reform increased from 26 percent to 38 percent of all core Jews.[5]

Two demographic factors have contributed to the stabilization or lack of growth in Conservative identification. One factor is the decline in the conventional family. Conservative Movement affiliation always has been built around the nuclear family—married couples who have or once had school-age children. Synagogue affiliation rises considerably when the first child reaches seven or eight years old. The postponement of marriage and childbearing meant significant losses for Conservative Judaism, especially in the under-forty age cohorts. It also meant that young singles and childless couples who were potentially serious Conservative Jews were further encouraged to join alternative prayer communities to avoid the older, conventional, family oriented mainstream congregations.

Another crucial factor is the passing of the second generation. As Marshall Sklare has so aptly demonstrated, the Conservative Movement is very much a second-generation phenomenon. The style, flavor, ethos, and mythos of the two (the generation and the movement) were a fortuitous match. Today we find proportionately fewer "inertial Conservatives" as the second generation has grown older (dominating the over-fifty-five age cohorts), and the third generation has taken its place. The generational shift then may have occasioned an erosion among less ideologically committed Conservative Jews; but those remaining may well consist of those more receptive to the official rhetoric and philosophy of Conservatism, a development similar to one in Orthodoxy.

This has to be looked at carefully, because if the Conservative Movement cannot continue to be the mass movement it is, it will either have to reorient itself as an elite movement, with all that that entails, or it will lose much of its vitality. This is true even with all of the problems inherent in the present gap between Movement standards and the religious behavior of most of the ordinary members of Conservative congregations. For some, Conservative Judaism was a kind of tribute that vice paid to virtue, in the sense that people who were not themselves sufficiently observant by the standards of their parents or grandparents recognized what they should be doing by identifying with Conservative congregations. For those who are middling, it has been a way to build a moderate involvement in Judaism. Nor was this surprising. So many Jews in the first generations shed their ritual practices as part of an unwanted Old World heritage, just as they changed their names. Even among those who had immigrated to the United States, many had relatively little or no Jewish education, and their children received even less.

The demographic trend suggests that many people who are not observant no longer feel uncomfortable or guilty about being nonobservant. Belonging to a generation that has few or no memories of authentic Jewish tradition from their families, they are quite willing to identify with a movement that does not make any more claims on them than they would make on themselves. In essence, the religious dimensions of Judaism do not interest them, except at special moments in the life cycle or the calendar.

In essence, when the vast majority of Jews are equally ignorant of things Jewish and lack Jewish experiences in their own lives or even memories of Jewish experiences with parents or grandparents, there is little to draw them to Conservative as distinct from Reform congregations or, for that matter, to any synagogue at all.

It is extremely difficult to combat this trend in conventional ways. What it comes down to is a competition among synagogues where the social environment, level of congregational prestige, and appeal of certain synagogue personalities or programs become the issue rather than larger ideological concerns. This is not to say that these were not always important, but there was a difference in the degree of their importance when sentimental and experiential ties existed of the kind that brought the second generation to Conservative Judaism.

Furthermore, the choice of a synagogue, especially on the part of younger couples and singles, is often based on the cost of membership dues and building fund commitments asked of new members. Young couples who might opt for membership in Conservative synagogues often turn away because of the higher costs that come at a time when they are having trouble buying a home and educating their children. Reform congregations that have paid for their buildings and do not require or provide as many hours of Jewish education often can settle for less dues, at least from younger members, and can rely upon their wealthier, older members to carry the burden. The Conservative Movement is suffering the consequences.

In addition, the Reform Movement has wisely provided seed money for new congregations in areas of expanding Jewish population, whether in the Sunbelt, in new suburbs, or even in new housing developments in the inner city. Thus they give their movement's local representatives a head start in developing congregations that continue to grow as the population shifts.

## ORTHODOXY RESURGENT[6]

The Conservative Movement faces a different kind of challenge from Orthodoxy. Earlier we cited the Elazar and Liebman estimate that there are no more than 40,000 to 50,000 Jews who live by the *halakhic* norms of the Movement. This means that when the Conservative mass is left out, the Movement is only the equivalent of a fair-sized Hassidic sect.

Moreover, the *hozrim b'tshuva* (newly observant Jews) phenomenon, carries some young people from the ranks of the potential Conservative elite, to Orthodoxy where *hozrim b'tshuva* are more visible and seem firmer and more active in their commitments. They are attracted by the presence of a supportive peer group of like-minded ideological stance and ritual observance.

Overall, the available demographic data shows that the percentage of Jews who define themselves as Orthodox in the United States has not grown, but there has been a transformation in the category whereby the nominally Orthodox have fallen by the wayside, and most of those who define themselves as Orthodox really are. They are part of an elite, in the sense that the distinction between the elite and the mass has virtually disappeared within Orthodox ranks. Moreover, the increase in the number of Orthodox has nearly doubled over what it was in earlier generations, even before factoring in the effects of today's high Orthodox birthrate, when compared to the low non-Orthodox birthrate.

Today, there are between 500,000 and 600,000 Orthodox Jews in the United States, plus another 850,000 in Israel, plus perhaps another 600,000 committed (as distinct from nominal) Orthodox in the rest of the world. This means that there are approximately 2 million Orthodox Jews who are wholly committed to Orthodoxy. That figure does not include non- and semi-observant Orthodox who otherwise identify with Orthodoxy as the right way to be Jewish, even if they do not live up to its precepts. Hence worldwide there are more committed Orthodox than the number of members claimed for the entire Conservative

Movement. As already indicated, the Conservative elite is infinitesimal in comparison. In fact, if the over 2 million affiliated or nominally Orthodox are added in when counting the Orthodox camp, worldwide there are nearly twice as many Orthodox as Conservative and Reform Jews combined. Even if we treat the nominal Orthodox as the equivalent of those who identify as Conservative, the latter are outnumbered by about two to one. Furthermore, the demographics are working for the Orthodox, since their birthrate is almost uniformly high and in some cases as high as any in the world.

The Conservative and Reform movements in the United States have been operating on very country-bound assumptions, namely, that since Orthodoxy is at most 10 percent of American Jewry and the vast majority of American Jews are Reform or Conservative, that that is the pattern in the diaspora as a whole. But the American scene can neither be extrapolated nor extracted from the world scene today, since most of the crucial decisions about religious life have worldwide impact—for example, "Who is a Jew?" legislation in the Israeli Knesset, patrilineal descent decisions in the Reform Movement, and other, similar constitutional issues.

The power of the Orthodox then is not only that of a determined minority, but it flows from numerical strength vis-à-vis the other movements, a worldwide scope that the others lack, and a real power base in Israel where, while a minority of the total Jewish population, Orthodoxy overwelmingly outnumbers the Masorti, Progressive and Liberal religious movements. Certainly the American Orthodox leadership understands what it means to have the base of strength that Orthodoxy has in Israel and even in Canada, Europe, Australia, and South Africa, and they play on it.

Taking into account defection from the Orthodox ranks, as shown in the 1990 NJPS tables, many more American Jewish adults who were raised in Orthodox homes now call themselves Conservative than vice versa, with nearly one-third of those currently Conservative coming from Orthodox homes but just five percent of those currently Orthodox coming from Conservative homes. However, this trend has now come to an end, as 89 percent of those currently Orthodox were raised in Orthodox homes. Currently the Orthodox are having more children and are retaining their allegiance, so their relative proportion and influence in American Jewry should continue to grow. In general, American Jews, like other Americans, do not think of themselves in a world context, but of the world in their context. And for American Jewry, in this case, Conservative Jewry, this can lead to erroneous decision making as it led to false triumphalism in the case of the Reform Movement in the 1980s and early 1990s.

The Conservative Movement really has no serious base of strength outside of North America, and indeed, it may be said outside of the United States, except in Argentina and Chile. Otherwise, it has only outposts (more on this later). Moreover, its base of strength in the United States is diminishing. If present trends continue, it may be unable to sustain the power its institutions presently have in Jewish circles.

In the United States there has been a radical shift in the situation, reflecting the reality of the concentric circles. The Orthodox form the majority of the innermost circle and a high percentage of the next one. This means that while in raw demographics the Orthodox may represent a mere 10 percent, plus or minus, of the American Jewish community, they actually count for much more within the active community. Though only 40 percent of American Jews are affiliated at any given time with the institutions of American Jewish life, the Orthodox are affiliated all of the time. Hence, at the very least, they represent 25 percent of the affiliated.

If we go beyond affiliation to activism, it is reasonable to estimate that Orthodox Jews now represent about one-third of the total of Jewish activists within the American Jewish community, albeit many of them in separatist rather than common activities. This reality is now beginning to be felt in the other institutions of the Jewish community, particularly in the federations and in federation-related bodies, since greater numbers of Orthodox Jews are successfully finding their way into the mainstream Jewish community.

In an age of resurgent fundamentalism in all religions throughout the world, it is a mistake to think of Orthodoxy as a stubborn anachronistic minority using certain levers of power to bring it more importance than it really has. It is both a direct and an indirect threat to the Conservative Movement because of its dynamism. Figures show that while most of those who leave the Conservative Movement go to Reform or to nothing, about 5 percent opt for Orthodoxy. Not surprisingly, the vast majority who do are from the Conservative elite or those who, having gone through the Ramah camps and the Schechter schools, would have opted for the elite. Thus while in overall percentage figures the "bleeding" to Orthodoxy may not be that significant, the percentage is a significant one for the elite cadres of the movement.

On the other hand, the Orthodox challenge should be taken as an opportunity to strengthen an alternative Conservative Jewish approach to tradition that will be as religiously compelling as Orthodoxy. At a time when the Orthodox Movement is moving to the right and adopting a "hard-line" approach to *halakhah* and Jewish life in general, which stands in antithesis to the Conservative approach to Jewish matters in so many ways, this is possible.

## THE CHANGING FAMILY[7]

The increase in one-person households, that is, of singles of all ages; later age at first marriage; delayed childbearing and a below-replacement-level birthrate; a higher divorce rate—with a resultant increase in single-parent families; and the small growth of single-parent families by choice—all of these create household types that do not fit into the demographic model of the ideal family toward which the vast majority of Conservative synagogues are "user-friendly." Membership goals and synagogue structures were designed for the suburban nuclear families of the post World War II era. Even dues and voting structures are predicated on households containing couples with school-age children at home (and, often, by including school fees, assume that these children do not go to day school).

Dual-career and two-job families find it difficult to fit into the division of labor based upon which synagogues have allocated the volunteer work so necessary for making their institutions function. Finally, the impact of intermarriage, even with conversion of the non-Jewish spouse, on parents and grandparents connected to synagogues has been incalculable. All of these, along with the movement away from all institutional ties and affiliations—for historical and sociological reasons—hit the Conservative Movement very hard. The Movement has already been battling for nearly two decades to confront these problems, particularly in its congregations, with varying degrees of success.

These are particularly acute problems, because the institutional life of the Conservative Movement is built upon the family as its nucleus. In this respect, it is like all Jewish movements that deal with long-term localistic and personal needs. The Jewish people and its religion are anchored in the family, and it is hard to think of Jewish survival without a strong familial base. It is like thinking of the American political system without strong local government. It might happen, but if it does, America will be an entirely different country. The same thing is true for the Jewish people: without families, the Jewish people may survive, but the family will be an entirely different entity. It is possible to change the shape of the family, as has been done several times over the course of Jewish history, but not to live without it.

The Conservative Movement is even more family centered than the Jewish people as a whole because of an accident of history. It was born and developed at a time in history when the nuclear family was at its strongest and most complete. A bit of historical background is necessary here. Prior to the twentieth century, most Jews lived within the framework of the extended family to a greater or a lesser degree. Even in quasi-traditional communities, one lived surrounded by grandparents, aunts, uncles, and cousins. Ironically, the single-parent situation also was not rare prior to the twentieth century. It seems that there was an even higher percentage of single-parent families in the nineteenth century and earlier because of early death, migration, desertion, and the like; but in most cases, other members of the extended family could step in to help. Only in the New World did this sometimes become a serious economic problem.

In the early twentieth century, as mortality rates changed, it became more likely that both parents would survive for many years. The Conservative Movement grew, as this phenomenon became widespread and built its congregations on the nuclear family and perhaps even more important its aspirations on the notion of multigenerational affiliation to the same congregation. As we move into another era, in which single-parent families and new family configurations are increasingly common, the Conservative Movement has a lot of adapting to do. At the very least, it has to consider the extent to which it wants to adapt to these new realities and the extent to which it wants to stand for older norms. These configurations, based as they are on the breakup of the original nuclear family, tend to lower Jewish affiliation and practice, partly because of the traumas involved and partly because of the family centered requisites of Jewish involvement. To this can be added the impact of the feminization of poverty and the cost of living Jewishly.

Widespread intermarriage poses both problems and opportunities. The problem of families based on intermarriages is a real one, even when the originally non-Jewish partner has converted. In many cases, the convert, even if devoted to Judaism, does not appreciate the peoplehood dimensions of being Jewish, but sees his or her conversion as essentially a religious matter in the limited American sense. Since identification with the Jewish people is far deeper and more complex, requiring a great deal more of the individual than the overtly religious dimensions, at some point this could make a difference in the strength of the newly undertaken Jewish commitment. The Conservative Movement, with its concern for Jewish peoplehood, must seek ways to foster a sense of Jewish wholeness among these new Jews.

Moreover, converts these days do not abandon their non-Jewish families. Hence their children are exposed to both Jewish and non-Jewish ways of life in a manner never before experienced in Jewish history, except perhaps among the Marranos, with all of the implications for influencing minority survival in the midst of a majority with a very attractive way of life. This is a problem less susceptible to being treated by organized effort.

All in all, interfaith marriage and conversion are likely to be with us for a long time. Hence the addition of Jews by choice should be viewed as an opportunity and a challenge. All Jewish movements have to rise to the occasion and transform what could be an erosion of Jewish strength into an overall gain. Here the synagogues are in the front line.

Migration, always a serious factor in Jewish life, has taken on new meaning for American Jewry and for the Conservative Movement in particular. Today it is increasingly unlikely that children who grow up in a particular congregation will stay in that congregation. The natural history is something as follows: originally there were congregations of families. At first, when the neighborhoods changed, the synagogue building was shifted, but most of the families went along because they moved at roughly the same time. Then there was a second stage when neighborhoods changed and synagogues moved and held onto only a portion of their earlier memberships as neighborhood outmigration led to scatteration over the metropolitan area. Now migration is more likely to involve children or even members moving from region to region within North America.

The Orthodox are less migratory than other groups, with about 5 percent ages eighteen to forty-four having moved interstate between 1985 and 1990, while almost 20 percent of self-designated Conservative and Reform Jews had done so. More traditional levels of observance are associated with greater residential stability. Over age forty-five, there is less mobility and less association of mobility with denominational affiliation. In fact, among the forty-five to sixty-four-year-olds, Conservative Jews were the most stable, followed by Orthodox and Reform Jews. Those ages sixty-five and over are the least mobile of all.

There is an association between shifting denominations and migration. Are "stayers" less mobile than "switchers," whose 1990 movement identification was different than that in which they were raised? The Goldsteins note that, "Considerable evidence supports the thesis that change in denomination is associated with geographic movement, especially when the distance of the move is taken into account" (p. 181). This is important data for the Conservative Movement, for if migration leads to a move from Conservative to Reform affiliation, then it is critical to find ways to enhance a Continent-wide sense of Movement allegiance. For instance, membership in a Conservative congregation in one city or state might automatically grant first-year membership in a new location. New electronic mail linkages should broadcast the arrival of potential congregants from rabbis in one city or state to another, and "welcome wagons" should follow.[8]

For at least two generations and perhaps longer, rabbis and synagogue leaders have geared their activities to the notion that they were producing the next generation of their own congregation. Indeed, part of their unwillingness to cooperate in community-wide or movement-wide activities, or even in intercongregational activities, was based upon this assumption, that they had to fight to retain their own people as members, assuming that this could happen. It cannot. If congregations emphasize that kind of continuity, they do not do themselves or the Movement any service.

Conservative congregations today have to educate people to be part of the Conservative Movement, wherever they happen to be. In return, they stand to gain from in-migration, and their children will remain within the Movement when they move elsewhere. If they do not do that, if they educate only for narrow congregationalism, then migration is as likely as not to result in membership decline. When people move to a new place, they look around to see where their new friends belong, and they join, regardless of the movement. That indeed is what has happened throughout the Sunbelt from the 1950s onward. Congregationalism on the basis of social network ties rather than movement concern became the norm.

All of this also has particular implications for the cathedral synagogue and its parallels. The cathedral synagogue was predicated on two things: intergenerational continuity and neighborhood stability. Both proved erroneous. For a while, cathedral synagogues could be sold when the time came to move on, but that has become increasingly difficult, as money has become tighter and interest rates have risen. Moreover, the cost of reproducing the cathedral synagogue has increased astronomically. While Jews have the money to pay for such synagogues, if they do not believe that their children and children's children will use them, their willingness to provide that money is likely to diminish, and indeed it probably has. The synagogue needs to become a portable institution again, not exactly to be housed in tents but certainly placing its emphasis on more modest buildings that are both more serviceable and, in fact, more disposable.

The importance of the demographic situation cannot be overestimated. The Conservative Movement after all is a popular, even mass, movement, and it gains its strength from that. If it is to be more than a transient phenomenon in Jewish history, even in American Jewish life, it will have to find ways to turn the present situation around.

Against this apparently gloomy portrait, we can see some positive resources for renewal. The numbers may have declined, but the principal reasons for the declines may have passed. The size of the Movement may have shrunk, but the quality of Jewish life for those remaining—in terms of ritual observance and perhaps commitment to Jewish education for themselves and their children—is certainly no worse and may in fact be better than Conservative Jews two and three decades ago. All of this adds up to a challenge and to an opportunity. The challenge lies in reversing decades of quantitative erosion. The opportunity lies in raising the quality of Conservative Jewish life to meet the needs of a still sizable and still Jewishly committed constituency.

## A NOTE ON REGIONALISM IN THE CONSERVATIVE MOVEMENT

American Jewry has been no less affected by the migrations that have shaped American society from its beginnings to the present than other Americans. The migrations westward and southward in this century have led to the establishment of major new Jewish centers west of the Mississippi and south of the Mason-Dixon line. Conservative Judaism has been much a part of these migrations.

Unlike Reform Judaism, which arose in the nineteenth century while Americans were settling what is now the Midwest and the West and offered Jewish settlers on the frontier who were abandoning much of traditional Judaism another religious vehicle that to them seemed American, Conservative Judaism came along after the close of the land frontier at a time when the United States was urbanizing. In a sense, it was the Americanizing movement of the Jewish settlers on the urban frontier as Reform had been on the land frontier. Hence it was rarely the first expression of Judaism in a particular locality, but often the first expression for many Eastern European Jews.

### The Northeast

Nevertheless, sectional differences have influenced and do influence the different expressions of Conservative Judaism in different parts of the United States. While there is no hard-and-fast rule, and one can find congregations of all kinds in the Movement's Northeastern heartland, it is not unfair to say that a more traditional Conservative

Judaism emerged and survived for longer in the Northeast than in other parts of the country. In part, this simply had to do with the characteristics of the Northeast compared to those elsewhere. For example, Jews in the Northeast lived in relatively compact neighborhoods more frequently and longer than they did elsewhere, so the possibility of walking to synagogue on Sabbaths and Holy Days remained a viable one until suburbanization after World War II, and for its religious elites until the 1980s. The more dispersed Jewish communities in other parts of the country out of necessity began to use their automobiles long before many of their counterparts living in the large Eastern cities did. Even the elites probably shifted to adjust to these realities earlier than their counterparts in the Northeast.

The dense Jewish population in the Northeast also meant that the Conservative Movement had to compete with other organized expressions of Judaism to secure its place. The idea of the synagogue center, first proposed by the late Mordecai Kaplan, was particularly useful under those conditions where synagogues felt the need to offer more comprehensive services to their members and not merely religious ones in order to compete for membership. This was much less true outside of the Northeast, where most Conservative synagogues were established in already reasonably well-structured communities in which many of the functions that the synagogue centers were called upon to perform in the Northeast were served by other Jewish organizations of a communal nature.

### The West

Efforts to build synagogue centers in the Midwest, West, and South were much less successful and were indeed looked upon by many congregants as an undesirable separation from the local Jewish community which, because the local Jewish populations were smaller, both in absolute numbers and percentage of the total population, felt the need to work together more intensely than in the Northeast. After World War II and the beginnings of massive suburbanization, synagogues in suburbs everywhere often were the first Jewish institutions on the ground in newly settled areas and were thus encouraged to provide services that no one else was.

This had particular consequences in the realm of Jewish education. In the Northeast, Conservative synagogues established their own schools from the first, and leading Jewish educators supported them in that effort, even though it meant the end of the older Talmud Torahs, which were independent. In the Midwest, the Talmud Torah system was communal, and it provided Jewish education for traditional Jews,

Conservative and Orthodox, or unaffiliated (only the Reform remained separated in their Sunday schools). Except for the largest cities, Conservative congregational efforts to establish independent schools were met with resistance until postwar suburbanization. Only then were congregations that wanted to have their own schools successful in doing so. In the West and the South, there were fewer Talmud Torah schools and relatively few congregations, often only one Conservative and one Reform in any particular community, so each established its own educational framework.

It was in the area of ritual innovation that regional differences may have been most pronounced. As in the case of traveling on the Sabbath, the difference in conditions between the Northeast and the rest of the country led to more and earlier ritual modifications or accommodations in other regions. This is not to say that there were no congregations that engaged in such experimentation in the Northeast as well, but they were the outliers and did not set the trends, whereas in the other regions they often were the leading congregations and pacesetters. For example, greater egalitarianism in ritual matters first developed west of the Mississippi, from Minneapolis to Los Angeles, where the rabbis who were spiritual leaders of leading congregations took steps in the early 1950s to increase women's role in the worship services, two decades before the overall Movement response.

Educational experimentation also was easier in the Midwest and the West. For example, while Camp Ramah was conceived at the Seminary (Kaplan again), the existence of Hebrew camps reduced the need for action in the Northeast, while in the Midwest the need for a Hebrew camp appeared more pressing to both the professional and voluntary leaders of the community. It was the Chicago leadership who took the initiative to establish the first of the Ramah camps in Wisconsin in 1947. For years there was a struggle between the local leadership and the Seminary over the course and nature of the camp. Similarly, USY was first developed in Minneapolis in 1947 by Rabbi Kassel Abelson.

When Mordecai Kaplan (again) proposed a university of Judaism to provide an integrated framework for transmitting Jewish civilization to Jews generally, not only to future rabbis and other professionals, Los Angeles, then a burgeoning community, seemed to be the most hospitable place to locate it. Here the Seminary was more directly involved, with Simon Greenberg, the Seminary's vice chancellor, spending several years in Los Angeles to launch the project.

Unfortunately, because of the weakness of Jewish scholarship in the West at the time and the particular characteristics of Jewish Los Angeles, the institution continued to function as an adult education program on a rather superficial basis for many years, and it has not been able to entirely transform itself, even now. It has made strides toward building more serious Judaic studies programs, culminating in the decision to establish an independent rabbinical school to train rabbis separately from the JTS, based on a curriculum that promises to be more innovative and change oriented than the JTS itself has advocated. Since the school is only in its early stages any serious consideration of it and its impact will have to await later treatment.

In sum, for Jews, as well as for non-Jews, the West (including the Midwest, the trans-Mississippi West, and the Far West) has been a region for religious innovation, primarily because necessity has forced change under different local conditions. Many of those innovations have since spread to the rest of the country and have been adopted as the formal position of the Conservative Movement. Informally, there is still a greater radicalism and separation from traditional Jewish norms and behavior of Jews specifically in the Far West, with people seeking ways to express their Jewishness that seem to be further removed from traditional sources and more attuned to religious and behavioral expectations of their environment. These often are perceived to shine alongside or in comparison to more traditional institutions.

## The South

The Conservative Movement came to the South relatively late, because Jews began moving southward in numbers to settle only in the 1960s, and then primarily to Florida.[9] The Jews in the rest of the South tended to be descendants of long-settled families whose congregations became Reform in the nineteenth century. If there are any special characteristics to Conservative Judaism in the South, they are to be found in Southeast Florida, where 630,000 Jews live from Miami to Palm Beach; over half of those identified religiously are classified Conservatives, and they form the third largest concentration of Jews in the country.[10] No one as yet has studied in depth the patterns of Jewish religiosity in South Florida, to the best of our knowledge.

In the first period, when "snowbirds" who were temporary sojourners and retirees dominated the migrants, Conservative congregations looked for rabbis who would be "stars," who could attract crowds of people who were either nostalgic for what they knew back home or were seeking something "dynamic" in a new place. What united them was their relative Jewish illiteracy, along with considerable experience with traditional Judaism. This was particularly true when the community consisted primarily of people who spent only part of the year in Florida. As the community has become more permanent and grounded in the region, congregations have come to be more like those elsewhere, with the need for "rabbis as stars" diminishing. The variety of congregations has come to resemble that of the rest of the country and the quest for Jewish knowledge, albeit still at a beginning stage, has been assisted by professors of Judaic studies at the local universities and not confined entirely to congregational rabbis. This is a national rather than a specifically regional phenomenon.

# Chapter 6

# *Leadership*

The subject of leadership in the Conservative Movement is a delicate and sensitive one. The discussion of the Movement's origin and history, institutions, ideology, and style is in the nature of structural issues in which only a few individuals come to mind, while the discussion of demographics is even further removed from the actions of individual leaders. But leadership as a subject is by definition intimately tied to individuals. Nevertheless, it is our intention here to set out general principles, not to reflect on the strengths or weaknesses of individuals who have played or continue to play leadership roles in the Movement.

## IN THE MOVEMENT

The fact is, the Conservative Movement in recent years has suffered from a paucity of compelling leaders able to confront its problems and motivate others to respond to them. This is perhaps most dramatically demonstrated in the Seminary's longtime reliance on certain very talented surviving members of its senior staff from the third generation of its rabbinical leadership (that is, those who served their apprenticeship immediately after World War I, becoming leaders by the end of the interwar generation) to reach out to the Movement in the congregations. Most continued until they died. Few of the fourth and even fifth generations have been able to do what they did.

This is not a question of competence. There are many competent people scattered throughout the Movement. The issue has been particularly crucial with regard to the top level of leadership, those who set the tone, guide its policies, and administer the Movement's affairs countrywide and in world arenas. In a sense, a generation of top leadership is missing, and its absence has not been felt until now.

This dearth of top-level leadership has several dimensions. One is the decline in the influence of the major figures at the JTS, both within the Movement and in the larger Jewish world. Because the Seminary has been entrusted with the leadership of the Movement since its founding, and in a real sense fathered the Movement, no alternative has emerged. Therefore, if it does not have leadership, the Movement does not have leadership.

Alternatives may emerge to Seminary leadership if the present situation continues. Over the last decade, the presidents of the Rabbinical Assembly have hesitatingly tried to step in to fill the vacuum, both personally and through the strengthening of the RA committees, but it is not the same, since they are essentially short-term leaders who continue to have all the congregational responsibilities of their colleagues while trying to play movement-wide roles. The RA as an institution could become more important as a source of leadership under the right circumstances, but that will require extensive institutional restructuring and even a change in the rabbinical roles of its leaders.

Most congregations resent having their rabbis spend too much time in activities outside of the congregational walls. Only very well established rabbis have that luxury, and then only in moderation. The localistic leadership of the congregations figures that it is paying for local services, not supporting statesmen to go further afield. That is one of the reasons for the decline in the visibility of great rabbinical figures, who were generally Reform rabbis of an earlier generation or rabbis serving Conservative congregations in the Reform mold, in the sense that their central activity was the weekly worship service and sermon. They were not called upon to do much else. Therefore, if a rabbi was a great preacher, he had the time and the vehicle for reaching a larger countrywide and even worldwide audience. Since even Reform synagogues now demand more attention from their rabbis, this phenomenon has disappeared.

We have already noted the difficulties in recruiting non-rabbinic leadership. The emergence of a stronger lay leadership in recent years is to be commended. The present leadership should be strengthened, and efforts should be made to supplement them through broad recruitment.

Except for the JTS board, both JTS and RA leadership almost by definition have to be rabbinical. Thus rabbinical predominance exacerbates the overall leadership problem. This is not an age for clericalism, and a movement that has to rely on people who emphasize that dimension is going to have perennial difficulties. The JTS escaped the problem somewhat in the past by elevating scholars who were scholar-statesmen and for whom the title rabbi was a source of authority, but not a particular source of power. All of this seems to suggest that there is a need for new channels of recruitment for both rabbinic and non-rabbinic leadership. These new channels must be able to overcome the limits of localistic congregationalism on the one hand and the problems of bureaucratization in the "central office" on the other hand.

## IN THE CONGREGATIONS

Just as the real strength of the Conservative Movement is in its congregations, so too is the strength of its leadership. Its many dedicated rabbinic and non-rabbinic leaders do excellent work in meeting the heavy demands placed upon them to serve their congregations in the variegated roles that they are expected to fill. Rabbis are called upon to be counselors, pastors, priests, and teachers, probably in that order, and from time to time, to be ambassadors to the larger community as well. They fulfill these roles even though the evidence indicates that they would prefer a different order of importance attached to them. In a democratic age, this kind of solid, middle-level democratic leadership is to be recognized as very important and valuable, but it is a leadership that will not rise above that station, even if it aspires to do so.

Leadership also is being affected by changes taking place in the broader American society. Thus the new-style business acumen of many board members, particularly those who undertake the conduct of negotiations with rabbis over salaries and terms of employment, has created an adversarial relationship to which the rabbis have responded by bringing in professional negotiators in an effort to get themselves the best deal possible, or simply in order to resist being taken advantage of by board members who are more skilled than they are in negotiations over such matters. This adversarial relationship has become common throughout American society, but it is new to most congregations where the ideal, if not the norm, was that board members had a certain respect for the rabbi and would not treat him as a negotiating adversary, and that the rabbi had a self-perception that did not permit entry into such an adversarial confrontation.[1]

Other changes taking place in American society have their impact on the rabbinate. More rabbis are committed to American notions of separating career and family and leisure time activities, and they are demanding more leisure time for themselves. In previous generations, many rabbis were frustrated because they personally had serious Jewish intellectual and religious concerns, not only more intense but often in advance of their congregants. Some even had to hide their true beliefs from congregations that could not appreciate them.[2]

Increasingly today, the tendency is for rabbis, while they may not be less serious about their Judaism, to share the views of their congregants. Many of these rabbis are successful in their own way, but they may conceptualize their role as professionals who pursue their careers. While they normally do so in an honorable way, this kind of self-definition does not lead people to make the choices or mount the challenges necessary to be leaders.

For example, now it has become professionally quite acceptable to negotiate the best salary and conditions possible for one's job, even turning the matter over to professional negotiators where necessary, but the result invariably must be a diminution of the spiritual standing of people meant to be spiritual leaders, even if it does not prevent them from doing a good, professional job. By the same token, the great rabbinical leaders of earlier times were almost always supported by wives who took seriously their roles as *rebbetzins* (Yiddish for a rabbi's wife).

At the same time, rabbis seem to be suffering even more than in the past from the stress and frustration associated with their positions, with the amount of stress and frustration growing in proportion to the dedication of the person involved.

These comments should not obscure the real difficulties inherent in the rabbinic role as it has developed in the United States. Rabbis have great difficulty because of the role conflicts that they find thrust upon them. Our research shows that most rabbis like to think of themselves as teachers, whereas their congregants see them either as pastors or counselors. In other words, rather than the educational function that they wish to fulfill, rabbis are required to perform the therapeutic functions that have become even more extensive in the therapeutic society of the United States today. As a result, rabbis who cannot perform that role are often dismissed as failures, while those who can are given recognition beyond their due.

In addition, the old days in which the rabbi's spouse was a *rebbetzin* who served the congregation hardly less than her husband are fast disappearing. Not only do rabbis' spouses, now men as well as women, pursue their own careers, but in some cases, they actively reject a share in their spouses' careers on the grounds that the congregation should not get for free what they are not willing to pay for. A few even pursue activities that stand diametrically opposed to the teachings that rabbis are presumed to espouse. All of this is consistent with the larger individualistic trends in American society, but it is hard to believe that it will not have a negative impact on Jewish life which, especially in its religious dimension, requires a strong spirit of dedication above and beyond the call of duty. All of this may be exacerbated when the spouse is a man or the rabbi is single.

Often, the non-rabbinic leadership in Conservative congregations is too far removed from the religious and educational dimension of congregational life. Such lay leaders confine themselves to what they know best, namely, worrying about the congregational budget and membership. They are not only not qualified to worry about programs, but they often are only minimally interested. While it is no longer the case that congregational presidents do not even show up for services, it is true that, except in those congregations geared to high involvement levels—such as the *bet midrash* (study hall) and *havurah* types—few congregational leaders are involved in continuing educational programs, unless an exceptional rabbi is able to establish that as a prerequisite for leadership.

To the extent that the latter models are spreading, this situation may be changing for the better. Whenever the *baalei batim* come from appropriate backgrounds, again emphasizing Ramah and the Schechter schools, and in some cases USY, they do have the requisite backgrounds to concern themselves with the substantive programs. Where this is the case, the quality of those programs is almost inevitably raised. The congregation is a more deeply serious enterprise, and the quality of its religious Jewish life is enhanced. The recruitment of such leadership should be encouraged.

In the last analysis, there is a strong tendency for rabbis to become chief executive officers (CEOs) and for congregational presidents to become chairmen of the board (COB). But even as the corporate world has discovered, to be a CEO or a COB is not necessarily to be a leader. Rather, it is a way of fitting into a management hierarchy that is something else entirely.

Conservative congregations are hardly alone in this phenomenon of substituting management for leadership. It has become a common complaint in American society, and congregations suffer from the results. Today, the business world is discovering, as are religious institutions, that good management is not enough.

## IN THE JEWISH WORLD

Outside of the synagogue, Conservative rabbis in particular have a different but no less acute problem. With their self-image as the heirs of the great rabbinic sages of *Talmud* (Oral Law), further reinforced, in many cases by the high status given to them by their congregations, rabbis seek special status in the larger community as the teachers of Israel, the guardians of the Torah. In fact, power in the community is elsewhere, and they are looked upon by those who hold the power, essentially high-level non-rabbinic voluntary leaders, or high-level Jewish civil servants in the federations, as another species of Jewish professional, indeed a professional whose main preoccupation is not cooperating with the larger community.

This seems to be more true of Conservative rabbis than of others. Reform rabbis never had expectations in the realm of Torah, but many did have expectations in the realm of community activity, seeing that as part of their function as bearers of the message of prophetic Judaism. Thus they easily fit into the communal framework outside of their congregations and the therapeutic framework inside. Orthodox rabbis knew where they stood in the hierarchy of *posekim*, and they had congregants who expected them to fit into that hierarchy in a certain way and who demanded little of them beyond their traditional functions. Moreover, they did not seek to participate in the general Jewish community, being involved in a rather separate Orthodox world. It is the Conservative rabbi who has suffered the most confusion of roles, a bearer of the *keter torah*, but not a *posek*, concerned with the community but unable to transcend rabbinic and localistic expectations and needs.

## VOLUNTARY LEADERSHIP IN THE EXISTING INSTITUTIONAL FRAMEWORK

The institutional leadership for the Conservative Movement as a whole is shared by a triumvirate of institutions—the Jewish Theological Seminary, the Rabbinical Assembly, and the United Synagogue of Conservative Judaism. As is normal, there is both cooperation and

competition among the three, and there also seems to be a certain hierarchy of influence with the JTS on top, then the RA, and finally the
United Synagogue. Previous chapters explained why the JTS stands at
the top of the pyramid.

The position of the RA was determined in two ways: through the
connection of its members to the JTS as former students, and through
the dominant role that came to be expected of individual rabbis within
their respective congregations. It should be noted that, while the leading rabbinical figures of the Movement were indeed powerful because
of their strong positions within their congregations, this situation was
far from being universally true. Most rabbis found themselves sharing
power with their congregational boards, and some even found themselves at the mercy of the lay leadership. All three of these models are
legitimate, in the sense that they have precedents in Jewish history, but
there is no question that the dominant voices in the Movement emphasized the first model, that of the rabbi as *mara d'atra*. Indeed, those rabbis in the last category were considered particularly unfortunate.

Despite the power of the *baalei batim* in particular congregations—
or perhaps because of it—the Movement as a whole did not develop a
strong non-rabbinic leadership. With some notable exceptions, lay
leaders were so poorly educated Jewishly that they could not even
engage in meaningful interaction with their rabbis on matters requiring Jewish knowledge. Synagogism encouraged and rewarded localistic as distinct from cosmopolitan lay leadership—those for whom their
synagogue was the sum and substance of their interest as Conservative
Jews (well described in colloquial terms as "shul Jews"). Those with
broader interests had little or no place to go in the Movement and its
institutions.

Hence, it is not surprising that, for most of its history, the United
Synagogue was dominated by rabbis. Its non-rabbinical leadership
consisted of people who emerged from the individual congregations,
usually under rabbinical tutelage, rather than as sophisticated leaders
capable of matching the rabbis. Often it simply was lack of Jewish
knowledge and observance that made the lay leaders dependent on the
rabbis. The really strong non-rabbinical leaders who were members of
Conservative synagogues often were drawn to other groups—first,
community relations organizations such as the American Jewish Committee, American Jewish Congress, or Anti-Defamation League, and
then to the federations and the United Jewish Appeal. Many of these
people have even been modestly active in their own congregations out
of a sense of noblesse oblige, but they did not rise to major positions in
the Movement because they did not seek them.

Only occasionally would a strong figure arise of his own initiative within the United Synagogue and succeed in establishing himself in an important role, usually for a very brief period before dropping out and going on to other things. Under such circumstances, the rabbis, who also had the advantage of being professionally committed to their careers and, hence, by definition, capable of being more fully involved than any voluntary leader, continued to hold the reins of power.

All of this should not obscure the existence of thousands of dedicated *baalei batim* active in Conservative congregations and in the United Synagogue who are committed to Judaism and Jewish life and strive to be thoughtful, observant, and knowledgeable Conservative Jews. While it would be desirable to attract some of the more cosmopolitan voluntary leadership of the Jewish world to leadership in the Movement, it is even more important to reinforce the ability of these responsible *baalei batim* to make their voices heard.

As is usually the case in such situations, the existing pattern became entrenched and self-fulfilling in all three bodies. The lay leadership that developed attracted others of similar background and interests and discouraged those of different character and orientation, just as in the time of Louis Finkelstein's stewardship of the Seminary, the members of the Talmud department let it be known that only Talmudists should be powerful. The only place where something similar to an egalitarian peer group system developed was in the RA, because most of the rabbis were indeed equals in status, observance, and knowledge.

In recent years, however, there have been changes in all three institutions. A new generation of more educated non-rabbinic leaders has developed within the United Synagogue, and it is beginning to make itself felt, albeit still hesitantly. At the JTS, the Talmud faculty has lost its privileged position to a broader faculty circle often led by members of the history department, now the other power center on the Seminary faculty. Egalitarianism in the RA has led to the development of contested elections for its leadership positions, with competition between two distinct factions. For a movement that prides itself on widespread participation across a broad base, all three of these developments are to be welcomed and should be encouraged. On the other hand, in each case, there is a concomitant loss of established authority that is having its impact on the balance between tradition and change within the Movement, something that will be considered in the following pages.

Beyond that, there is the issue of representation of the Movement in other Jewish forums. This is a delicate matter, since it involves drawing the line between necessary partisanship and simple power play.

Many observers of the Federation and community relations worlds suggest that activists in those spheres of communal activity who identify as Orthodox display an overt sense of loyalty and obligation to Orthodoxy in their roles as communal leaders. Many Orthodox *baalei batim* enter the wider communal world in part out of a strong sense of Orthodox partisanship. They often are seeking communal support to further Orthodox institutional interests, or they try to shape the agenda of the Federation or community relations agency in ways that are consistent with their understanding of the political and social concerns of Orthodoxy. Some (though certainly not most) leaders in communal life who identify as Reform Jews also participate in Federation and community relations agency affairs with Reform institutional or social agendas in mind.

In contrast, the impression of most observers is that few activists identified with Conservative Judaism participate in Jewish communal life as Conservative partisans. The vast majority have little sense of the relationship between Conservative Judaism and most of the issues they confront—from Jewish philanthropic priorities to domestic American concerns. Even if they were aware of Conservative concerns, it is questionable whether their support for the Conservative agenda would be as fervent as that found today among many of their Orthodox and some of their Reform counterparts. According to Ismar Schorsch, the current chancellor, this is a hallmark of Conservative Judaism, at least since Schechter's concern for "catholic Israel." Part of the task of the Movement is to educate these community leaders. This also is a great opportunity to mobilize them and others hitherto peripheral to the Movement's decision-making core to explore the meaning of Conservative Judaism outside of the synagogue. If Conservative Judaism takes seriously its claim to include human issues within *halakhah*, then this is one vehicle for making that claim real.

# Chapter 7

# *The World Movement*

As of 1996, there were an estimated 13,025,000 Jews in the world. Approximately 5.7 million live in the United States, and 362,000 live in Canada. An additional 4,567,700 live in Israel, about 595,000 in the former Soviet Union, and well over 1 million in Western European countries. The largest of these Jewish communities is found in France, with 524,000 Jews, the United Kingdom, with 291,000, and Germany, with 70,000. Nearly another half-million are in Central and South America (440,000), with the largest concentrations in Argentina (205,000) and Brazil (100,000). As noted by Sergio DellaPergola, "Just about half of the world's Jews reside in the Americas, with over 46% in North America. Over 35% live in Asia . . . most of them in Israel. Europe . . . accounts for over 13% of the total. Less than 2% of the world's Jews live in Africa and Oceania."[1]

While the United States has the largest Jewish community, it contains less than half of world Jewry, and the ratio between it and Israel is rapidly narrowing. In 1914, there were forty Jews in the United States for every one in Israel. By 1948, that ratio had shifted to 10:1; by 1963, to 3:1; by 1975, to 2:1; and today, approximately to 5:4. If the demographers' median projections for the next generation are correct, sometime around 2010 Israel will pass the United States to become the largest Jewish community in the world as a result of the decline in the number of American Jews and the growth rate in the state. Needless to say, if that or something approximating it occurs, American Jewry will lose some of its special position on the world Jewish scene.

## THE NEW CONTEXT OF WORLD JEWRY

One of the most important phenomena of our times has been the reemergence of an increasingly well-integrated world Jewish community with its own polity, focused on the State of Israel but embodied in a network of "national institutions" centered on the Jewish Agency (we use the term in the Zionist sense, referring to the Jewish nation, not to any particular country) and Jewish multi-country organizations such as the World Jewish Congress in which Israel and the diaspora Jewish community are represented and work together on common tasks. This world Jewish polity represents a restoration of *Adat B'nai Yisrael* (the community of the children of Israel), in the sense of the assembly of Israelites, embodied in concrete institutions to serve *Am Yisrael* (the Nation of Israel), which is held together by a common faith, a common religious tradition, and a shared history, but which until recently did not have the institutional structure required to function as a body.

There is no doubt that Zionism and the establishment of the State of Israel contributed decisively to the reemergence of a world Jewish polity. In addition, changes in transportation and communications technology and the increase in Jewish wealth and leisure time were crucial to making this possible. Today, hardly any Jew is more than one day's flight away from any other, give or take a few hours, or from Israel, and the vast majority of Jews are in closer proximity. This is reflected in the fact that an estimated 26 percent of all American Jews have visited Israel at least once. Among those who consider themselves Jewish by religion, the percentage is 31 percent, of the secular Jews it is 11 percent, and of the Jews by choice it is 11 percent. This is a very high figure when it is recognized that over 40 percent of all American Jews have never left the United States.[2] Moreover, virtually all Jews in the world are just seconds away from their brethren through the telephone and increasingly through electronic communication devices such as the Internet, produced by the cybernetic revolution.

These interconnections are bound to increase as the cybernetic frontier advances. Hence, world Jewry is becoming increasingly inter-related on every level. Whereas even a few years ago contacts between the various Jewish communities of the world occurred almost exclusively at the top leadership level, as though the tips of different pyramids would occasionally touch, today there are networks of relationships, including family and interpersonal ones, that are rapidly turning all of the Jewish world into a single matrix, all of whose cells are interconnected. This was already apparent by the Yom Kippur War, when every Jewish community of over 7,500 in the United States and many smaller ones absorbed casualties from among its sons who had settled in Israel.

What is happening to American Jewry in this regard is similar to what is happening to the United States as a whole. Until a few years ago, Americans, no matter how involved their government was in international affairs, could feel that the United States was more or less insulated from the rest of the world, except to the extent that it wanted to absorb foreign immigrants and foreign capital or enjoy foreign climes through investment and tourism abroad. Today, the United States, with a huge trade deficit and with a dollar that fluctuates against other currencies, has become almost fully integrated into the world economy. Under such circumstances, no less can be expected of its Jews, especially since the American Jewish community wants to be connected with Israel and other Jews elsewhere.

This situation opens up whole new vistas for the Jewish people and creates new challenges for those movements in Jewish life that were most indigenous to and even confined to the United States, the Conservative Movement being first and foremost among them.

## THE SCOPE OF THE WORLD CONSERVATIVE/MASORTI MOVEMENT

Technically, the Conservative Movement is worldwide in scope. In fact, it is overwhelmingly a U. S. movement, with some overlap into Canada. As of 1992, the diaspora comprised 67 percent (8,704, 900) of world Jewry, with just over 3 million of these outside of the United States.[3] In all of that sea of Jews outside of the United States, more than 7 million all told, there are probably fewer than 60,000 affiliated or identified with the Conservative Movement.

The Movement's greatest successes outside of the United States and Israel (where there are now forty congregations, the Tali school movement, a kibbutz, a moshav, the Noam youth movement, and a thriving *Beit Midrash*, now known as Machon Schechter, to train rabbis and teachers) have been in South America, especially in Argentina, and in Great Britain. In Argentina, there is a whole network of Conservative institutions founded by the late Rabbi Marshall Meyer when he was rabbi of Congregation Bet-El in Buenos Aires. These include five congregations, a rabbinical school, a youth movement, and a Camp Ramah. When Rabbi Meyer moved to New York, he brought graduates of the Seminario Rabbinico to work at Congregation B'nai Jeshurun in Manhattan and created greater interaction between the Seminario in Buenos Aires and the JTS in New York. JTS faculty teach there regularly, as they now do in Budapest as well.

Elsewhere, in Central and Latin America, there are Masorti congregations in Chile, Colombia, Brazil, and Mexico. (Technically, the United Synagogue considers Canadian, Central American, and those synagogues in U.S. possessions such as Puerto Rico part of the North American organization rather than the World Council of Synagogues.) In England, mostly in London and its environs, there is a network of congregations. Rabbi Louis Jacobs is considered the nominal "chief rabbi" of the Masorti Movement in Britain. Several of the Masorti rabbis in England were ordained at Machon Schechter in Jerusalem. Rabbis from Machon Schechter also are serving in the former Soviet Union and in reconstituted communities elsewhere in Europe. Efforts are now underway to establish a presence in Germany, and a new French *machzor* (High Holiday or Festival prayerbook) has been commissioned from the Rabbinical Assembly. In Denmark, Norway, and Sweden, the mainstream synagogues are de facto, if not dejure, part of the Conservative Movement. There also is an affiliated synagogue in Johannesburg, South Africa.

In fact, contrary to its position in the United States, the Conservative Movement is the third of the three main branches of Judaism on the world scene. Orthodoxy, which is third in the United States, subject to the qualifications mentioned above, is clearly first. It is established almost everywhere outside of the United States, and even in the two or three small communities where it is not (Sweden, Denmark, and perhaps Hungary), its presence is strong. It also has the numbers to back up its official or quasi-official status. Indeed, there are usually more breakaway right-wing Orthodox in those communities than organized non-Orthodox.

The Reform Movement also is moderately strong outside of the United States. There are Liberal, Progressive, or Reform synagogues (the terms mean different things in different places, including traditional or

Conservative in some places) in almost every country with even a modest Jewish community, and they are generally well established, although clearly no more than minority expressions within a predominantly Orthodox scene. Moreover, they also have a world movement headquartered in Jerusalem that has some meaning and that draws serious leadership from countries other than the United States.

Given the greater integration of the world in all of its facets and the reemergence of a world Jewish polity bound by increasingly intense interaction among its parts, the weakness of the worldwide movement is a serious problem for Conservative Judaism, one that has generally been ignored because of the American centeredness of the Movement. It is not only that there is very little out there, but what there is has very little voice in the Movement, in part because of the Movement's American-centered orientation and style and in part because of its present leadership structures. There is a real question about whether the Movement is too American to move much beyond the United States. Certainly it will not be able to do so unless it continues to develop leadership outside of the United States.

Here too the Conservative Movement is up against one of Orthodoxy's strengths. Orthodoxy is a world movement in its leadership as well as in its membership. There are major Orthodox leaders in Israel, the United States, and even in Europe, figures who command large battalions even among the nominally Orthodox.

It is true that most of those outside of the United States who are affiliated with Orthodox congregations practice their Judaism like Conservative Jews, but for whatever reason, up to now they have not wanted to formally identify with a group that actually says that it changes *halakhah* and makes things easier (for that is how it is perceived in their minds) and does not simply close its eyes to individual practice while maintaining a certain public standard of observance.

This attitude reflects a basic difference in outlook separating the United States from the rest of the world. Americans take pride in being pragmatic, that is, in trying hard to bring ideals into convergence with reality and to despise "hypocrisy," or, any endorsement of ideals that is very different from the expected reality. Most of the rest of the world, on the other hand, being more pessimistic about human nature, has lower expectations of reality, but most believe that higher ideals are important in order to keep human beings from losing sight of a better way of life. This has its carryover into the religious sphere, where many Jews outside of the United States consider it perfectly proper to view traditional Orthodoxy (as distinct from fundamentalist Orthodoxy) as the ideal, even if they expect to fall short of Orthodox standards and do not have any intention of changing their ways. They believe that public recognition of what is right has its own virtues and is not hypocritical.

The Conservative Movement's success in the United States has been a result of its more or less pragmatic American approach. That is precisely why it is of less interest outside of the United States, where pragmatism is often considered to reflect a lack of real standards, or worse, mindlessness.

In recent years, there has been some improvement in this regard. The emergence of a strong and vital Conservative Movement in Argentina began over a quarter of a century ago. The history of the Argentinian movement, which by now is the strongest and most vital Jewish religious force in that country (even though still nominally a minority in confrontation with an Orthodox establishment whose power is preserved by its alliance with a highly secular community structure), is instructive. When the late Rabbi Marshall Meyer, the builder of Conservative Judaism in Argentina, went to Buenos Aires, he did so essentially on his own initiative. That is, there was no deliberate effort on the part of the Movement to build an Argentinian base. It was he and he alone who was able to establish a network of Conservative congregations, a rabbinical seminary, a day school, a Ramah camp, a youth movement, and the other paraphernalia of a movement in that country. While the American Movement gave Meyer Rabbi its blessing, that was about the extent of its support.

Rabbi Meyer spoke to the hearts of many of the younger generation of Argentinian Jewry, earning their respect and affection, which redounded to the benefit of his movement. As a result, Argentinian Jewry was not only revived in a religious sense, but it began to "export" Conservative rabbis to other parts of Latin America, particularly to Chile, its next-door neighbor. A small community facing difficulties as a result of political upheaval within the country, it invariably turns to Argentina for help in securing professionally trained Jewish leadership in the rabbinical and educational spheres.

Several congregations in Brazil and other Latin American countries also have drawn upon graduates of the Seminario Rabinico. This gives the Conservative Movement new opportunities for developing a real Latin American base. The Seminary had been sending a few faculty members to the Seminario since its founding. Over the last decade, this number has increased, as has the export of Seminary faculty as visiting professors to teach in the former Soviet Union.

The situation in Scandinavia was much the same. In Sweden, Morton Narrowe, a graduate of the JTS, became the rabbi of the Jewish Community of Stockholm and was later granted the title of Chief Rabbi of Stockholm.[4] From there, he led the community into nominal affiliation with the Conservative Movement, although basically he embodies the connection. As of his retirement, Rabbi Philip Spectre has filled that position. An *oleh* (immigrant to Israel) and graduate of the Jewish Theological Seminary, he had formerly served as a pulpit rabbi in Ashkelon and as the director of the United Synagogue in Israel. In Denmark, the Melchior family, which for several generations has led the community, found their way into the Conservative Movement for reasons of religious principle. The Norwegian community also is led by a member of the Melchior family.

Recently, modest, concerted efforts have been made by the Movement under the aegis of the World Union to strengthen its presence outside of the United States. Even Canada has remained predominantly Orthodox. In Great Britain, efforts were initiated to capitalize on the break between Rabbi Louis Jacobs and the British Orthodox establishment to bring him and his congregation into the Conservative fold. There are now nearly a *minyan* of Masorti congregations, some with rabbis who are graduates of Machon Schechter in Jerusalem. In fact, Jonathan Sacks, the chief rabbi of the United Synagogue there, has begun attacking the Masorti congregations with vehemence. And the critique and strategic plan for the future of the United Synagogue—*A Time for Change*, published under the leadership of David Sacks in 1992—continually contrasts losses in United Synagogue membership to the growth of Masorti congregations. Beginning to be taken seriously as competition is tacit acknowledgment of the growing strength of the movement in the United Kingdom. An indigenous Masorti movement developed in Hungary a century ago in the form of the Neolog community, which today is the largest Jewish community in the Soviet bloc outside of Russia and the only one with a rabbinical seminary. Yet there has been little or no contact between that community and the World Council of Synagogues.

Outside of the United States, the Movement confronts a new problem. There is no question that even those who want to adhere to Conservative or Masorti Judaism want a more traditional form of Jewish religion than is now the norm in the United States. Machon Schechter is therefore particularly well equipped to provide for these congregations. In this respect, they are more like the Conservative Jews of the interwar period than the Conservative avant-garde in the contemporary United States. Thus efforts to increase Conservative strength outside of the United States are likely to interject more traditional elements into the Movement.

## THE MOVEMENT IN ISRAEL

The (rather slim) ray of hope in all of this is that in Israel the Masorti Movement is number two—a distant number two, but clearly more attractive than Reform Judaism. Neve Schechter is now the home of the flourishing Machon Schechter (Schechter Institute for Jewish Studies), with some 350, mostly Israeli, students. Today there are forty Masorti congregations in Israel that are sufficiently well established to have telephones with listed telephone numbers, a good measure of permanence in the Israeli environment. It is reasonable to assume that the Movement has some 10,000 adherents in Israel, along with an umbrella congregational organization and a branch of the Rabbinical Assembly. It has organized its own Law Committee, which published its first volume of responsa in 1986.

There is a Ramah camp that serves the Movement in the diaspora through summer and half-year programs and also runs day and overnight camps for Israelis. Neve Schechter continues to serve rabbinical students from the JTS and some others, but in addition there is a *Bet Midrash l'Rabbanim* (seminary for rabbinical studies) for Israelis, while the Schocken Institute gives the Movement a certain presence on the scholarly scene. The Movement also has an active youth group, Noam, with over 1,000 members and its first kibbutz, Hanaton, as well as connections with other veteran kibbutzim whose members are looking to the Conservative Movement to foster stronger links to Judaism.

Although it is still overwhelmingly what in the United States is referred to as an "immigrant church," in the last few years the Movement has tried to reach out to the children of the immigrants with limited results. But however weak the Masorti Movement is, it does have more of a popular base than does Reform. However, Reform has a far more visible institutional base that is getting stronger, as the massive new World Union for Progressive Judaism-Hebrew Union College-Jewish Institute of Religion complex, near the King David Hotel overlooking the Old City in Jerusalem, continues to grow in physical size and programming.

There is a real paradox confronting the Masorti Movement in Israel. On the one hand, somewhere between 40 percent and 55 percent of the Jewish population in that country define themselves as traditional, but very few of them have been attracted to Masorti institutions. In great part, that is because the Masorti Movement is still perceived as a *landsmanschaft* [immigrant association] for *olim* from the West. Beyond that, its Ashkenazi Litvak origins give it a ritual and style that is quite at variance with the mass of organically (as distinct from ideologically) Masorti Jews who are Sephardim. In order to reach out to that Masorti population, it is necessary to develop a Sephardic Conservative movement or at least a wing that is rooted in Sephardic custom, ritual, and style. This is what the ultra-Orthodox have done in Israel out of necessity, if not out of love. The ultra-Orthodox *yeshivot* are all extremely Ashkenazi in the old-fashioned way. The religious Zionists and the institutions of the National Religious Party originally ignored the difference in customs and rituals between Ashkenazim and Sephardim and forced all Sephardim who came to their institutions to become Ashkenazified, leading to a great deal of resentment among many of those same Sephardim after they became adults. The ultra-Orthodox only began to reach out to more than a handful of Sephardim somewhat later. They, because of their traditionalism, encouraged their Sephardi adherents to follow their own religious rituals, which the *haredim* (fervently Orthodox) saw as *halakhically* required of every Jew under the theory of *minhag avot* (the custom of one's ancestors). While in other respects they also pursued a course of Ashkenazification, by keeping the Sephardim separate in ritual matters (something that was often reinforced by their prejudices against Sephardim), they opened the way for the development of a separate ultra-Orthodox movement, today embodied in the Shas (the Sephardic Torah Guardians) party. They also gained many Sephardic adherents for ultra-Orthodoxy. Despite the encouragements, the Masorti Movement in Israel has, whether by choice or default, followed the pattern of the National Religious Party (NRP) rather than of the *haredim* in this matter, to their loss.

A new, perhaps more likely, group to target for outreach are the hundreds of thousands of immigrants from the former Soviet Union. Few of them come with any religious ties. A handful are attracted to Orthodoxy in percentages apparently not different from those who are so attracted in the West. Most seek no religious identification, but some have been attracted to the Masorti Movement, and the opportunity may exist to attract more.

A survey conducted by the Jerusalem Center for Public Affairs in 1986 for the Masorti Movement in Israel discovered that while less than 10 percent of Israelis claimed to have heard of the Masorti Movement, as many as one-third of them were interested in learning more about it and perhaps in investigating the possibilities of making use of one or another of its institutions. Two groups in particular stand out as expressing such interest—Sephardim of the first generation and Israeli-born children of Israeli-born parents, that is, third generation and beyond, some of whom are seeking their way back to tradition. Thus, all in all, the data shows that the Movement has a field of opportunity in Israel that offers a challenge to it.

In 1992, the Guttman Institute for Applied Social Research conducted a survey funded by the Avihai Foundation exploring the religious heritage and behavior of Israelis (see Table 7.1). The survey again demonstrated what every previous survey had revealed, that rather than polarization into *dati* (religious) and *hiloni* (secular) camps, Israeli society actually consists of a continuum of religious attitudes and behaviors, with only 20 percent defining themselves as secular and 25 percent as religious in the Orthodox or ultra-Orthodox sense. The other 55 percent maintained various degrees of Jewish observance and belief, ranging from mainly Orthodox to the maintenance of a few historic Jewish customs.

Commentators on the study have suggested that while it is generally accurate on the patterns of observance, it emphasizes some points requiring serious consideration and ignores others. For example, the Ashkenazim are far more likely to be secular than the Sephardim. Moreover, the younger generation of the Ashkenazim is drifting further from observance or belief. The general thrust of Israeli society, while it can be interpreted as relatively stable over the time that studies of this kind have been undertaken, shows a clear, if slow, trend toward growing secularization. Finally, the critical question of the division between those who feel religiously obligated to observe and those who simply follow habit or custom is not made clear.

In this respect, Israel seems to be developing the kind of Judaism that has benefitted the Conservative Movement in the United States. At the same time, the idea of Conservative Judaism, that is, that people can legitimize changes in traditional religion to reflect their own preferred behavior patterns, which is considered absolutely necessary in the United States by so many people, is much less possible in Israel, where the fixed character of religious ritual is generally accepted by many, regardless of their personal practices. People from the Mediterranean world are especially prone to a different view, holding that

TABLE 7.1
Religious Observance and Belief among Israeli Jews (1991)

| Religious Practice | Always | Sometimes | Never |
|---|---|---|---|
| Light *Shabbat* candles | 56% | 24% | 20% |
| Recite *Kiddush* (Friday night) | 46% | 21% | 32% |
| Synagogue Saturday morning | 23% | 22% | 56% |
| Do not work [in public] | 42% | 19% | 39% |
| Do not turn on electricity | 22% | 14% | 64% |
| Participate in *Seder* | 78% | 17% | 5% |
| Light Hanukkah candles | 71% | 20% | 9% |
| Fast on Yom Kippur | 70% | 11% | 19% |
| Bless *Lulav* (Sukkot) | 26% | 15% | 59% |
| Observe *Kashrut* at home | 69% | 18% | 14% |
| No pork, shellfish, etc. | 63% | 16% | 21% |
| Brit Milah | 92% | | |
| Bar Mitzvah | 83% | | |
| Wedding | 87% | | |
| Burial/*Shiva*/*Kaddish* | 88-91% | | |
| *Mezuzah* on front door | 98% | | |
| Contribute to charity | 74% | | |

| Religious Belief | Believe | Doubt | Do not Believe |
|---|---|---|---|
| God exists | 62% | 25% | 13% |
| Torah is from Sinai | 54% | 32% | 14% |
| Non-observance punished | 27% | 36% | 37% |

*Source*: S. Levy, H. Levinsohn, and E. Katz, *Beliefs, Observances and Social Interaction among Israeli Jews* (Jerusalem: L. Guttman Institute of Applied Social Research, 1993)

human behavior is not necessarily expected to match human aspirations; that is, they accept religious standards as eternal ones, but they also accept that individual humans live up to those standards as best they can or as they are moved to do so. This latter reality militates against accepting any non-Orthodox definition of Judaism, no matter what one's behavior.[5]

Israel gave the Masorti Movement a great opportunity when, in 1977, the Ministry of Education launched an experiment in developing individual schools within the state school network that emphasized the study and practice of traditional Judaism in a non-Orthodox way, in the manner of the well-known Masorti school in the French Hill neighborhood of Jerusalem. These schools are known as Tali (an acronym for *Tigboret Limudei Yahadut*, in English, Supplementary Studies in Judaism) schools. The Ministry recognized that since a minority of Israeli children attend the NRP-dominated state religious schools, which normally do not take in children who are not observant in an Orthodox manner, there was a need for developing a vehicle to teach Jewish religion as tradition to interested non-Orthodox Jews. Using provisions in Israeli education law that allow principals and parents to determine up to 25 percent of the curriculum of their schools on the basis of the specialized needs of their constituency, the experiment opened up the possibility for schools within the state school network to reorganize their programs and curricula to teach what is, in effect, Masorti Judaism. While these schools have no formal relationship with the Masorti Movement, they are clearly parallel to it.

Initially the Conservative Movement did not take advantage of this opportunity. Each of these schools had (and has) to be organized separately, and the Movement left the organization to haphazard coalitions of interested parents and teachers. For the most part, it still does. The most successful school, in French Hill in Jerusalem, while organized by a Conservative Jewish educator with the support of members of the French Hill congregation, emerged prior to the Education Ministry's initiative, fully independent of the Movement in every respect, including its own fund-raising in the United States. Indeed, its leadership feels the need to put distance between it and the Movement to this day. The same is true of the other schools.

Even when the Ministry of Education established the position of coordinator of Tali schools and appointed two Conservative Jewish educators in succession to the post, the Conservative Movement did nothing to facilitate their work, nor did it even encourage them to remain in the position. Subsequently, control at the ministry level passed into the hands of the Orthodox. The whole story is one of missed and perhaps lost opportunities. One bright spot is that Noam, the Masorti youth movement, has now been recognized as the youth movement for the French Hill school (in Israel, particular youth movements are accredited to particular schools), which will create necessary school-movement cooperation, at least in that form.

The other bright spot is the rapid growth of Machon Schechter, organized by the Movement to be the Masorti rabbinical and teachers' seminary in Israel. With strong, energetic, and aggressive leadership, the Machon has expanded rapidly in its first decade, attracting students in Israel, both native Israelis and others, serving Conservative/Masorti rabbinical students from elsewhere in the world (e.g., the Latin American Seminario in Buenos Aires has a year-long program at Machon Schechter, and the Machon has essentially assumed responsibility for the JTS program in Israel). Machon Schechter also has worked to extend its services beyond rabbinical training and beyond Israel's borders to Russia, with some success. This expansion has resulted in the training of teachers as well as rabbis for the Tali schools. The extent of its activities has brought it into conflict with the Masorti Movement leadership in Israel, and to some extent, that conflict has been the price of its growth.

In general, building the Masorti Movement in Israel is more a matter of building schools than of building synagogues. This cannot be overemphasized. The Movement has to adapt to the Israeli scene, where the role of both the synagogue and the rabbi is much less important than in the diaspora. Congregations meeting for prayer are necessary, but in Israel, they are led by knowledgeable *baalei batim*, because most Israelis who are going to seek out a synagogue are likely to be trained enough to play a role in the services. In a Hebrew-speaking and Hebrew-reading country, rabbis are not needed to announce pages or even to give sermons. Hence, a successful religious movement is contingent upon developing a cadre of educated Jews that is Masorti in its orientation, something that can only be done through Masorti schools. Obviously there will be a need for synagogues in the diaspora mold for those who have been raised away from tradition and who need professional assistance to be brought into Jewish ways. But if the Movement comes to be known only as that, in the Israeli environment it will never be considered as serious as one rooted in stringent traditional study and knowledge of sources.

There can only be Masorti schools if there are appropriate teachers for those schools. It is far easier to establish a school today than to find the personnel to staff it who can teach in a Masorti way. Having a rabbinical seminary in Israel fits in with the orientation of the Movement in the United States, but it is much less important in the Israeli context than having a *bet midrash l'morim* (seminary for teachers). Fortunately, Machon Schechter is currently flourishing as a teacher training school, having derived permission to grant an M.A. based on its affiliation with the Seminary. The Orthodox have learned this lesson very well, concentrating their efforts and public resources on building several networks of schools and *yeshivot* and leaving prayer groups to private initiative. Build schools and one builds a community from which everything else flows. Without schools, there is no community, and nothing flows.

Israel offers a great challenge to the Conservative Movement, since in our times any Jewish movement that does not have a strong presence in Israel will never be part of the overall Jewish picture in a serious way. Today, the Masorti Movement in Israel is still struggling. It is not getting the support that it deserves from its big brother in America, yet it is making strides. Moreover, it has a potential constituency if it can learn how to reach out to it. This has to be a matter of great concern to the entire Movement.

## A MISSED DIRECTION

During the first post-World War II generation, the Conservative Movement concentrated heavily on its internal development, and as noted earlier, on a certain competition with other Jewish institutions. Institutional needs, ideology, and style all reinforced these tendencies, which led to an increasingly isolated movement, obviously important and acknowledged as such on the American scene and even to some extent beyond the United States, but not really connected to the larger Jewish world. The Conservative Movement took this course at precisely the time when the Jewish world was breaking out of the old congregational-plus-community relations pattern, whereby both Jewish activists and rank and file identified with some synagogue, while the activists also identified with a community relations group and the rank and file with some fraternal or women's group.

A new, more complex organizational network was developing, framed by the Jewish community federations locally and by the Council of Jewish Federations and the United Jewish Appeal countrywide. New opportunities for activity and leadership were opening up that offered increasingly attractive possibilities of becoming involved in events of historic significance, particularly those related to the founding and development of the State of Israel.

It is as though the Conservative Movement deliberately decided to stay out of those exciting activities. As a result, its leaders did not and do not play leadership roles in other bodies, and even those members who do rarely see themselves as really attached to, much less representing, the Conservative Movement in any way. Where there has been contact, there appears to have been confrontation and conflict, usually more in rhetoric than in reality, but it is the rhetoric that creates the image.

Many bodies outside of the religious sphere also have failed in this regard—B'nai B'rith and some of the community relations organizations come to mind. To the extent that they have failed, they are declining. There is no question about it. They continue to exist because institutions have a momentum of their own, but they are no longer vital, except insofar as they can link themselves to the larger whole.

## A New Partnership

This kind of isolation is never good. It is even worse at a time when the Jewish people are actually reconstituting their worldwide and countrywide polities to reflect the new epoch that emerged after the Holocaust and the reestablishment of the State of Israel.

It is now time to overcome that isolation. A new philosophy of federation-synagogue partnership should be developed to take the place of the competitive outlook of the 1950s and 1960s, whereby the federations are recognized as the framing institutions of the Jewish community and the synagogues are recognized as the most important local cells within it, with other institutions providing specialized services within the Federation framework to both. The emphasis on Jewish continuity and the recognition by the Council of Jewish Federations, at least since the late 1970s and especially since the 1990 National Jewish Population Study, that religious identification in general and synagogue membership in particular are highly related to being a contributor to Federation fund-raising, will frame and enhance such efforts.

Such an approach could lead to synagogue partnerships with Jewish community centers, a development in a number of communities for joint work with youth groups and senior citizens, among others, and joint sponsorship of cultural and educational events. In recent years, federations have become involved in adult education in partnership with synagogues in jointly sponsored programs that utilize the teaching skills of rabbis, cantors, and other synagogue staff, with positive consequences. Jewish family and children's service agencies also should join congregations in sponsoring various kinds of support groups utilizing synagogue facilities, once the concept of the synagogue as a vital cell within the overall Jewish community is accepted.

There are many other implications and relationships that can be explored and developed. A broadened conception of the congregation's role in the overall Jewish community would give greater scope to the activities of its non-rabbinic leadership. It is a conception of the future that offers great possibilities for all Jewish institutions and can restore Conservative institutions to an active role within the Jewish community as a whole.

Worldwide, the results of this reconstitution will shape Jewish life for the indefinite future. That larger whole is dominated by the State of Israel, the Jewish Agency, the World Zionist Organization, Keren Hayesod, the United Jewish Appeal, the United Israel Appeal, the Joint Distribution Committee, the Council of Jewish Federations and its constituent federations, and equivalent bodies linked to the Jewish Agency-State of Israel network in other countries. That network is where the action is, where decisions are made, insofar as there is any single network in which decisions are made for the Jewish people. On one level, these bodies, except for the State of Israel, do not get involved with religious activities per se. On another level, as the instrumentalities of governance of the world Jewish polity, they make decisions and allocate money, which affects religious activities. They also control the major share of the funds spent for Jewish public purposes. The Jerusalem Center for Public Affairs has calculated that the Jewish people, including the State of Israel, now spend approximately $36 billion a year for public purposes, 90 percent of which passes through that network. Thus the Conservative Movement must seek to build bridges to that network, not simply come to it from time to time demanding its fair share but become an involved part of it in some appropriate way.

Is there a turnabout in the world movement? Since 1986, the Conservative Movement has become more aware of the Jewish world outside of North America. It has made some effort to strengthen its position in Israel, and it has become more active through Mercaz—the Zionist Organization for Conservative/Masorti Judaism in the World Zionist Organization and the Jewish Agency—principally to press for its interests in that arena and to gain funding (what the non-Orthodox

Jewish leadership believes is funding equivalent to Orthodoxy) for the development of Conservative Movement programs in Israel and in the rest of the world.

The Movement leadership also has begun paying more attention to the rest of the world. When the states of the former USSR opened up to Jewish activity, the Conservative Movement quickly made some effort to move into them. Due to indigenous developments stimulated by the late Rabbi Marshall Meyer in the many years that he was in Argentina, the Conservative Movement in Latin America has moved steadily ahead. A small but greater Conservative presence has been fostered in Western Europe as well. There seems to be a new realization on the part of the very top movement leadership in the United States that the Jewish world is more than their predecessors thought it was. How far this will go is not immediately clear, but it is a sign of response, of recognition, and of an effort to respond to the new reality.

# Chapter 8

# *What the Movement's Leadership Seeks*

Interviews with Movement leaders reveal certain commonalities. Many agree with the statement of the problems presented thus far. They all had a sense that a great deal needs to be done to address those problems, but they also shared a sense that few of the other prominent figures in the Movement would agree with the solutions they individually proposed. They tended to define the central problem of the Movement as one of developing, recruiting, and retaining the passionate loyalty of the most serious Jews. Finally, they prescribed solutions that would bring to the Movement serious and passionate Jews who share their own individual styles of seriousness and passion.

For the most part, the suggestions they advanced are complementary, sometimes they are competing, and only in a few instances would anyone regard them as conflicting. Many are complementary in that they contribute to advancing several goals simultaneously; some are competing in that a movement's intellectual, personnel, and financial resources are limited, and decision makers will need to choose among the several approaches; and a few are conflicting in that some leaders may prefer to promote recruitment of their own type of serious and passionate Jew to the exclusion of others.

The major types of serious Jews of which the leaders spoke can be grouped as follows:

- the *Halakhic*
- the Intellectual
- the Spiritual
- the Communal
- the Zionist

A discussion of the suggestions for revitalizing the Movement generally can be organized by grouping them under these five rubrics.

## RAISING THE *HALAKHIC* PROFILE

Some leaders suggested that a substantial commitment to elevating the consciousness of and commitment to *halakhah* should be undertaken in all parts of the Movement. In so doing, they argued, Conservatism can lay claim to an authenticity that many Jews are seeking, while bringing a genuine aura of seriousness to the Movement. It would, over time, provide the Movement with an enlarged ideologically committed inner core who, in their daily lives, would exemplify Conservative Judaism at its best, thereby setting an implicit standard for others.

Advocates of this approach stress that they see the major cleavage within the Movement not so much in terms of a "left/right" ideological split but more in terms of a *"halakhic*/non-*halakhic"* orientation. Those committed to *halakhah* may be liberal or conservative, *makail* (lenient) or *machmir* (stringent), but the key concern for them is to evolve norms and practices from within a *halakhic* framework.

The application of such an approach would have ramifications throughout the Movement. Here are some suggestions we heard:

1. The Seminary should make a clear distinction between academic and religious thinkers. Currently the academic and religious missions of the Seminary are confused with the consequence that non-*halakhic* academicians are in the position (willingly or not) of shaping the religious norms of the Movement.

2. The Seminary faculty with expertise in *halakhah* should be encouraged to involve themselves more directly and frequently in contemporary issues affecting Conservative Jews and their congregations. In particular, they should be encouraged to publish and lecture about their distinctive and some-

times competing views on the application of a Conservative understanding of *halakhah*.

3.  Pulpit rabbis should be encouraged to emphasize the authority of *halakhah* to their congregants, congratulating them on whatever affirmations of Jewish law they practice reminding them of additional precepts that they should follow.[1]

4.  Ritual observance should constitute a criterion for positions of leadership in the Movement. One person we spoke to even suggested a gradually expanding requirement for lay leaders to commit themselves to observing *halakhic* regulations, as is already done in USY.

5.  The observant—or perhaps the newly observant—should be recognized and honored by the Movement in explicit ways. Perhaps rabbis or schools or congregations that have been extraordinarily successful in stimulating observance should be singled out for recognition.

6.  Schechter school students should learn more rabbinics relative to the other aspects of Judaica that currently constitute their curriculum.

## ENHANCING CONSERVATIVE INTELLECTUAL LIFE

Other leaders with whom we spoke, while not necessarily rejecting the elevation of *halakhic* consciousness as a worthwhile policy, nevertheless placed greater emphasis on what, in essence, must be seen as a policy of enhancing the intellectual life of Conservative Jewry. They are concerned that many of the most intellectually aware Conservative Jews in America conduct their Judaic intellectual lives outside of the orbit of Conservative Jewry. Perhaps even more important, now that most Jews under age forty have graduate degrees, Conservative Judaism cannot survive unless it can stimulate and appeal to the most intellectually gifted and involved congregants.

A policy of enhancing the quality of Conservative Jewish intellectual life would have many components, including the following:

1.  The all-movement publication that is informative about the Seminary (*masoret*) is a reworking of a public relations/fundraising piece. A more zippy but intellectual one such as *Reform Judaism* is still needed, and/or *Conservative Judaism* should be sent to more people or subscriptions to it should be marketed.

2. The Movement should promote the publication of major works that articulate its philosophy. As a notable example, one leader suggested, the Movement failed to capitalize on the publication of Rabbi Isaac Klein's *A Guide to Jewish Religious Practice*. At least its congregations and institutions should actively promote sales of a "bookshelf" of these books that already exists (Isaac Klein, Seymour Siegal, Elliot Dorff, Robert Gordis, and now the books of the new generation, such as Daniel Wolpe and Daniel Gordis), along with the Movement's Siddur, Mahzor, Geffen's *Celebration and Renewal*, Heschel's *The Sabbath*, and the set *The Art of Jewish Living*, published by the Federation of Jewish Men's Clubs, on Jewish customs and observances.[2] They could be sold as a package in synagogue gift shops, and the whole bookshelf could be encouraged for use as bar mitzvah or bat mitzvah and wedding gifts. The Movement-wide *Luach* (calendar) *for the Synagogue* also has been a successful endeavor. The USCJ Book Service has begun to function as a Movement bookstore. The JTS now has a web page linked to Amazon.com which sells its own publications.

3. The Movement should identify those intellectual areas where scholarly work would make an important contribution to the substance of Conservative Judaism. For example, no single work documents, traces, and analyzes trends in *halakhic* development over the centuries. Such a work would substantiate the Conservative claim that *halakhah* (or at least its interpretation) is ever changing in response to social circumstances.

4. Rabbis should involve intellectually sophisticated lay people in the intellectual and cultural lives of their congregations. Several observers report that the insecurity of some rabbis leads them to resist sharing the spotlight with those who, they believe, would diminish their reputation.

5. Just as some might set observance requirements for Conservative leadership, so others would set (de facto) requirements of intellectual involvement. Conservative leaders would be expected, if only implicitly, to be literate, to be committed to study, to be involved with some of the leading issues of the day, and to participate in weekend or summertime conferences and retreats. Synagogues can replicate the Wexner Heritage programs for adults or the Florence Melton Mini-School model. The Beit Midrash Talmud program, which went

national in 1995–1996, is a good first attempt at this type of focus. First it was tried in the New York area at the Seminary, and after two years of great success, it was "mainstreamed" to congregations all over the country under the coordination of the Seminary in cooperation with the Rabbinical Assembly.

6. The Movement should organize regional or countrywide learning institutes where lay people, rabbis, and seminarians might study texts, discuss important books or articles, and exchange views on contemporary events in the Jewish world.

## ADDRESSING THE SPIRITUAL NEEDS OF CONSERVATIVE JEWS

Some leaders with whom we spoke voiced little objection to the *halakhic* or intellectual approaches; they thought that these approaches would influence only limited numbers of Conservative Jews. They said that most of the potentially serious and passionate laity is neither *halakhic* nor predisposed to intellectual discourse. Rather, they suggested, the *halakhic* discussions prevalent among rabbis and Seminary faculty may be regarded by many as "a-theological," that is, lacking a passion for discerning the nature of God and what is expected of those created in God's image. These advocates voice a classic complaint against the *halakhists*, saying that they emphasize ritual performance as a standard of Jewish commitment to the exclusion of *mitzvot bayn adam l'chavero* (commandments regulating human relationships).

Moreover, what we may call the "spiritualists" argued that the intellectually oriented approach often puts the text ahead of the learner. In fact, they claim, too much of Conservative Judaism is intellectualized, and not enough is passionate and emotional. They say that the Movement has failed to convey a vision of Judaism that speaks to real people's lives. Instead, congregants should be shown how their private and personal human needs and everyday ethical decisions can be informed and enhanced by serious study of the sacred texts. Educationally we may refer to this emphasis as a "learner-centered" rather than a "text-centered" approach. The new University of Judaism rabbinical school curriculum, as announced, seems to follow this new "learner-centered" approach. It is also market oriented to teaching rabbis to do outreach work.

The spiritualists' critique and program, at its broadest, also focuses on the changing nature of Conservative synagogue life. During the 1960s and 1970s, a significant segment of committed Conservative Jews expressed their lack of enthusiasm for the prevalent, conventional congregational model. If we may oversimplify, some saw the rabbis of their parents' generation as pompous, distant, and authoritarian. They saw the large congregations they grew up in as cold, bureaucratic, impersonal, and overwhelming. They no longer saw the need to impress the Gentiles with the permanence of the Jewish presence in America, as conveyed by massive synagogue structures or well-spoken rabbis. Rather, the congregations they would join ideally would address their needs for community, warmth, intimacy, meaning, and transcendence.[3]

The implementation of a spiritually oriented Conservative Jewish agenda would affect several parts of the Movement simultaneously, in subtle and systemic ways. For example:

1.  It would imply significant changes in the training of rabbis, hence in the ethos of the Seminary. Spiritualists complain: (a) that the Seminary has long taken its purely academic mission more seriously than its responsibility to train rabbis and otherwise service the Movement; (b) that the Seminary's faculty is overly oriented toward rationalism and legalism rather than emotion and inspiration, both in teaching style and course content; (c) that relations between faculty and students smack of a hierarchical authoritarianism rather than a collegial quasi-egalitarianism that typifies many professional and graduate schools in other fields; and (d) that few, if any, faculty members project an integrated program, a vision for the future of Conservative Judaism in America. These criticisms imply a number of changes, both subtle and overt, large and small. They may range from examining the way in which professors treat students to something as simple as adding courses on Hassidism and mysticism.

2.  The spiritualists' critique also has ramifications for the Movement's schools and summer camps. All of the tools of education and communication—sermons, journals, conferences, formal and informal education—should try to demonstrate the importance of Jewish texts for addressing the major spiritual questions. Where does one find meaning in life? How should we treat our family, friends, and colleagues? Where do we fit into the scheme of history and the Divine Plan?

3.  The Movement should sponsor more learning institutes for various age and family groupings. These institutes would fuse aspects of community building with text study, directed at people's spiritual needs.

4. The Movement should showcase its most gifted inspirational leaders and give them a platform on which to air their views about the ethical issues of the day.

5. Jewish tradition speaks to many issues. The Movement should systematically tackle some of the key social and political issues and demonstrate how Conservative Judaism addresses questions such as the economy, abortion policy, homosexuality, nuclear disarmament, homelessness, hunger, and matters of similar currency and magnitude. Toward that end, it might want to commission several vehicles for taking the tradition and applying it in practical ways, combining lay and rabbinic figures. A model of such an effort, though not through a lay commission, was the cooperative work done by Chancellor Schorsch and the late Dr. Carl Sagan in a public symposium and, more privately, under the aegis of Vice President Gore in an interfaith coalition to save the environment.

## THE COMMUNAL APPROACH

For some, the key problem facing the Movement is not so much one of defining its mission or philosophy, or of doing a better job at projecting its ideology. Rather, the main challenge is a people problem, in particular, the Movement's failure to attract and to engage a large number of the most talented Jews involved in Jewish life.

The implicit critique here is that for far too long the task of shaping Conservative Judaism, of speaking on its behalf, and of running its institutions has been in the hands of rabbis, in particular, the rabbinical leadership at the Seminary. As a result, the Movement has had difficulty in attracting a talented, wealthy, and culturally sophisticated non-rabbinic leadership. In contrast, the Reform Movement has invested heavily in its laity and has established several formal and informal networks of lay leaders on regional and national levels.

This state of affairs relates to a distinct though related critique. Orthodox Jews who want to express their support for a traditionally minded American social agenda can do so within an Orthodox framework, albeit through the informal networks of the Orthodox community. Reform Jews who want to campaign for civil rights or for nuclear disarmament find a well-financed, professionally staffed sub-agency in their Movement that is prepared to help. In contrast, politically and socially minded Conservative Jews have no place within the Conservative

Movement or community where they can express their Jewishly inspired commitment to social action of one stripe or another.

The Conservative Movement should be a place where talented laity can expect to find other influential, and stimulating leaders. Unfortunately, the Movement currently suffers from reputational and morale problems that discourage some of the most potentially valuable laity from participating.

To remedy this situation, interviewees suggested two broad programmatic ideas:

1. The Movement should establish a variety of task forces dedicated both to addressing the problems of the Movement and to charting directions in social and political areas heretofore largely neglected by Conservative Jewry as such. Thus one may contemplate task forces on finance, public relations, publications, and the major social political issues of the day.

2. The synagogues should sponsor—regionally and country-wide—conferences for leading lay people on social, political, and religious issues. Such conferences would not only provide a context for political and socially motivated Conservative Jews to express themselves, they also would serve as vehicles to establish informal networks among the laity and to provide a training ground and springboard for the identification, recruitment, and training of high-caliber lay leadership.

## THE ZIONIST APPROACH

Those Conservative leaders who see themselves as more passionate about Israel argue that Movement leaders have failed to appreciate the extent to which both Israel and the Masorti Movement there can benefit Conservative Judaism in the United States. A deeper involvement with Israel, they maintain, can have several important benefits. It can motivate idealistic Conservative youth; it can serve as a rallying cause for Conservative laity; and it can help legitimate Conservative Jewry as a world religious movement in world Jewish contexts.

Instead, they complain, the Movement's leaders have heretofore seen Israel as a diversion from more important tasks. They argue that genuine and extensive Conservative involvement in Israel is a worthwhile investment that will "pay off" in terms of a deeper commitment, a more educated laity, and even (and not least) more productive fundraising for the Movement as a whole.

In response, most of the American-based leadership evidenced true and genuine warmth toward the Israeli enterprise. They themselves volunteered the view that Israel can offer the locale for the greatest growth in Conservative Judaism and that such an eventuality can only help legitimate and strengthen Conservative Judaism in the United States. The problem, one leader suggested, is not ideological but financial. How can the Movement allocate scarce resources at a time when its major institutions in the United States and Israel are facing mounting deficits?

Among the concrete steps that the more self-avowedly, Zionist-oriented Conservative leaders suggested are:

1. Improve both the reality and the image of Conservative involvement in Israel. This suggestion would initially entail more investment in strengthening the Masorti Movement, but it also implies greater attention to Masorti Judaism in the Movement's publications.

2. Increase the number of Movement-organized trips to Israel. These could include programs especially for youth, synagogue leaders, or major contributors. Some suggest that the activities of the Masorti Movement can serve as an inspiration for increased contributions on the part of major donors to Conservative Judaism generally.

3. Create ongoing dialogue groups with Masorti peers in Israel that examine new models of Israel-Diaspora relationships, which could be crucial to the development of in-depth, people-to-people relationships. This would be patterned after the UJA's Israel Forum groups. These groups could even begin as Internet forums or chat groups, then they could actually meet in actual rather than virtual space.

4. Nurture and create new relationships between synagogues. A program twinning American and Israeli synagogues already exists. In like fashion, perhaps Tali schools could be twinned with Schechter schools and USY to Noam groups as well.

## RESOLVING CONFLICTS, SETTING PRIORITIES

In our discussions, some of the most prominent and ostensibly influential members of the leadership ranks of Conservative Jewry began their conversations by noting how their views were shared by few if any others, how no one listens to them, how few leaders talk to one another, and how no one else recognizes the need to change. These comments suggest that one of the important prerequisites to change is present: the leadership already recognizes problems in the Conservative Movement. But the comments also imply that leaders need to start talking to one another about the state of the Movement much more than they now do. Were they to do so, they would find that they share many insights, and that they are much more willing to support innovation than they give each other credit for.

Of course, once leadership begins serious deliberations, they will need to sort out priorities, and in so doing, they will bring to the fore the cleavages that divide themselves and the Movement generally. It is here that some of our experiences and observations may prove helpful.

The controversy on the ordination of women as rabbis and as cantors, followed more recently by the debate over the role of out-of-the-closet gay men and lesbian women, focused considerable attention on the "left-right" ideological cleavage within Conservative Judaism. Unfortunately, that attention has obscured other cleavages that may well merit as much attention. Perhaps the most significant is the rationalist-spiritualist dimension. Those we have called the "spiritualists" believe—rightly or wrongly—that the so-called rationalists fail to appreciate the emotional side to learning, community, and religious commitment. Another cleavage that impressed us was that between the "Zionists" and "Diasporists."

Insiders of any movement have a tendency to react to cleavages as sources of division and weakness. In the interests of the movement, they search for ways to diminish cleavages, to narrow gaps, and to suppress or at least dampen minority protest. However, the risks of deep division, of internecine conflict, have to be weighed against the opportunities for Movement revitalization. In other words, strategies that are designed to avoid conflict and its appearance also often serve to cut off channels of expression, to preclude the emergence of new and vital subgroups within the Movement.

Rather than resolving conflicts, and rather than trying to decide upon the single or dominant course Conservative Judaism should take, leaders ought to explicitly foster the development of the various trends within the Movement. In other words, the so-called rationalists have a stake in the development of a non-rationalist (or emotion-oriented) version of Conservative Judaism, just as those more spiritually inclined must recognize the value of an intellectually, *halakhically* oriented trend.

The problem for leaders trying to decide among the alternate directions and programs outlined above is, therefore, much less ideological than it would first appear. In making these decisions, in considering which program and policies should advance, leaders need to ask pragmatic questions such as "How much of whose time and which money needs to be invested in these policies and programs, and what benefit to the Movement can we project?" Generally we found leaders willing to allow other parts of the Movement to pursue their own most valued programs, as long as those efforts did not preclude others.

In sum, we found that there is more good will and good thinking than most leaders commonly suppose. If so, then a concerted effort to forge a deliberative community stands a good chance of producing a mandate for change in several areas.

While this book emphasizes problems, it is important to understand that the Conservative Movement has begun its second century with great pluses as well as minuses. On the one hand, it starts with the great advantage of having provided the religious framework for the largest single segment of American Jewry, so much so that the Reform Movement has had to imitate it in a number of decisive ways. At the same time, there is a minus here in that the Reform Movement has apparently done so with sufficient success to attract a fair share of the next generation of Conservative Jews to its ranks, while at the same time Conservative Judaism has not articulated a sufficiently firm position on religious matters to stem a certain bleeding of its elite to Orthodoxy.

On another level, precisely those things that may make Conservative Judaism the religious framework for a large segment of American Jewry may also keep it from being able to be easily spread to other parts of the world, thereby confining it to the United States, which, as indicated above, is becoming a serious problem.

The Conservative Movement also has the plus of having begun to articulate an ideology of modern traditionalism. The minus is that this ideology has never been sufficiently articulated and conveyed either to the Movement's activists or to its members to be clearly and persuasively understood. Recent developments in all three branches of Judaism may have helped sharpen the clarity of the Conservative position, but there is much to be done to enhance that clarity. Whether the Movement can do it, given its tendency toward pragmatism and "every-congregation-for-itself" behavior, is one of the challenges to be faced.

The Movement comes with the strength of being in the center of American Jewish life. As such, it eschews the simplicity of Orthodoxy, which claims to be Torah-true, and of Reform, which asserts the primacy of the modern experience in judging the appropriateness of the tradition. Instead, Conservatism speaks of balance, of fusion, of integration, of tension, of struggle, and ultimately of (and in) ambiguity.

Encompassing the center is both a strength and a weakness. It is a strength because there are usually more people attracted to the center than to either extreme. On the other hand, it is a weakness because it is hard for the center, however vital, to articulate clear positions. Hence, the excitement tends to gravitate to the extremes and to be well expressed by people who embrace extremes. In our opinion, it is harder to take a moderate centrist position than an extremist one, but more correct. The problem is how to convey the essential correctness of the vital center in the face of extremists who can capitalize on natural human inclinations to go for comprehensive, even magical, solutions to their problems, which the extremists can promise (but not fulfill) but the center cannot.

For many years, prominent figures in the Movement implicitly, if not explicitly, conveyed a disdain for its central mission. Their words and actions portrayed Orthodoxy as legitimate and authentic, while Conservatism was merely a necessary compromise with a partially assimilated American Jewry. One very prominent leader, on visits to local congregations, is reported to have frequently taken his honored position on the *bimah* having already prayed privately, suggesting not so subtly that something was lacking in the congregations' *davening*. Rabbinical school graduates report that the pulpit rabbinate—for which most were ostensibly being trained—was held in low esteem, in contrast to far more prestigious pure scholarly pursuits.

To a large extent, the Movement has already begun to address some of these difficulties. Now, perhaps more than ever before, the Movement's leaders have come to grips with the limits to the growth of Conservative Judaism. Orthodoxy refuses to wither away, and Reform will not assimilate away, while Reconstructionism eats away at the edges. If so, then Conservatism needs to and largely has dropped its aspirations for encompassing all of committed American Jewry. Once that is the case, some constraints on movement building are dropped as well. A Conservative Judaism aspiring to serve—and serve well—only that large fraction of American Jewry that accepts its basic message is a movement that can contemplate setting sharper boundaries, not so much as to fence others out as to give its most demanding adherents something to which to adhere. In short, as one of our prominent interviewees said, "We need to be more militant!"

Thus the third plus is that the Movement has crystallized as a party within Jewish religious life, with a well-developed institutional structure, albeit with problems; with some ideological distinctiveness, albeit with problems; and with a style all of its own, albeit with problems. The minus is that, as a party, it demands party discipline in institutional matters. This may change if the Movement moves from being a party to a camp that offers a variety of ways to be a Conservative Jew. The Movement would have to reconcile itself to not being coterminous with Conservative Judaism under such circumstances, which would require a real adjustment and would also have to build a network with the other movements or parties within the Conservative camp. This should be seen as an opportunity for growth and intensification of the Masorti approach to Judaism.

This movement from party to camp seemed more likely in the 1980s, when different ways of expressing Masorti Judaism had not only emerged but began to be articulated. Since then, however, several of those ways have either diminished or have severed their relationship with the Movement. For example, the Union for Traditional Judaism, once known as the Union for Traditional Conservative Judaism, has separated itself entirely from its Conservative roots, as the Reconstructionist Movement did in the other direction even earlier. It may be that the movement of so many Conservative Jews, including Movement leadership, toward a non-*halakhic* Judaism will lead Masorti Judaism in a different direction, although for the moment it seems as though the opportunity for the Masorti Movement to become a moderate or liberal *halakhic* camp in and of itself may have passed.

The problems of the ideological center continue to play themselves out. In particular, conflicts between the so-called left and right and between the *halakhic* and non-*halakhic* (and the two dimensions are not identical) leaders have come to the fore. In the past, the institutional decision-makers of the Movement sought to downplay these conflicts, to shield them from the public eye. That was a minus, however. In conversations with various prominent figures, all suggested that the proper ventilation of these conflicts could go far toward educating the Conservative public and could project an image of an intellectually aware and vital movement. That is a plus.

The age when Conservative Judaism was portrayed as a means to a more authentic end, as a compromise rather than a value in and of itself, seems to have passed. Those who are choosing the Conservative Movement—whether as rabbis, seminarians, synagogue presidents, parents, or campers—are doing so for reasons more positive than their predecessors may have had in the past. In an odd sort of way, the strength of Orthodoxy has left Conservatism with a more confident, self-assured leadership than in the past. That is, since Orthodoxy is now seen as more legitimate, enduring, tenable, and even authentic than it once was, far fewer (if any) younger Conservative leaders—lay or rabbinic—are choosing Conservatism as a fallback or compromise. Thus as daunting as the problems are, the Movement is in the process of generating its own answers and solutions.

One of the Movement's strengths in the past was its cadre of rabbinical leaders. However, this led to the weakness of rabbinical predominance. The Movement now must decide whether it wants to continue to be basically in the hands of the rabbis or to become multifaceted in its leadership. Given the comprehensive and quite anticlericalist character of Judaism, in the authors' view, the move toward more multifaceted leadership is a necessity.

Finally, the Movement faces a real irony. Its entire orientation is based on the need for consistency in life, that is, that Judaism must reflect not only the eternal values and norms of the Torah but also the way in which contemporary Jews understand and fit into the world around them. One would think that this demand for consistency, a major contribution to Jewish life, would be a source of strength among a people that has always been committed to both tradition and change within its mainstream. The irony is that paradox rather than consistency may also be a source of strength. The resurgence of Orthodoxy, which on the one hand has become much less modern in its approach to life, and on the other hand is attracting some Jews who are engaged in many facets of the contemporary world, is a reflection of this.

The Reform Movement also is changing in paradoxical ways. While approaching tradition with few absolute demands, it becomes more traditional in its behavior, and pulls away some formerly Conservative Jews. This should surprise no one. Many movements have started in opposition to the establishment and have succeeded only to the extent that they have adopted the establishment's ways.

On balance, these pluses and minuses lead to the conclusion that the Conservative Movement faces real problems, but that it does so with a strong basis for dealing with them.

# Part II

# Next Steps

Chapter 9

# *Ideology,* Halakhah, *and a Broadened Base*

This chapter suggests that there is much that is dynamic in the Conservative Movement and much ferment that contributes to that dynamism. The emergence of different congregational styles, the institutionalization of the *havurot*, and the growth of the Solomon Schechter schools are all examples of basic strengths within Conservative Judaism. The division between the mainstream of the Movement and its right wing over *halakhic* issues also could have contributed to this dynamism but led to separation rather than a standoff. The fact that *halakhic* issues can stimulate such serious and intense concern is all to the good. Equally impressive is the revitalization, or perhaps the vitalization, of the Committee on Jewish Law and Standards of the Rabbinical Assembly and the establishment of a parallel law committee in Israel.

Perhaps most exciting of all, there are new non-rabbinical voices being raised in the Movement that are serious and have something to say. While the number of adherents who are ideologically and behaviorally consistent with Conservative norms remains relatively small, there is a growing number who are outside of the rabbinate or other synagogue-related professions. Some are professors of Jewish studies.

161

Some have built their careers in the Jewish community in other capacities with Jewish federations, community relations agencies, or the like. Others are to be found in all walks of life. Many are relatively well educated Jewishly, hence their contributions are couched in the same Jewish language as the rabbinical leadership.

Finally, the growth of the Movement in Israel and in Latin America offers new possibilities for a worldwide Masorti approach to Judaism that can, in time, acquire an appropriate ideology and institutional framework. These are the Movement's strengths, and it should seek to build on them.

At the same time, it is important to identify several problem areas that merit the close scrutiny of the leaders of Conservative Judaism. In most such cases, it is possible to identify one or more policy directions through which to address those problem areas. A serious grappling with the issues articulated below can serve to generate fresh thinking and action. Finally, it is important to note that the problems outlined below vary widely. All are important, though some are more concrete; others are more abstract; some may involve all parts of the Movement; and others may be restricted to one institution or set of individuals.

## THE NEED FOR IDEOLOGICAL CLARIFICATION

The Conservative Movement starts from the ideological and intellectual premise that Judaism is normative yet has a strong developmental dimension. Unfortunately, that premise has become more of a slogan to be repeated than a reality to be studied and understood, so the Movement will find appropriate ways to combine both in its thought and practice. The slogan "tradition and change" may help pinpoint the issue, but there needs to be much more systematic thought about what it means to espouse a normative system with a strong developmental dimension. It is also misleading in the sense that tradition need not be normative, while change need not be progressive.

If the authors understand the Conservative Movement correctly, it is this sense of tradition as normative and change as developmental that differentiates the Movement from Orthodoxy on the one hand and Reform on the other hand. Earlier it was suggested that the distinction, phrased in political-legal terms, is between the Torah as constitution and the Torah as code. Conservative Jews view the Torah as a constitution that can be interpreted according to certain canons and along certain developmental lines, but they do not feel bound hand and foot by the codes that have, in Conservative eyes, ossified the constitution.

Nor is the Torah merely a guide as it is for the right wing of the Reform Movement. Since it is normative and a constitution, it is in some sense binding, even when Jews are not altogether pleased or comfortable with the bonds. Yet since the beginning of modernity, citizens of the Jewish polity have had to voluntarily decide that the constitution is binding for themselves, since the human power to bind, once vested in the Jewish community, no longer exists in any coercive way.

It is important to maintain a continuing exploration of the tradition as normative yet developmental. In part, this would involve an articulation of the original meaning of *masoret* (tradition), namely, bond (cf. Ezekiel 20:37, "*masoret ha-brit*"—tradition of the Covenant), a meaning that is reflected in the Latin *religio*, the source of the word "religion," which also means bond.

An empirical assessment of the present state of the Movement reinforces the need for such an effort, among others. Once there was a very large number of Jews who had come to the United States from the Old World who wanted to preserve traditional Judaism but also wanted to integrate into American society. They and their children became the Movement's constituency. The Movement won them over by harmonizing their Jewishness with characteristics of American society such as the nuclear family, the widespread acceptance of religious pluralism, and the harmonization of American language, dress, and diet (within limits) with the Jewish religion.

Today, when the majority of American Jewry is fourth generation or beyond, that original synthesis is not sufficient and, indeed, is not holding. The synthesis that constituted Conservative Judaism shows signs of unraveling because of changes in the external environment as much as changes within the Movement itself. Let it be clear what is meant when we say that the synthesis is unraveling:

- It means that the suburban synagogue model is no longer adequate, and even if particular synagogues are coherent and holding together, the model is on the brink.
- It means that the Rabbinical Assembly, which in the past could paper over differences and the lack of decision making by pretending that the lack did not depart from Orthodox norms, even if it departed from Orthodox results, is, by taking stands, now also sharpening its internal differences. In this context, the women's ordination, patrilineal descent, and legitimization of homosexuality issues are only the most paramount and visible ones.

- It means that the Seminary-centered rabbinic dominance of the Movement is weakening its ability to attract voluntary leadership or to play a proper role in contemporary Jewish life.

Moreover, the end results of the earlier synthesis have been disappointing to those who have been the pacesetters of the Conservative Movement intellectually and ideologically, in the sense that only a small percentage of those who have affiliated with the Movement have really become normative Conservative Jews in their Jewish observance and practice. On the other hand, the Movement does make a difference within the full spectrum of American Jewry. Today, the spectrum ranges from Haredi-Orthodox-Traditional-Conservative-Reform through Reconstructionist forms of commitment by individuals who are Jewishly affiliated and who care about self-perpetuation. Survey research on the subject consistently shows that those who identify with Conservative Judaism are to be found between Orthodox and Reform on almost any measure of Jewish identity, belief, or practice and are almost invariably closer to the latter. Thus there is a sharp separation between Orthodox and non-Orthodox and a narrower one between the two major non-Orthodox movements.

As a result of the foregoing, and other factors discussed in the body of this analysis, the Conservative Movement now faces a situation in which it must seriously reconsider many of the premises it implicitly accepted, the approaches adopted and used over the past sixty to eighty years, and the institutions that have developed to reflect these premises and to implement these approaches.

In part, this has to do with clarifying the ideological position of the Conservative Movement and presenting it in better ways to the public it seeks to reach. This will mean more clear-cut ideological self-definition. The mission of Conservative Judaism is poorly understood, not only by the laity but by many of the Movement's professionals. Some of the most involved Conservative Jews are Conservative by default. They know that they are neither Orthodox nor Reform, so they must be Conservative. Studies of social movements and organizations document that a clear understanding of their meaning and purpose is vital to their cohesiveness and ultimate success. Thus the ambiguity about the substance of Conservative Judaism has negative ramifications in many ways.

Approaches, on several levels, are needed to address the problem of ideological ambiguity. These include, but are not limited to, the following:

1. *The Movement should establish a broad-based, worldwide ideological study group, drawing on its best brains, rabbinic and non-rab-*

*binic, with local and regional branches throughout the world to explore this issue in a serious, text-oriented way, to come up with a systematic statement of what Conservative Judaism stands for and a set of canons to be used when interpreting halakhah liberally.* The ideological task force appointed in 1985 was a first step in that direction, but it needs to be institutionalized and broadened in its composition, geographically and otherwise. Such study groups would help both the articulation of an ideological basis for Conservative Judaism and would also deal with the problem of trendiness in *halakhic* interpretation within the Movement.

2. In contrast to Orthodoxy and Reform, the code words or slogans of the Conservative Movement are little utilized. Orthodox leaders speak of "Torah-true" Jews and the "traditional *halakhah*"; Reform leaders speak of "prophetic Judaism" as well as of "social action" and "social justice." *Conservative Judaism should develop and popularize its own slogans and code words that convey its meaning.* The dual commitments of the Movement can be conveyed in expressions such as "modern traditional," "traditional egalitarian," "normative development," "authenticity and integration," and "the dynamic *halakhah*."[1]

3. Within the pluralistic framework of contemporary Jewish life, *Conservative leaders should be willing to contrast their Movement's stance with the shortcomings of Orthodoxy, Traditional, Reform, and Reconstructionist.* In clear language, they should state that Reform is in some senses "unauthentic"; it is all too frequently insensitive to the demands of the Jewish past—the decision on patrilineal descent is a good case in point. High-volume denunciations of this decision should not be left to the Orthodox. Pluralism means acceptance of the legitimacy of other groups, but also willingness to criticize them when seen as unauthentic.

   At the same time, Conservative leaders should point out how Orthodoxy has failed to develop the tools with which to relate Judaism to modernity. Insular reaction to modernity is a confession of Jewish weakness rather than a celebration of Jewish richness. Conservative leaders should attack some of the less attractive results of the Orthodox worldview for which the Orthodox should be held accountable, those activities that are the direct consequences of Orthodoxy's failure to properly and adequately integrate into the modern world.

This is not easy to do in a sufficiently straightforward yet diplomatic way, one that will preserve the unity of the Jewish people, also a very important norm given the Movement's historic and abiding concern for *Klal Yisrael*. But Orthodox spokesmen certainly attack Conservative Judaism as well as Reform Judaism for what they see as deviations from Jewish tradition, and they do so in the most vigorous ways. By the same token, because of their common stance on behalf of a more liberal religion, the Conservative Movement is easily lumped together with the Reform Movement even on matters where the two Movements differ as sharply as Orthodox and Reform. If the Conservative Movement wants to develop its own identity, it has to articulate its uniqueness in a heightened manner, albeit in such a way as to preserve respect for Jewish unity. Indeed, Conservative Judaism, as a movement of the center, can play a vital role as an intermediary between Orthodox and Reform extremes.

4. *The internal debates over halakhah and social policy within the Conservative Movement should be communicated to the larger Conservative public, to give them a sense of the importance of the halakhic and normative issues in the Movement.* This should be done in a timely fashion, when issues are controversial, and in a way that the public can appreciate and understand.

5. Since its inception, scholarly research has played a role in shaping and legitimating the Movement. In each period, certain lines of scholarly inquiry and publication have contributed to the richness and the case of Conservative Judaism. *Leading scholars, rabbis, and lay people should jointly try to identify the types of research and publications that will advance the understanding of Conservative Judaism, to encourage JTS faculty and other scholars to pursue those lines of inquiry, and to widely disseminate the products of their efforts.* In this, the Movement should follow the model of the American Enterprise Institute or the Brookings Institution in developing a series of forums whose proceedings are edited and published in pamphlet form, disseminating reprints and digests of seminal articles, and in general publishing and distributing focused materials that will strengthen Conservative Judaism. *Conservative Judaism* should be made more widely available, both within the Movement and beyond it (perhaps with a change in name), reaching out to the lay leadership and to the academic and intellectual communities. The *United Synagogue Review*

should be published more frequently and used as a channel of dissemination of ideas, principles, and especially concrete *halakhic* information for the Movement's membership. *Masoret* is a limited step in this direction.

The Movement has claimed that *halakhah* has developed over time and responded to changing social circumstances. As of yet, to our knowledge, no synthesizing social-historical work has documented these changes and the forces behind them. A well-articulated, fully elaborated presentation of the Conservative/Masorti approach, including *halakhic* positions and the textual-historical grounds on which they are based, is vitally needed.[2]

The change of the Movement's name to Masorti has several advantages. In the first place, it is a Hebrew name and thus can be comfortably used by Jews affiliated with the Movement and others worldwide. Having a Hebrew name, also gives the Movement a certain advantage. At the same time, it is more than adequately descriptive of the character and thrust of the movement that is to be traditional in thought and practice, not Orthodox, which implies a fixed, rather rigid body of thought; nor seemingly unconcerned with Jewish tradtion by placing liberalism first, as do the Reform and Reconstructionist movements. In that connection, the original name "Conservative Judaism" was useful when the Movement was founded, because it emphasized conserving Jewish tradition and practice at a time when Reform seemed to be moving to change everything. Now, however, the main thrust of the Masorti argument is not that it is conservative but that it is traditional, yet with a spirit of change.

## FOSTERING A MORE SERIOUS *HALAKHIC* MOVEMENT

This brings us to the issue of how seriously committed the Conservative Movement really is to *halakhah*, and how much it feels either committed or obliged to adjust *halakhah* to every current trend.

In the present situation, there seems to be a great ambivalence towards *halakhah*. The Movement is indeed "Conservative," in that it wants to conserve its *halakhic* commitments and responsibilities, but many of its members and some of its leaders are not really prepared to face up to the implications of those commitments and responsibilities in its day-to-day affairs. In short, it presents a public face as a *halakhic* movement, but with much private inconsistency.

The rhetoric of the Movement speaks of loyalty to a developing *halakhah*. As is well known, the majority of the membership has little serious commitment to *halakhah*, developing or otherwise. In recent years, the *halakhic* position of the Movement as a whole has been presented by the RA Committee on Jewish Law and Standards. Now some rabbis are articulating a challenge to the *halakhic* basis of the Movement. Some are saying that the Movement is already post-*halakhic* and should recognize that development. Others argue that the Movement should develop several distinct networks of Conservative *halakhic* authority. Perhaps even more serious is to claim undying loyalty to *halakhah* but also to side in favor of whatever is "in." They render the *halakhah* as unserious as those Orthodox who always decide against change. This ambivalence is easily picked up by Movement adherents and observers, and it is frequently pointed to as a form of hypocrisy. Every effort must be made to overcome that ambivalence, so that appropriate action can be taken to make *halakhah* a living reality in the Conservative Movement.

Another problem to be confronted in this regard is the distinction in reality between public positions and private behavior. While a certain gap between the two can be expected under any circumstances, that gap is presently too great for the Movement as a whole. In dealing with this problem, several contradictory policy alternatives should be considered. These include the following:

1.  Do nothing. All religious movements abide deviations from codified norms. Deviation in practice should not be the basis for revolutionary change in official standards of behavior.
2.  Raise the *halakhic* profile of the Movement. Demand adherence to the Conservative understanding of *halakhah* as a condition for leadership—lay or rabbinic—in the Movement.
3.  Recognize several circles of *halakhic* development within the Conservative framework. One may represent thinking at the Seminary; another may arise in Israel; a third may reflect the views of more traditional Conservative Jews; and still another may reflect the opinions of more liberal Conservative rabbis.[3]

The Conservative Movement should use its *halakhic* position to strengthen its identity and its members' adherence to *halakhic* norms by taking tough *halakhic* stands where necessary and moderate ones where desirable. The *halakhic* decision makers in the Movement have to be as prepared to argue on behalf of firm *halakhic* decisions when they decide in favor of or against change, and have to tell their constituents why they are doing so. This model has been followed in the cases of patrilineal descent and the role of openly practicing homosexuals being admitted to rabbinical school and/or being placed in United Synagogue congregations by the Rabbinical Assembly Placement Service.

There are two dimensions to all *halakhic* decisions: (1) the dimension of *halakhic* precedent considered simply; and (2) the historical-sociological dimension. In recent years, the latter has been understood in trendy terms and has often influenced the former. Both need to be understood from a longer-range perspective. Moreover, they need to be considered in light of the internal norms of the Movement, not simply in terms of the Movement's competition with other movements. To this end, the norms of the Movement need to be better defined.

If Conservative *halakhah* is to be meaningful, it must be widely available. There needs to be a manual presented in *halakhic* terms, not simply a guide to practice or an empirical discussion of mainstream Conservative practices and their variations. The development of such a handbook or manual will have to reflect the difference between Torah as constitution and *halakhah* as code, to leave room for variance in practice, but it should be *halakhic* in character and design. Granted, Rabbi Klein's position represents the right wing of Conservative Judaism today, but still his book offers a handbook of Conservative *halakhic* practice. All Conservative Jews should be encouraged to have it in their homes and to refer to it.

More easily used guides to *halakhah* and Jewish life from a Conservative perspective could be produced and distributed. The excellent and accessible Joint Federation of Jewish Men's Clubs and the University of Judaism's *Art of Jewish Living Series* by Ron Wolfson, including the volumes on *Shabbat*, Passover, and Jewish Mourning, should be given wide dissemination. Similarly, the reissuance of the manual on observance of *The Dietary Laws* by Samuel Dresner and Seymour Siegel is very welcome.

Following on that theme, *halakhic* decisions should be widely circulated to all members of the Movement. They should be reprinted in Movement journals and in congregational bulletins as a matter of course, and discussion with regard to them should be solicited, both written and oral. In other words, *halakhah* has to become a living part of the Movement.

## BROADENING THE BASE

In many respects, the demographic situation is working against the Conservative Movement, whether with regard to the changing family structure, the declining birthrate, the tendency of Jews of the fourth generation and beyond to shift away from Conservative Judaism to Reform or to disaffiliate altogether, or, on the other hand, the growing worldwide and local strength of Orthodoxy. The Conservative Movement must take major, even drastic, steps to deal with this changing situation, otherwise it will fall victim to its earlier success.

In contrast to Orthodoxy, Conservative Judaism employs an overly restrictive definition of affiliation: a Conservative Jew is someone affiliated with a Conservative synagogue.[4] As a result, the Movement fails to cultivate institutional loyalty among many who might see themselves as Conservative Jews for reasons of ideology, practice, family tradition, or connections to Conservative institutions other than the synagogue.

The existence of a Conservative community that is the logical outgrowth of the Conservative Movement as it originally developed is now inevitable. Once the Movement accepts this, it can make room for Jews who identify themselves as Conservative for whatever reason, or who are connected to Conservative institutions other than the synagogue. It will enable the arms of the Conservative Movement to pursue a larger population and to open connections to it for individuals who see themselves as part of the community but may want only specific, formal linkages to the institutions that serve that community.

This is especially important since new Conservative institutions have emerged with their own constituencies, who in many respects represent the cutting edge of Conservative Jewish development today. These institutions should become channels of Movement affiliation and participation, no less than congregations. They include the Solomon Schechter schools, the independent *havurot*, and the Ramah camps through a national alumni association.

Adding these constituencies to the Movement in a recognized and an active way also will open up possibilities for attacking some of the other problems of broadening the Movement's leadership by opening up new channels of recruitment; raising the level of formal Jewish involvement of its membership; overcoming rabbinic predominance; and limiting the negative effects of synagogism. It will help confront the demographic situation, especially since *havurot* are geared to the singles and new-style families in many cases, and even offer channels for strengthening links to other Jewish bodies.

Part of the broadening of the base of the Movement will involve outreach to new constituencies or old ones that are in danger of abandoning Conservative Judaism. As it happens, all three of the Movement's new non-congregational institutions have that capability. The Schechter schools have already become, for all intents and purposes, the non-Orthodox community day schools in many communities, with special ties to the Federations. In many communities, the Schechter schools are the only real bridge between the Conservative Movement and the Federations. At times, the leadership of the Conservative Movement has not been happy about this whereas, in fact, it should be encouraged as a source of recruitment and linkage to the larger community. The task is to build the kinds of bridges that keep the schools identified with Conservative Judaism, yet at the same time to encourage wider involvement of their leadership.

*Havurot* represent the obverse of the Schechter schools in the sense that they are not linking institutions as much as they are highly personal and localistic ones. But they perform an outreach function in that respect as well, one that addresses the demographic problems of the Movement, since they are geared to precisely those groups—singles, new-style families, and elites dissatisfied with ordinary congregational ways—to which congregations are not.

The Movement needs to develop academic cadres in addition to the JTS faculty or JTS graduates who teach Jewish studies at other institutions. An extraordinarily high percentage of the alumni of the Ramah camps has entered the academic world. They should constitute a fertile base for building such cadres, albeit not an exclusive one.

1. *The Movement should think of and utilize a broader institutional definition of the Conservative constituency, embracing Schechter school families, Ramah families, and independent havurot members, as well as other quasi-affiliated groups that share the Conservative approach to Jewish life.* True, most members of Conservative networks outside of the synagogue are currently, have been, or will be synagogue members. But failing to see their current involvement as a basis of affiliation as valid as synagogue membership deprives the Movement of additional sources of energy, passion, and new recruits.

2. It would be good to encourage new forms of extra-congregational expression despite the tensions inherent in doing so. For example, those parents who want to form *minyanim* in their Schechter schools should be able to do so without opprobrium. Important Conservative congregations of today grew out of school *minyanim* in the past, and the Movement has lost something without that channel of congregational development. USY and Kadima chapters should operate or be available through the schools.

3. Instead of being attacked or discouraged, as they all too often are, and thus driven out of synagogues, *havurot* should be

encouraged to remain independent yet more a part of the overall Movement framework.

4.  The Movement should invest in a series of countrywide and regional academic conferences and seminars on the future of the Conservative Movement, emphasizing the ideological and *halakhic* dimensions. Conferences could be convened that could then be used as a means to identify as broad a base of interested academics as possible. They in turn would be encouraged and assisted in creating an academic forum parallel to the other institutions in the Conservative Movement. Academics have some of the same needs as everyone else, and they will find their way to Conservative congregations, Schechter schools, *havurot* or whatever, provided that suitable opportunities exist. As we have seen, where they are given free reign and have reasonable leadership from their own ranks, they will create such institutions. But they also are different from non-academics and thus need vehicles of their own. The Movement should make every effort to provide such vehicles.

5.  Concomitant with the foregoing, *the Movement should consider changing its commonly used name from Conservative to Masorti (already its official Hebrew name) in North America to give dramatic impetus to these changes.*

## CONFRONTING THE DEMOGRAPHIC CHALLENGE

As indicated in Part I of this book, the evidence points to a decline in Conservative affiliation as American Jews become more rooted in the United States and in a more hostile environment to Conservative Judaism in almost every respect. Many, if not most, of the recommendations proposed here address those problems in some way, but none can suggest a clear, decisive way to attack the negative demographic situation. The ideological and *halakhic* clarifications and institutional changes suggested can be of help by offering new grounds and new vehicles for identification with Conservative Judaism that are more compatible with contemporary Jewish life. These will not halt the decline, but they can help make those who remain Conservative Jews more serious, knowledgeable, and observant. Below are some recommendations with regard to strengthening the world Movement, through which Conservative Judaism may be able to overcome some of its demographic weaknesses in the United States by capitalizing on possibilities for growth in the other diaspora communities and in Israel. Beyond that, there may be very little that can be done.

1. Rabbis and other leaders of the Movement can and should encourage Conservative Jews to have more children, even though they can do no more than encourage them.

2. There are limits to the degree to which any *halakhic* movement can accommodate intermarriage, especially mixed marriages, but what can be done short of those limits should be explored. The *Keruv* project should be enlarged.

3. The Movement should step up its efforts to recruit from both Orthodoxy and Reform. Thus, for example, it is a mistake for the Conservative Movement to abandon the *hazara b'tshuvah* (becoming religiously observant) phenomenon to Orthodoxy. It should develop vehicles for people who wish to become *ba'alei t'shuvah* (newly observant) to do so through Conservative frameworks, including Conservative versions of *ba'al t'shuvah yeshivot* in Israel and perhaps even in the United States. The Jerusalem-based *yeshiva* program of the Conservative Movement, which was modeled on Pardes, is the first step toward such Masorti *yeshiva* frameworks. Established in 1995–1996 in Jerusalem with two students, it grew to fourteen in 1996–1997, thirty-three full-time and fifteen part-time students in 1997–1998, and forty-two full-time and fifteen part-time students in 1998–1999. The program encourages college students and graduate students to immerse themselves in Torah study. Most of the students in the full-time egalitarian program for college graduates have deferred graduate school while immersing themselves in traditional Jewish texts. As of Fall 1998, the *yeshiva* established by the United Synagogue officially came under the academic auspices of the JTS, thus enabling students to earn credit for course work at the JTS, defer repayment of previous loans taken for university studies, and qualify for new federal loans. Similarly, as Reform Judaism has become more traditional, there may be more Reform Jews exposed to Jewish tradition who can be brought to see its inauthenticity in Reform hands. This kind of competition in Jewish life is healthy, since it is based on offering real choices in way-of-life matters in which the Conservative Movement has a point of view and much to offer and not merely institutional duplication and competition. The Movement should strongly encourage such efforts to counteract the demographic situation. Needless to say, the Conservative

Movement can only go on the offensive if it has a clear base from which to launch its effort, in this case, a clear ideological and *halakhic* base of the type that we have recommended the Movement pursue.

## BUILDING A REAL WORLD MOVEMENT

If the Conservative Movement confines itself to its American base, it will be bound to continue to grow weaker. In an increasingly interdependent world, this kind of national isolation is no longer possible for anyone. It is particularly impossible for Jews, for whom Israel is a central magnet and the only source of a comprehensive, authentic Jewish experience of any kind in our time.

1. The Conservative Movement must take immediate, active steps to strengthen its position in other diaspora communities, most especially in Israel. This means, in the first place, to recast the thinking of the Movement from a parochial American approach to a worldwide one.

2. It means seeking out links to existing non-Orthodox but *halakhic* movements in the other diaspora countries such as has been done with the Neologs in Hungary and the Reform congregations in Great Britain, and as was done virtually by accident in the established Jewish communities of Scandinavia.

3. The Movement must build Conservative/Masorti institutions wherever possible, as was done in Argentina. The possibilities for this are increasing for two reasons. First, the fallout from Orthodox institutions on the part of those who cannot see themselves connected with such extremism is increasing, and there is every legitimate reason to provide such people with a religious substitute. Second, if Orthodoxy continues to move to the right, it will be increasingly difficult for those who were content to be nominally Orthodox to remain within Orthodox congregations. Hence, more and more of them are likely to seek a home in a *halakhic* movement that retains those aspects of tradition that they have found attractive in the past, while at the same time being modern.

An active, aggressive program of this nature will have two benefits. First, it is likely to increase the size of the Movement. Second, it will restore the Movement's esprit, as is always the case when a group is on the offensive rather than the defensive and where there is growth rather than retreat, or even a stabilized status quo. Such efforts will require dedicated leadership that in itself will be an enriching force for the Movement.

4. While this new effort is being launched, or perhaps prior to it, there must be a thorough, honest study of what exists in the world Movement at the present time and of what the possibilities are for expanding in the diaspora. Such a study should be undertaken at the earliest opportunity.

5. If a world movement is to succeed, leaders and institutions from outside of the United States will have to play a serious role in it. It cannot simply be a matter of American efforts abroad, in part, because of differences in the Jewish condition in the United States and elsewhere and, in part, because of the problems associated with any American efforts abroad, which, in many countries, are perceived to be imperialism even when they involve Jews working with other Jews. This will mean a reduction in the exclusively American character of the Movement, even before its world character becomes as pronounced as may be hoped. It may also require something of a brake on religious change, since many Jews in the rest of the world are not affected by the same trends that have brought the most radical changes to the Conservative Movement in the United States. Precisely what that means remains to be seen. But the Movement must be willing and prepared to accept this de-Americanization in terms of institutions, leadership, and behavior.

## BUILDING A MASORTI MOVEMENT IN ISRAEL

In the last analysis, given the importance of Israel in the Jewish world today, no Jewish movement can hope to survive, much less flourish, without an appropriate presence in the Jewish state. In the case of a movement such as the Conservative Movement, appropriate means substantial, not simply an "immigrant church" able to serve those of its members from the diaspora who happen to find their way to Israel, temporarily or permanently. Building a Masorti Movement in Israel may require even more of a shift from the American model than building one in the other diaspora communities. But unless such a movement is built and the shift is made to the degree necessary, Conservative Judaism will, in our opinion, be more subject to attrition and attenuation everywhere.

First, the basis for building a Masorti Movement in Israel must be in the schools, not in the congregations. Second, it must focus on a population of educated *baalei batim*, not on a narrow elite of *klei kodesh*. In other words, the elite-mass division common in the United States cannot be allowed to emerge in Israel. Third, it will have to be more ideological and more *halakhic* because of the character of Israeli society that sees real movements as those that have ideologies and that views Jewish religion in more traditional terms. Fourth, it will have to be more involved in the public institutions of Israeli society in some way, perhaps even to the point of becoming "political" in the Israeli context, again, because of the nature of Israeli society.

1. The Conservative Movement should devote major attention to building a larger network of Masorti or Tali schools in Israel in conjunction with the Ministry of Education, taking advantage of whatever is left of the opportunity offered by the Ministry to do so. Building these schools, providing them with extra support, and fighting for their existence is the single most important activity that the Conservative Movement can undertake to enhance its Israeli presence.

2. The Conservative Movement must focus its attention on preparing appropriate teachers for those schools, either through Machon Schechter or through capturing some of the existing teachers seminaries, or both. It is far more important to have teachers in the Masorti schools who are committed to teaching a Masorti approach to Judaism than anything else. Indeed, without such teachers, it will be impossible to have meaningful Masorti schools. Over the last five years, the teacher-training part of Machon Schechter and its Masters Program has become more fully developed and has many more students in the education track than in the rabbinical one.

3. The development of an indigenous rabbinate is important, if not as important, as the first two. It must be accompanied, however, not only by training in an appropriate rabbinical seminary but by appropriate requirements for general education and appropriate ideological content in Jewish education.

4. The Conservative Movement should reach out to the Sephardic population of Israel, the natural reservoir of Masorti Jews, by recruiting Sephardim, not to Ashkenazify them as the other Israeli movements, Orthodox and secular, have done, but to help them build Sephardic Conservative congregations based upon the Sephardic *minhag*.

Only congregations that preserve the Sephardic *minhag* are likely to have a chance to attract large numbers of Sephardim. It is true that individual Sephardim, especially upwardly mobile ones who think that being Ashkenazic is being better, will join Conservative congregations as they are now constituted, but that will not begin to tap the large population of Masorti Jews that exists in Israel today. There are three concrete steps that can be taken in this regard. One is to develop Conservative congregations using Sephardic ritual and custom. The second is to appoint Sephardim to major leadership posts in the Masorti Movement in Israel and the world. A third is to have the Masorti schools emphasize Sephardic ritual and custom. All three of these steps go against the ethnocentrism of the Masorti Movement in Israel and Conservative Judaism generally. The first is the least difficult in a sense, although even so it would require Western *olim* to help out, and they would have to become familiar with and part of the Sephardic *minhag.* The second is a bit more difficult, although still not impossible. The third requires taking a risk, in the sense that it means downplaying the school's role in serving the children of Western *olim* in the religious sphere and going out to attract a population that most Western *olim* do not seem to want in their schools, since they share many of the local Ashkenazi prejudices on the subject. In our opinion, without bold measures like these, the Masorti Movement will continue to limp along with a couple of dozen functioning congregations, a handful of schools, and a few other institutions that primarily serve Conservative Jews from elsewhere.[5]

One of the greatest possibilities lying before the Masorti Movement in Israel and the Conservative Movement generally is that of the reunion of its Litvak and Sephardi dimensions. However difficult it might be to forge this alliance, objective political circumstances make it a logical one, especially in Israel but equally in the United States, where Orthodoxy is increasingly dominated by its Hassidic elements that are interested in repealing most of the style changes introduced by modernization, rejecting any concern for aesthetics and a modulated, more classical approach to religion in favor of a certain wild *shtetlized* romanticism. In fact, this Hassidic influence is to be found in non-Orthodox movements, particularly the Conservative Movement as well, in a kind of neo-pseudo-Hassidism that has properly tempered some of the excesses of Conservative behavioral rigidity but too often offers only a romanticized nostalgia in its place.

An alliance of Litvaks and Sephardim has indeed taken place in Israel in the form of the Shas party. It is a curious one in some respects, and its future is by no means clear, but it is an object lesson for more moderate representatives of both traditions to examine.

5.  With regard to the Masorti Movement's involvement in Israeli politics, there are several possibilities. One is to preserve what had been the status quo, namely, an almost totally apolitical posture in practice and a political involvement opposed to posture in theory. The other is to pursue the course that was undertaken in the wake of the Reform Movement, namely, a continuation of the previous theoretical position along with a de facto entry into politics to demand a share of the spoils, in this case, the politics of the World Zionist Organization and the Jewish Agency, which is no less politics for being outside of the formal state apparatus. A third possibility is commitment to political involvement in such a way as to pursue the larger goals of the Masorti Movement. To the extent that it is possible to make a recommendation, we would recommend that the Movement prepare for the third course, but to wait until it has gained sufficient strength to be effective before more fully entering the political arena. This does not mean that the second course should be discontinued. However, if it continues as it is currently unfolding, the Conservative Movement will soon come to be viewed as being no better than any of the other spoils seekers gathered around the trough, however justified their claim to support may be.

The Movement might find getting involved in the Jewish Agency-World Zionist Organization (WZO) arena on substantive issues, and not only through requesting funds, a useful intermediate step, perhaps even a sufficient one in terms of political involvement. The world Conservative Movement is already represented in those forums. It simply has to make its representation more effective and develop a realistic program for them to advocate and pursue with regard to the issues confronting the Jewish Agency and the WZO.

In the last elections, there was a dramatic result in the United States with the Conservative (Merkaz) and Reform

(ARZA) parties supplanting the traditional Zionist parties. This is a major step in the right direction.

Statesmanlike thinking on the part of the representatives of the world Conservative Movement would do much to enhance credibility in the eyes of those who dominate the *keter malkhut* of world Jewry, thereby legitimizing the Movement as an active part of world Jewry and strengthening its requests for a share of the financial resources available to the Jewish Agency and the WZO.

6. *The Conservative Movement must upgrade its presence in Israel and use Israel as an educational and even a fund-raising instrument in the United States.* The world Conservative Movement lags behind both its Reform and Orthodox counterparts in providing financial support for its presence in Israel. This state of affairs has not only weakened the ability of the Masorti Movement to move ahead at a time when it is too small to generate sufficient resources of its own but has lowered the Conservative Movement's claim to legitimacy in the context of world Jewry. Most important, it has weakened the ability of Conservative Judaism to utilize Israel as an instrument for building commitment to Conservative Judaism in the diaspora.

## Is Conservative Judaism Best Served through a Single Movement or a Multi-Movement Community?

In the past, streams within the Conservative Movement that diverged from its central tendencies have taken their leave of Conservative Judaism. The Reconstructionists and the independent *havurot* are two prominent examples. More recently, the Union for Traditional Conservative Judaism has broken away. To a lesser extent, the Masorti Movement in Israel is a potential breakaway, five, ten, or twenty years hence. If such a development would be viewed as unwelcome, then the Movement's leaders need to consider policies that would forestall the losses of emerging streams.

There are three possibilities:
1. The Conservative Movement can insist on the maintenance of a single, unitary movement as it presently does, with institutional divisions along functional, rather than ideological or religious, lines and fight all efforts to provide multiple choices in the ideological or religious sphere.

2.  The Conservative Movement can accept the reality of multiple approaches to Conservative Judaism and reorganize accordingly to accommodate as many of those approaches as possible within its ranks, thereby maintaining a common organizational structure for Conservative Jews.

3.  The Conservative Movement can recognize that it is part of a larger Conservative community or camp and simply allow other members of that camp to form their own movements or institutions within or outside of the present movement as they wish, recognizing them as equally entitled to be considered Conservative Jews.

While the Conservative Movement does not have to foster such separate organizations, it should not be afraid to take the kinds of stands that will lead to the development of other organizational structures within the Masorti camp that may or may not be connected with the present Conservative Movement's organizational structure.

## LINKS TO THE JEWISH PEOPLE

Until the 1980s, the Conservative Movement was largely isolated from the rest of organized Jewry in the world. The Movement's leaders were rarely visible on the world scene and then almost exclusively in matters involving the Movement alone. Locally, Conservative congregations sought to be even more self-contained than any others. Leaders of the Jewish world did not find the JTS a stopping place unless they were specifically invited for a particular event, which was rare. The importance of overcoming this isolation can hardly be overemphasized. If the Movement is to grow, it must try to overcome the problems associated with that.

1.  Pursuit of a more active role in those bodies within the WZO-Jewish Agency is one good and relatively easy way to overcome that isolation.

2.  Locally, Conservative rabbis and other leaders have to make an active effort to become involved in the larger community, to make their presence felt as contributing members of the community on an individual basis, since that will redound to the credit of the Movement as a whole.

3.  Locally and countrywide, the Movement's leadership must correct the image of being the spearhead of criticisms of the organizations that have emerged as the dominant element in

the organizational matrix of American Jewry, such as the Council of Jewish Federations [now merged with the UJA to form the United Jewish Communities (UJC)] especially since much of that criticism is ill informed and relies upon images developed fifty years ago that are no longer accurate. In that arena as well, the Conservative Movement should seek to find ways to become more involved.

The growth of Continuity Commissions and synagogue program funding by local federations has fostered this process. For example, in 1997, Barry Shrage, president of the Combined Jewish Philanthropies of Boston, went on record at the Bienniel Convention of the United Synagogue of Conservative Judaism, stating that, "The Boston Federation will help any synagogue pay for a full-time parent and family educator to create a culture in which educating children is supported. . . . We are also creating a heritage program with the Boston Hebrew College and area congregations to bring a full two-year intensive Jewish literacy course to every young family in every congregation in Greater Boston. Federation pays for it, but the congregations are putting money into it too, notwithstanding that everyone began by saying there was no money available."

4.  Here, the Jewish Theological Seminary can be a tremendous asset. Like the Hebrew Union College-Jewish Institute of Religion (HUC-JIR), it should seek ways in which it can contribute as an institution of higher learning to the American Jewish community beyond the limits of institutionalism or the vagaries of individual career choice. The fact that the HUC-JIR has developed one of the two most successful schools of Jewish communal service in the United States, and that its founding director was a Conservative Jew in his personal practice and affiliation all his life and continues to be, is just one example, but it is one that is worth emulating, not by trying to compete with existing programs but by finding underdeveloped areas of communal concern. It is true that the JTS-Columbia Joint Social Work Program now has more than seventy-five alumni. This is a useful contribution to Jewish life, but it remains to be seen how many of the graduates will work in Federation and organizational settings in which they will be professionals who play leadership roles in Jewish communities. Since most of the graduates have been in the field for less than ten years, it is, as yet, impossible to assess their impact.

In addition, the Seminary as a scholarly institution, can host various kinds of conferences, seminars, colloquia, and consultations on issues of concern to American and world Jewry to which people of all persuasions, viewpoints, and affiliations are invited, so that the JTS becomes known as a center of community-oriented and concerned intellectual ferment. Finally, the Seminary also can set up task forces on issues of common Jewish concern, perhaps with a more "religious" bent.

# Chapter 10

# *Internal Unity*

## From Congregationalism to Community

Too many synagogue leaders (rabbis and board members) maintain an overly institutional definition of their mission, often to the exclusion of the purpose of building a Conservative Judaism broadly conceived. In some instances, leaders react less than enthusiastically to developments that represent more intensive forms of Conservative Jewish identity but which they think detract from the strength of their synagogue. These instances include: opposition to the emergence of smaller *minyanim* of more learned or traditional worshipers, unease over perceived competition from Schechter schools, failure to build on the Ramah camp experience, and the mixed reaction to *aliya*.

By now it should be clear that the congregation is not a *kehillah*, but it is one entity (albeit the cornerstone) in a larger *kehillah*. It should be equally clear that most congregations are not synagogue-centers, because most of the center-type activities are provided elsewhere in settings considered more attractive, for whatever reasons, whether the local Federation, the Jewish community center, or independent or communally sponsored Jewish schools or private clubs. Therefore, different kinds of congregations should be encouraged to serve the range of

183

interests to be found within today's Conservative community rather than to focus on building comprehensive synagogue-centers.

1.  *Strong metropolitan councils for Conservative Judaism that would embrace all local Conservative institutions should be established.* It would be easy to establish such councils as paper organizations to satisfy the symbolic need. They should be given real purpose and the power to carry out those purposes. In other words, the councils need teeth. They need to be able to take steps to implement and encourage collaboration in regard to staff and funding to minimize unnecessary duplication in order to become effective instruments of the Conservative Movement and hopefully even the Conservative community in each locality.

2.  Leaders and activists should make a concerted effort to spend time among the various institutions, not only synagogues, so that they develop a loyalty to the furtherance of Conservative Judaism in all of its manifestations.

3.  *Social mechanisms should be developed that would recognize achievements in one sphere (such as a Schechter board) as a stepping-stone to leadership in another sphere (such as a synagogue or regional United Synagogue board).*

4.  *There needs to be a great strengthening of the independence of the schools, particularly the day schools, within the Movement's structure.* One of the consequences of excessive synagogism has been to reduce much of Jewish education to an appendage of individual congregations, designed or redesigned to suit the perceived needs of that particular congregation rather than the larger needs of educating a new generation for active Jewish involvement.

This is an educational necessity to enable educators to pursue their tasks with minimum deflection to serve other needs, however legitimate, and to develop cadres of full-time teachers for Jewish schools instead of relying upon a non-professional or at best a semi-professional, part-time staff. It also is necessitated by demographic realities that have reduced the number of Jewish children available in any community and have even further reduced the number available for Conservative schools to the point where simply to have viable schools, there must be transcongregational and intercongregational efforts. The proliferation of congregationally based day schools is repeating all of the mistakes of the earlier synagogization of supplementary Jewish education.

These ideas usually provoke the response that many synagogues remain alive primarily through the memberships generated by their schools. There is enough evidence from communities where community and intercongregational schools exist that partnerships can be developed between school and synagogue that will achieve the same goal. As long as congregations maintain their synagogue skills, bar mitzvah and bat mitzvah requirements, junior congregations, and/or youth groups, and as long as they maintain close relations with the schools so that the latter reinforce congregational demands and interests in this respect, they reap benefits similar to when schools were physically part of the congregations.

Such independence offers several possibilities: (1) the development of intercongregational, movement, or community schools with enough of a critical mass to provide a reasonable Jewish education; (2) the reestablishment of a Jewish education profession, with full-time professional teachers able to secure sufficient employment to make Jewish education their only career; and (3) the restoration of self-respect to Jewish educational administrators who are now third or fourth on the congregational totem pole but who need to become more significant figures in the Conservative Movement in their own right, comparable to congregational rabbis.

Excessive synagogism often has meant that families who send their children to Schechter schools yet are active members of congregations are treated as though somehow they have abandoned the synagogue in some crucial way. Congregations should make a special effort to include and recognize children who attend Schechter schools and their parents, giving them no less recognition than those who attend their own congregational schools, and even more recognition for taking upon themselves the burdens and joys of more intensive Jewish education.

*Informal Jewish education also should be encouraged on a community-wide as well as a congregational basis, with USY and Kadima linked where possible to the day schools as their youth movement arms.*

## REDUCING THE GAP BETWEEN THE CIRCLES

Broadening the base of the Movement means broadening the leadership and raising the level of the membership to reduce the distinction between them. Given the realities of American Jewish life, it is unlikely that the Conservative Movement can entirely overcome the elite-mass distinction. But it very much needs to do what it can to reduce it and at the very least to expand the elite beyond the estimated 40,000 to 50,000 presently included within it—to reach out and pull more people into the inner circles of Jewish life. The present number cannot sustain a world movement that will be able to compete with Orthodoxy especially outside of the United States.

The degree to which a serious transformation is required here cannot be overemphasized. Efforts that have been initiated in the past have not been perceived as serious by potential candidates for the Conservative elite. Compounding the problem of self-definition is the "old school tie" that unites alumni of the same institution, as would be expected, into a very close-knit group. Added to this is the reality of familial interconnections within that relatively small group. Thus we have a situation in which Conservative rabbis, educators, cantors, and professors of Jewish studies and their families may have come to know each other in their early teens at Camp Ramah, may have studied together at the Jewish Theological Seminary, may have graduated to service in a common occupation, may have married into each other's families, and may have raised children who do the same. This is a source of great strength to the Conservative inner elite, but it also tends to make that elite even more insular and exclusivist than it might otherwise have been, thereby working against any substantial increase in its size.

In general, the Conservative Movement has not placed enough emphasis on using its schools to reduce this gap because of its extreme congregationalism, yet the development of a viable and serious movement with a base of educated Jews beyond *klei kodesh* requires an extensive and a comprehensive school system, elementary and secondary. There is enough evidence from the Ramah experience (which needs to be systematically studied—such a longitudinal effort was begun at Ramah Darom in 1998) to suggest how this is so. It is folly for the Conservative Movement to ignore that evidence and to not build on this reality.

1. In that connection, *it is vitally important for the Conservative Movement to develop an extensive network of Schechter high schools*. A good beginning has been made at the JTS, in Caldwell, New Jersey, on Long Island, and now in Westchester. Independent but related schools such as the Charles E. Smith School in Rockville, Maryland, and the Akiba Hebrew Academy in Philadelphia are models of community high schools that can and do serve Schechter graduates.

Reluctance on the part of American Jews to develop day high schools is singular. Although the cost of such schools is far greater than day elementary schools, the issue is not limited to that of cost as much as it is an irrational fear that children who attend such schools will not be admitted to the best colleges, even though the evidence is strongly to the contrary. But the Movement must make a major effort, including making a major commitment to provide the funds necessary for changing the situation.

It is nothing new to state that it is in the high school years that both Jewish identity and knowledge are deepened. Losing its children in those years cannot help but hurt the Movement as a movement as well as the Jewish people in general. Expanding such high schools would be a form of parent retention as well.

2. There may be a need to create yet another institution, a *bet midrash* in every locality that can sustain one, either within existing congregations, linked with the other local institutions of the Movement referred to above, or preferably as an independent institution, where adults can go to study topics of substantive Jewish interest across the spectrum of Judaism and Jewish concerns at a serious level. Such an institution would be another point of identification, this one geared to adults who are likely to become the most committed to Conservative Judaism.

3. The use of conference centers such as that of the University of Judaism in Ojai, California, for learning purposes is not entirely new, but it needs to be expanded with more such centers, and deeper learning experiences must be made available. These centers also could be used for the academic conferences and seminars recommended above on a year-round basis.

4. The role of Camp Ramah should be further strengthened. It should continue to be a camp where Masorti Judaism is taught and practiced, but one that draws from as wide a population as possible, not merely from Conservative congregations. The Ramah camps need to strengthen their Hebrew dimension and give it new emphasis. In their present state, several of the Ramah camps have become the equivalent of the brief experiment with a USY camp conducted some thirty years ago. It would be more useful for the Movement to restore the special demands required of Ramah campers, as in

the early days of the Ramah movement, and to develop other camps, perhaps under the auspices of USY, for those who cannot meet the Hebrew and other Jewish educational standards, which will be able to do for such young people what Ramah has traditionally done for the more qualified. The Ramah camps should be seen as an extension of the Schechter schools, with lower fees and funding provided accordingly.

5.  USY should be encouraged to expand its short-term encampments, which fill an important function. Where feasible, encouragement should be given to holding such encampments during the year as well as in the summer. These could join the already successful USY Pilgrimages to Israel and Eastern Europe, and the USY on Wheels and Nativ year-long programs, especially to reach those children who do not attend day school. It also would be useful in developing teen-oriented camping programs that have suffered in recent years because of the shifting interests of American Jewish teens.

6.  *The Conservative youth movements should be tied in with the Schechter schools*, developing a link between school and movement similar to that in Israel. The combination of day school, youth movement, and Camp Ramah would provide a framework for developing and keeping Movement loyalty.

7.  *The Jewish Theological Seminary should give serious thought to developing more intensive continuing education programs for non-rabbis.* There have been recommendations in the past that the JTS and the University of Judaism develop general undergraduate and graduate programs, such as at Lee College, with Jewish content to reach out to young people who are not planning to be rabbis but who wish to add a Jewish dimension to their general studies. These programs are not only costly but problematic, since most people go to college to achieve their career ends, and it is hard to see which career ends would be fostered by such institutions other than Jewish ones, which brings us back to the same problem. But it is possible to develop serious continuing education on a high level, if not for large numbers, at least for significant numbers of them, who in the process will continue their Jewish learning and build the social networks that will make them part of the Movement's inner circles. This program might be modeled on the highly successful Wexner Heritage Program, the Florence Melton mini-schools or the Boston Hebrew College's Meah program.

The use of the dormitories of the Jewish Theological Seminary and the University of Judaism for this purpose, or for a movement-wide *midrasha masortit* (traditional seminary) program, is desirable. They also can be used as hostels for elderhostel-like study programs, an activity that can be developed on a self-supporting basis. The Women's League for Conservative Judaism has pioneered in Elder Hostels, and the Lehrhaus program at the JTS is expanding nicely. The close of the twentieth century saw the development and implimentation of an outstanding set of distance learning courses on the internet taught by JTS faculty.

## INTEGRATING THE MOVEMENT'S PARTS INTO A WHOLE

The Jewish Theological Seminary, the Rabbinical Assembly, the United Synagogue of Conservative Judaism, the Women's League for Conservative Judaism, and the Federation of Jewish Men's Clubs—all are arms of the Conservative Movement, and representatives of each regularly comment on the lack of coordination and coherence among the parts that make up the whole. A look at the bylaws and articles of incorporation of these constituents of the Movement shows them to be completely compatible regarding goals and the promotion of traditional Judaism as understood by the historical school. Yet, in day-to-day operation, these groups do not work together smoothly. Some voluntary and professional leaders attribute the lack of coordination and even knowledge of each other's activities to competition over the campaign or financial structure of the constituent groups. Others say that it is the historic centrality and attitude of the JTS and its leaders toward all of the other arms of the Movement that cause the problem. Whatever the cause, the situation requires a remedy.

1. *Masoret*, the Movement-wide magazine, should be strengthened. In addition, *Conservative Judaism* should be expanded and sent to all Movement affiliates (at least to all presidents of Conservative congregations and other institutions) rather than just to the rabbis, as it is presently. Each of the constituent groups would have a section at the end of the magazine to serve the "house organ" function.

2. A Movement-wide calendar should be developed. Presently, the United Synagogue and the Women's League publish daily diaries, and individual Men's Club chapters publish calendars. Moreover, the United Synagogue has undertaken the publication of a wall calendar for the past decade. A

Movement-wide calendar with special events of all constituents and anniversary death dates of lay and professional Movement "greats" could be a unifying symbol. (Thus far, the only such joint project has been a shortened form of the Grace After Meals, which bears the insignia of each of the constituents—and many are unhappy with the particular formulation of the short Grace.) Also, full Hebrew editions of Conservative liturgical publications should be published for use in appropriate venues.

3. The *Luah Beit Haknesset* (the synagogue calendar) is a pioneering joint effort that gives the Movement a common scheduling framework.

4. The new Movement-wide Torah Commentary project (with the JPS) to replace the Hertz Chumash in all of the Conservative synagogues, under David Lieber as general editor, with Chaim Potok, Harold Kushner, and Adele Berlin, should be a model of a unifying intellectual project. It will aid Movement consciousness as the proliferation of the use of the Movement prayerbook *Sim Shalom* has already done.

5. In addition to a calendar for home use, a central clearinghouse calendar should be kept for major Movement functions across constituent groups. This has not been done in the past and has led to embarrassing conflicts for Movement activists (e.g., a Seminary board of overseers meeting is scheduled opposite a United Synagogue convention or board meeting).

6. In metropolitan areas where the Movement is large enough to have one or more full-time regional professionals employed, all should be housed in the same central office, which should be designated as the office of the Conservative Movement. All work for Ramah camps, Women's League, Men's Clubs, United Synagogue, Seminary Campaign, United Synagogue Youth, and the like would be centralized in this office. The Conservative Movement council recommended above should be organized and should function out of this office.

7. A long-range planning committee made up of the representatives of each of the constituent groups should meet at least quarterly to plan and coordinate the future of the Movement.

8. Other countrywide projects could become Movement symbols. For example, the Rabbinical Assembly and the United

Synagogue each publish Movement directories, and the Federation of Men's Clubs sells New Year's cards every year as a major fund-raising project. The directories should be Movement wide. If the cards were a Movement project, the illustrations might be from the Jewish Museum's collection or from the display books from the rare book room of the JTS library. The cards could display on their backs the logos of all constituent groups. This would shift a significant fund-raising project from a constituent to the Movement, so the profits would have to be apportioned to various groups as would those from the calendars and diaries.

9.  The Seminary remains the nexus of the Movement. Therefore, it must be sensitive to including all of the Movement's institutions and constituencies in its governance and programs. For instance, neither the Women's League nor the Men's Clubs used to have representatives on the JTS Board of Directors. In the 1980s a representative of the Women's League and early in the 1990s a representative of the Federation of Men's Clubs were finally added to that board. The same was true of the search committee for the present chancellor. A true sense of worth and cooperation will not be achieved as long as the Seminary is thought to have disdain for one or another of the constituent organizations of the Movement. For example, the United Synagogue may expel a congregation for failure to pay dues or live up to its educational standards, but the Seminary may keep leaders of that congregation on its board or honor them in other ways. This kind of action or inaction leads to a feeling among leaders of the USCJ that they are stepchildren of the Seminary to be exploited when useful and to be ignored when that is to the benefit of the Seminary or its campaign. The Seminary is to be commended for its recent efforts to overcome this historic problem and encouraged to increase those efforts.

10. There needs to be some coordinating group that will look into the duplication of programs among constituents. For example, for several decades, the Seminary's Melton Research Center and the Department of Education of the United Synagogue produced competing Hebrew language programs for congregational schools. Each constituent group is interested in adult education, and no one is coordinating their efforts. The Men's Clubs publication of *Shabbat*

*Seder*, in its excellent *The Art of Jewish Living* series, is to be commended as a necessary effort to work together with the University of Judaism, another arm of the Movement, on an educational project. On the other hand, the Women's League published a Passover guide almost simultaneously with the Seder guide from the *Art of Jewish Living* series. How much more effective would one publication, with the insignias of both groups, have been in terms of marketing the books themselves and greater Movement consciousness?

Another example of duplicative programming is in the area of Israel trips. The United Synagogue, the National Ramah Commission, and individual rabbis and their congregations plan yearly trips to Israel for teenagers and adults. Not only is there no coordination among the programs, there is rivalry among them! The Masorti Movement in the United States has established a travel arm, in the form of "Travel Dialogues," that tries to bring about coordination in travel programs that include substance as well as the trip itself. This needs to be strengthened. Here the Foundation for Conservative Judaism may be able to play a coordinating role.

11.    Just as the constituent agencies of the Movement need to pay close attention to greater interaction, so too do all of them need to consider other organizations and constituencies within the purview of the Movement. For instance, there is the National Ramah Commission (which relates to the JTS much as the United Synagogue Youth Commission relates to the United Synagogue, although individual camps are owned locally, so there is much less central control); the JYDA (association of youth directors); the Educators Assembly; the Cantors Assembly; and the Association of Solomon Schechter Day Schools. Each of these constituencies must be taken into consideration when and if a Conservative Movement office is established or a Conservative council is formed for a metropolitan area. If all are included, those who have formerly held sway will have to share power, but many more Jews will have a stake in the Movement as a whole. Such a "simple" tool as stationery bearing the names of all of the relevant constituent groups in a metropolitan area under the heading of a Movement office would be one symbol important to the support of any function or project discussed in a letter sent out on it.

## BROADENING THE LEADERSHIP

The non-rabbinic leadership of the Movement draws heavily upon those who have distinguished themselves in Conservative synagogues. But as a direct result of this recruitment pattern, several other sources of leadership recruitment have been underutilized. These consist of two broad categories: leaders from Conservative institutions other than synagogues (Schechter schools and Camp Ramah boards are the most apt examples) and leaders in Jewish life outside of the Conservative Movement per se (such as Federation or defense agency activists, Jewish studies academicians, and other academics and intellectuals). In short, the problem here is to create structures and to institute other changes that will result in a more variegated leadership.

Part of the reason for the absence of a certain style of voluntary leadership is that rabbis have tended to dominate Movement policy making in areas where *baalei batim* might otherwise choose to be active. In contrast, even the most prominent professional leaders in other contexts (the Federation movement, the defense agencies) view themselves as administrators or as organizations and communities ultimately responsible to the voluntary leadership. This striking difference in the attitude of the top professional leadership of the Conservative Movement (namely, the rabbis) and those elsewhere (usually "executive directors" or "executive vice presidents") may explain the comparative success of the latter in recruiting and retaining energetic, talented, affluent, and intelligent voluntary leaders.

Rabbis, not inappropriately, do not view themselves as "professionals" but as teachers and representatives of Torah, which puts them in a category by themselves. Moreover, the gap between elite and mass in the Movement does not encourage rabbis to share power with a laity that they see as inferior to them in knowledge and commitment. This perception, however accurate, also creates a vicious circle of self-fulfilling prophecies, one that is no longer functional in a world where the general education of Jews has risen as high as it has and participatory involvement has become the expectation.

Volunteers who have the equivalent or even more secular education than rabbis and who are used to being involved only where they can actively participate are simply not going to consider the Conservative Movement a viable alternative for the investment of their time, energy, and commitment. At one time, this group was essentially confined to academics. Today, it includes members of the liberal professions and businesspeople as well. Hence, the Movement will have to choose. If it wants to broaden the base of its leadership and reduce the great gap between elite and mass, it will have to break the vicious circle.

One other adverse consequence of rabbinical preeminence in leadership ranks is that rabbis, very understandably, respond as educators to social problems within the Movement. Thus their response is to devise ways to better articulate values. Politicians, community organizers, and businesspeople think in different ways. They think of incentives, of reward structures, of constructing social settings, and of a variety of other techniques to manipulate opportunities and interests rather than simply articulating values. In short, it is our impression that the leadership of the Movement has been remarkably short of political and communal organizing savvy (even though it may be far stronger in the development and nurturance of ideas).

1. The Movement should establish a variety of national task forces on both Movement problems and larger Jewish and general issues. These should serve as forums for Conservative Jews who have distinguished themselves in areas other than leading Conservative synagogues. The Movement's regional and national meetings and retreats could be designed explicitly to appeal to non-synagogue leaders.

2. The Movement should consider the formation of political and social action committees of Conservative Jews for certain causes.

3. In connection with these and other Movement-oriented activities, the Movement should recruit proven leaders who are themselves Conservative Jews from other spheres of Jewish life into positions of leadership within the Conservative Movement. Such leaders might be reluctant to spend many years on synagogue boards, but they may be prepared to become active in regional or Movement affairs. National and international movement assemblies should not be scheduled opposite major *Kehillah*-wide meetings.

4. The Movement's rabbinate must give careful consideration to redefining its role to reaffirm its *halakhic* and educational responsibilities, while at the same time encouraging lay people to become part of the common leadership pool. In essence, they should drop the clericalist model to which the Conservative Movement has succumbed and readopt the three *ketarim* model (see Chapter 4). The goal should be to transfer as many of the functions of the *keter kehunah* to congregation members as possible, whether leading services or visiting the sick, while strengthening the role of all rabbis,

including congregational rabbis, as representatives of the *keter torah*. Efforts also should be made to build Movement connections with the *keter malkhut* that will give the non-rabbinical cosmopolitan leadership elements incentive to lead within the Movement and to learn what is necessary to be good or at least adequate Jewish leaders.

Emphasizing that model is important, because it is the first step in achieving this reconceptualization of the rabbinical role, a breaking away from the one borrowed from Reform Judaism (this is another way in which the Conservative Movement can distinguish itself from Reform and even point to Reform inauthenticity), to restore a more traditional conception of the role of the rabbinate. If successful, this also would help set apart the Conservative Movement from Orthodoxy. A declericalized Conservative Movement also can point out the flaws in Orthodoxy's tendency to shift toward the enhancement of the power of its rabbinate at the expense of the *keter malkhut*. In other words, the Conservative rabbinate could form a more appropriate alliance with *keter malkhut* leaders, both within and outside of the Movement, but this would require a major reeducation and a revolutionary change, including the incorporation of the teaching of the new rabbinical role into the Seminary curriculum.

## THE ROLE OF THE JEWISH THEOLOGICAL SEMINARY

As much as the rest of the Movement, the Jewish Theological Seminary is at a crossroads. If it is no longer to be a neo-*yeshiva*, guiding the Movement *halakhically* or at least setting the highest *halakhic* standards for the Movement to follow, then it must at least remain a significant graduate school for Jewish studies that is also capable of providing appropriate service for the Movement. This means that faculty standards have to be maintained. The appointment and promotion of the faculty must continue to be on the basis of criteria accepted in universities all over the world as major ones, especially contributions to scholarship. Today, there is intense competition among the major institutions of higher education for serious Jewish studies faculty. Hence, the JTS no longer has the near monopoly it once had. Promotion standards also are high. The weakest area has been that of search committees, but even this improved in the 1990s.

On the other hand, there is no reason not to strengthen a division of continuing education in which faculty would be encouraged, even assigned, to participate as part of their overall responsibilities to the Movement. Faculty members of a theological seminary must play a dual role—maintaining their scholarship at the highest levels, while demonstrating commitment to the movement they serve. The level of involvement will obviously differ from faculty member to faculty member, based on individual talent and personality, but the expectation should be there and should be, as a general rule, translated into action, even though there is some implicit conflict of roles. After all is said and done, the Seminary differs and will continue to differ from secular universities through its commitment to religious ideological norms. Its faculty must (and do) recognize that and respond accordingly.

This still leaves the question of what role the Seminary should play in guiding the Movement *halakhically*. In part, this will depend on the faculty's emphasis. In the days when the core of the faculty consisted of the Talmud department, it was easier to assume the primacy of the Seminary role. Once it shifted to the historians, there was less legitimacy in such a role. Still, it would be appropriate for key members of the Seminary faculty to continue to play at least an anchoring role in *halakhic* matters through participation in the Committee and on Law and Standards through teaching and writing on *halakhic* matters in concrete ways.

1.    The faculty and academic leadership of the Jewish Theological Seminary should initiate an exploration of what they perceive their role to be in the Conservative Movement as it is now developing. Once they have developed a common position, they should act to share it with other institutions of the Movement, and ultimately they should forge a consensus on the appropriate role of the Seminary and its faculty.

2.    In the interim, the Movement should continue its practice of encouraging appropriate Seminary faculty to participate in the Movement's decision-making forums, especially the RA Committee on Jewish Law and Standards.

3.    A Seminary fund should be established to encourage faculty members to pursue scholarly and public activities of direct benefit to the Conservative Movement of the kind to which we have referred in other recommendations in this book. In that connection, special attention should be paid to the teaching and diffusion of the distinctive historical critical method that constitutes the intellectual undergirding of the Conservative approach to Judaism.

## STRENGTHENING RABBINIC LEADERSHIP

Rabbis, for the most part, devote themselves wholeheartedly to their congregations and spend long hours working on their congregation's behalf. Most choose the rabbinate because they are inspired by Jewish values and want to devote their lives to serving the Jewish people. Nevertheless, there appears to have been a drop in the sense of vocation among some Conservative rabbis. This has been inspired in great part by the external environment in which the reference groups from which most rabbis are drawn have tended to make work a matter of career rather than vocation. Careers are then secondary to some overall American sense of "the good life" as one that offers considerable leisure time and that has divided families into congeries of individuals, each pursuing their individualistic versions of that life. Such a situation poses problems with regard to Jewish values in connection with the rabbinate and community leadership in general. On the other hand, dedication to one's vocation does not preclude the need to provide for one's family. Day school education, Camp Ramah, university education, and pensions are all substantial, albeit legitimate, expenses. Hence, the fact that Conservative (and Reform) rabbis have attained better living conditions is not only right and proper, but it is the only possible way in which a self-respecting Jewish community can function. The question needs to be raised, however, about whether these trends are beginning to come at the expense of a vigorous and dynamic movement.

On the other side of the coin, rabbinic "burnout" seems to be a growing problem. Why are young, idealistic, and once highly motivated rabbis leaving the pulpit rabbinate? Are there ways of encouraging good rabbis to remain in the pulpit? The answers to these questions lie both in the rabbis and in the congregations. It would certainly seem to be in the spirit of Jewish values to move away from adversarial confrontation between rabbis and congregational boards on all issues other than those *l'shem shamayim* (for the sake of Heaven), but this must be done in such a way that all parties are protected.

It is no accident that the *Habad* Lubavitch Movement has grown in strength in the way that it has. Its leaders, major and minor, are palpably dedicated to the cause of *Habad* Lubavitch and Judaism as they understand it, and they are willing to make great sacrifices to attain their goals. In this respect, Habad is only one among several such vigorous movements—the non-Hassidic *yeshiva* world offers other examples—and is only one in a long line of such movements, Orthodox and non-Orthodox. The Zionist Movement, for example, was like that in its early days. Some people question whether the Conservative Movement ever had as much of that élan vital as these other movements, but it certainly had more in its earlier days.

It is possible to understand the present situation as a matter of institutionalization and routinization, but that only helps to understand the problem, not to deal with it. If the Conservative Movement were as dominant as its leaders perceived it to be, then it could live on the basis of that institutionalization and routinization for some time. But since it is now faced with real competition, it dare not and cannot.

1. Recruitment to the rabbinate has to emphasize the sense of calling, even at the price of drawing in fewer rabbis. Rabbis who feel a vocational responsibility in the original sense of the term will be better, more effective spiritual and *halakhic* leaders in any case.[1]

2. If this is impossible, then there has to be some separation between the "called rabbinate" and those who simply follow convenient careers of choice with appropriately different titles for each group. Major gifts in the 1990s of $15,000,000 to fund a Davidson School of Education and $5,000,000 to endow the Miller Cantor's Institute have already led and will continue to lead to evaluation of the spiritual and vocational development of contemporary *klei kodesh*. Acknowledging as valid the task of nurturing rabbis, cantors, and educators to work on the front lines and training scholars to preserve the sacred texts and uncover new knowledge are key to the future growth of the JTS as a whole. Ambivalence about the relative merits of these multiple tasks has sometimes led the morale of alumni to flounder in their allegience.

3. This entire matter needs serious additional study to determine exactly what motivates rabbis (and their spouses) and how motivated they are to do what they are doing. Such a study should be undertaken as soon as possible.

## LEARNING FROM HISTORY: A SUMMARY AND FINAL WORD

The Conservative Movement, which had such auspicious beginnings in the early part of the twentieth century, has now been caught in a more difficult situation because of changes in the environment and situation in which it finds itself and over which it had little or no control. These changes rendered some of the patterns established by the Movement in its salad days considerably less relevant and in some cases even counterproductive. Thus the Movement faces great challenges.

The challenges that face the Conservative Movement are in one sense part and parcel of the challenges that face all of American Jewry and indeed the Jewish world as a whole. However, enough of them are uniquely challenges to the Movement within that larger context. Social science, which is often better at picking up weaknesses than strengths, would have no difficulty painting a gloomy portrait of the future of the Movement. However, social science, like any other form of forecasting, can be and often is confounded by changes in the situation, and even more so by the powers of the human spirit. Thus, in the last analysis, it is up to the people to decide their own future by their thoughts and actions. In this respect, the Conservative Movement has the institutional strength to respond. If its members and leaders have the spiritual strength and the will to do so, then they can meet the challenges that face the Movement and confound gloomy forecasters.

This examination of the Movement has tried to view it, in the words of Oliver Cromwell, "warts and all." It has not tried to pull its punches, because it is believed that the Jewish world will be better if it has a strong Masorti center and that the Conservative Movement could continue to provide that center as it once did. With proper ideas and effort, it will again.

When the Conservative Movement emerged out of the historical school in the latter half of the nineteenth century and the early part of the twentieth century, the avowed purpose of its leaders and leading adherents was to continue to blaze a path for traditional Judaism in the modern world by holding onto both the religious and national dimensions of Jewish life as complementary to one another, no less under conditions of modernity than in earlier times. In this, they rejected Reform Judaism that had broken with *halakhah* and *mitzvot* and renounced the national dimension of Jewish civilization in favor of an exclusively religious Judaism in which congregational rabbis were the predominant figures. By the same token, unlike ultra-Orthodoxy which, like Reform, was equally a response to modernity, dating from the conclusion of the Napoleonic Wars, the historical school and the Conservative Movement recognized the legitimacy of change based upon the adaptation of Torah to contemporary conditions, as long as the fundamentals of Torah were not compromised by the adaptations.

The ultra-Orthodox accepted a multifaceted definition of Jewish civilization but, like the Reform, they too vested the greatest power and authority in the hands of the rabbis, albeit a new kind of rabbinical authority figure, whether a Hassidic *rebbe*, the head of a *yeshiva*, or a *posek*.

When the first institutional manifestation of the historical school took form in the United States, there was no indigenous American Orthodox movement. It was not until the arrival of the Eastern European Jewish masses after 1880 that a separate Orthodoxy developed. It was at that time that a majority of the older traditional congregations in the United States were identifying with the new Jewish Theological Seminary. Only after the reorganization of the JTS and the appointment of Solomon Schechter did some of those congregations drop away and return to a by-then identifiable Orthodox Movement with its own institutions. The others continued their adherence to the JTS, taking its graduates to their pulpits.

Other JTS graduates began to organize new Conservative congregations, separate from the first. What was common in both cases, however, was a continued identification with traditional *halakhic* Judaism, only within a historical perspective that allowed for and encouraged certain kinds of changes and resisted others. Until after World War II, the Conservative Movement saw itself as a wing of traditional Judaism, adhering as much to the *halakhic* interpretation of Torah as Orthodoxy. Indeed, its leaders were fully prepared to argue that their historical approach was more correct from a *halakhic* perspective.

Only after World War II and the migration of Jews to the suburbs and to the South and West during the years of greatest growth of the Conservative Movement did there begin to develop a radical wing that sought to go beyond the evolutionary changes fostered by the Seminary and most of its graduates. That radical wing was led by rabbis trained in new doctrines in the Seminary of the 1930s and 1940s, coupled with a lay leadership that saw its connection to Conservative Judaism as one based upon nostalgia as to which was the "right" Judaism, manifested mostly in their expectations from their rabbis than in their own religious thought and behavior.

Moreover, as American Orthodoxy was reinvigorated by the influx of ultra-Orthodox refugees from Europe after World War II, the Orthodox themselves were less willing to recognize the Conservative Movement, even de facto, as part of the traditionally Jewish *halakhic* camp, pushing the Movement further away from *halakhic* Judaism as Orthodoxy defined it.

Meanwhile, the new and expanding Conservative Movement had made an excellent short-term adaptation to the United States without taking the radical steps of the Reform Movement. It discovered what was acceptable in the American pattern and incorporated that pattern

into the structure and orientation of Conservative Judaism—congregationalism, a special role for a pastoral leadership, and the other dimensions discussed in the preceding pages were all part of that short-term
adaptation. In a very real sense, Conservative Judaism made a form of
traditional Judaism acceptable and even desirable on the American
scene, so it was no wonder that it became the largest Jewish religious
movement in the postwar years.

The transformation began in the mid-1960s. The children of the
pioneers of Conservative Judaism on the suburban frontier, who had
been raised in an atmosphere that saw Judaism as essentially congregational and confined to "synagogue skills," revolted against that kind of
religion, either finding it lacking in the spirituality they were seeking or
too parochial for the world which they encountered in the universities
and on television. Countrywide and worldwide social change rendered
many, if not most, of the short-term solutions that the Conservative
Movement had earlier adopted inadequate for the times.

Within the Movement itself, the younger, committed adherents
began to demand the incorporation of the changes of the 1960s into
the Movement's ways. Many of those reforms were achieved in the
1970s, particularly in the realm of women's rights and gender equality in the synagogue and Judaism as a whole, but also in other areas of
traditional *halakhic* practice. By the 1980s, the Conservative Movement
was increasingly seen as a camp within liberal Judaism rather than
within *halakhic* or traditional Judaism. Faced with ever stronger rejection by the Orthodox and the pulls of its own young people, the
Movement's leadership took as its primary referent the liberal thinking of the day, whether it squared with *halakhic* reasoning or not. All of
this was made clear in the various surveys and studies done during
that decade. Conservative Judaism, which had always been almost
exactly in the middle between Reform and Orthodoxy, began to shift
further toward Reform, opening up a greater chasm between Conservatism and Orthodoxy than had ever been intended by the Movement's founders.

This was accompanied by an increased, and even a new, sense of
denominationalism. Whereas the Conservative Movement had been
very careful in earlier years to avoid any symbolic acts or declarations
that would make the Movement seem to be more than a *branch* of the
Jewish people as a whole (indeed, its leaders had been criticized by
the Movement's left for that), now a new leadership began making the
symbolic identifications and necessary declarations to assert the *denominational* separateness of Conservative Judaism. This was reinforced by
the emergence of an identifiable Conservative Jewish lifestyle. For only

a few was that lifestyle formally advocated by the Movement. For most, it was more a synthesis between traditional religious practices in some areas and what most of the rabbinical leadership of the Movement would easily identify as excessive accommodation to the American scene. The effective norm in Conservative Judaism became one of observing *kashrut* (the dietary laws) at home but maintaining fewer restrictions on eating outside; or attending services on Saturday morning and then going out to lunch and going shopping. These patterns, however they may have fallen short of the highest Conservative expectations, clearly separated the approximately one-third of the members of Conservative congregations that followed them from both Orthodoxy and Reform.

For the two-thirds that were not so clearly identifiable, many had identified with the Movement because of their nostalgia for familiar customs. Without that nostalgia, many of their children moved to the Reform Movement, whose resurgence was largely based on Reform becoming more traditional in its customs, though not in its commitment to the idea of Jewish religious obligation. Thus the Reform Movement passed the Conservative Movement in size and became the largest of the movements on the American scene by a small number, while the Conservative Movement suffered a measurable decline.

Given the reality of this situation, this book argues that the Conservative Movement must find a way to modify those of its survival techniques developed for past generations that have now been rendered obsolete and to develop new strategies for the medium and long term. Those new strategies must be based on the demands of traditional Judaism involving Jewish peoplehood, the maintenance of Jewish norms and obligations, and the establishment of reasonable boundaries between Jews and non-Jews. What this means is that Conservative Judaism and its adherents must move back into the traditional camp.

Conservative Judaism cannot be both *halakhic* and responsive to every politically correct demand of contemporary liberalism. It must place the requirements of Jewish law and tradition and Jewish peoplehood first and foremost. This does not mean becoming Orthodox with a different name. There is or should be a place in the world of traditional Judaism for those who do not accept the contemporary Orthodox view of *humrot* (stringencies), that is, who measure Jewish fidelity by making Jewish observance more difficult. There also should be a "historical" path for traditional Judaism, one that holds that the Torah does recognize changing times. And while it does not believe that adaptation to those times unexceptionally or uncritically is correct, adaptation remains within the four ells of Torah and *halakhah*, and reasonable and meaningful adaptations are *halakhically* possible as well as humanly necessary.

Expressed in other terms, this means that for Conservative as well as for Orthodox Jews, the Torah is and remains the Jewish constitution. As Saadia Gaon said, Jews are Jews by virtue of the Torah (as their constitution). As we noted earlier, the difference between Conservatism and Orthodoxy is that Orthodoxy treats the Torah not only as a constitution but as a sacred code, whereas Conservatism draws a distinction between the sacred constitution and the codes that have developed in response to different situations and can be modified as situations change.

The problem of Orthodoxy is that by making the code itself sacred, it is rendered immobile on a host of issues. The trouble with Conservative Judaism is that it has expanded its flexible attitude toward the codes to make the constitution more flexible than tradition allows it to be. A Conservative Judaism that properly embodies a firm attitude toward the Torah as a sacred constitution, along with a flexible attitude toward its codes, will be in a position that will enable the Movement to maintain genuine *halakhic* demands as norms and boundary setters for its members.

This shall strengthen the Movement in the long run. Evidence from scientific studies of religion points clearly to the fact that in matters religious, the greater the demands, the more faithful and dynamic are the adherents who accept them. We believe that the Conservative Movement will become stronger as it becomes more demanding, even if it has to become somewhat smaller in numbers in the process.

Comparisons to contemporary Orthodoxy are instructive. By all accounts, no more than 10 percent of American Jews are Orthodox. That percentage has remained constant for a long time, but the composition of Orthodoxy has changed from many who are nominally Orthodox and few who are actually so to one in which just about all who claim to be Orthodox actually are. This has given Orthodoxy a strength in the United States and on the world scene far beyond what its percentage of the U.S. or even of the world Jewish population would suggest. Even a reduced Conservative Movement of twice that size, filled with adherents mobilized on behalf of Jewish life in the Conservative manner, would do the same and even more for the Conservative Movement.

In this last section there were many suggestions for institutional developments that would foster intensive Jewish commitment on the part of serious Conservative Jews, by combining spirituality, *mitzvot*, and a sense of the richness of Jewish civilization. Fostering such institutional changes will offer the Movement a chance to move back into a position of strength inside of the traditional camp rather than to increase its weaknesses by remaining outside of that camp. Further, it is in the spirit and nature of the Conservative Movement to do so.

# Glossary

*Adat B'nai Yisrael*—the community of the children of Israel

*Ahdut Avodah*—Labor Unity, an Israeli political party, now part of the Israel Labor Party

*Am Yisrael*—the nation of Israel

*ARZA*—Association of Reform Zionists

*Ashkenazic*—Jews from European countries

*Ba'alei T'filah*—prayer leaders

*Ba'alei T'shuvah*—newly observant Jews

*Baalei batim*—householders (i.e., lay leaders)

*Bar/Bat mitzvah*—(pl. b'nai or b'not mitzvah) age of majority when Jewish girls (at twelve) and boys (at thirteen) become personally responsible for fulfilling commandments. Marked by a public ceremony.

*Bet*—the house of

*Bet Midrash*—study hall

*Bet Midrash l'Limudei HaYahadut*—seminary for Jewish studies

*Bet Midrash l'Morim*—seminary for teachers

*Bet Midrash l'Rabbanim*—seminary for rabbinical studies

*Bimah*—podium

*Dati*—religious

*Daven*—pray

*Davening*—prayer

*Dayanim*—judges

*Dinim*—laws

*Edah Haredit*—ultra-Orthodox

*"Emet Ve-Emunah"*—Truth and Belief, the most recent official statement of Conservative Movement ideology

*Eretz Yisrael*—the Land of Israel

*Habad*—one of the names of the Hassidim from Lubavitch. An acronym derived from the Hebrew words *hochma* (wisdom), *binah* (understanding), and *deyah* (knowledge).

*Halakhah*—Jewish law

*Havdalah*—ceremony marking the end of the Sabbath

*Havurah*—fellowship

*Havurot*—fellowships

*Hazarah b'Tshuvah*—becoming religiously observant

*Hazzanim*—cantors

*Hevrot*—task groups

*Hiloni*—secular

*Hozrim B'tshuva*—newly observant Jews

*Humrot*—stringencies

*Kabalat Shabbat*—prayers recited at the beginning of the Sabbath on Friday night

*Kabbalistic*—mystical

*Kahal*—congregation

*Kallot*—learning assemblies

*Kashrut*—the dietary laws

*Kehillah*—community

*Keruv*—literally to bring closer. A project encouraging conversion to Judaism of non-Jewish partners in interfaith households and then greater involvement of these families in synagogue life.

*Kehunah*—priesthood

*Keter* (pl. *ketar'im*—crown (literal)

*Keter kehunah*—priestly domain (rule)

*Keter malkhut*—civil domain (rule)

*Keter torah*—Torah domain (rule)

*Kiddush*—blessing over the wine recited on Sabbath and major Festivals

*Kippot*—skull caps

*Klal Yisrael*—the whole community of Israel

*Klei kodesh*—religious officiants

*Kosher*—permitted to be eaten according to the Jewish dietary laws (literally: ritually fit)

*L'shem Shamayim*—for the sake of Heaven

*Litvaks*—Jews of Lithuanian ancestry

*Luach*—calendar (also Luah)

*Machmir*—stringent

*Makil*—lenient

*Mara d'atra*—authoritative leader

*Masoret*—tradition

*Masoret Ha-brit*—tradition of the Covenant

*Masorti*—traditional (here used as the Hebrew name of the Conservative movement)

*Midrasha Masortit*—traditional seminary

*Mikva*—ritual bath

*Mikvaot*—ritual baths

*Minhag*—custom

*Minyan*—group of ten Jews over the age of bar or bat mitzvah that constitutes a quorum for formal prayer

*Mitzvot*—commandments

*Moetzet Gedolai Hatorah*—Council of Torah Sages

*Mohelim*—circumcision specialists

*Musmahim*—fully ordained rabbis

*Negidim*—commissioners

*Nesi'im*—magistrates

*Nusah*—style of prayer, liturgy

*Olim*—new immigrants to Israel

*Parnassim*—officers, usually of congregations or communities

*Pesach Seder*—traditional feast at beginning of Passover

*Posekim*—religious decision makers, arbiters of Jewish Law.

*Rav*—rabbi

*Rebbe*—spiritual mentor

*Rebbetzin*—Yiddish for a rabbi's wife

*Rosh Hashanah*—the Jewish New Year

*Sephardim*—Jews from Middle Eastern or North African countries

*Shabbat*—the Sabbath

*Shaliah tzibbur*—prayer leader

*Shiva*—the seven-day mourning period

*Shochtim*—ritual slaughterers

*Shtetl*—small town in Eastern Europe with an organized Jewish community

*Shul*—synagogue

*Shushan Purim*—the day after Purim, observed as Purim by Jews living in cities that were walled at the time the events took place.

*Siddur*—prayer book

*Sofrim*—scribes

*Talmidei Hakhamim*—religious scholars

*Talmud*—oral law

*Teshuvot*—rabbinic responsa

*Torah*—usually refers to the five Books of Moses or the entire body of religiously authoritative Jewish teachings

*Yeshiva*—institution of religious study

*Yeshivot*—institutions of religious study

# Notes

## INTRODUCTION

1. Marshall Sklare, *Conservative Judaism—An American Religious Movement* (Glencoe, Ill.: Free Press, 1955, 1972).

2. Jack Wertheimer, "Recent Trends in American Judaism," *American Jewish Year Book* (New York and Philadelphia: American Jewish Committee and Jewish Publication Society, 1989), pp. 63–162.

3. Charles Liebman, *The Ambivalent American Jew: Politics, Religion and Family in American Jewish Life* (Philadelphia: Jewish Publication Society, 1973).

4. Neil Gillman, *Conservative Judaism: The New Century* (West Orange, N.J.: Behrman House, 1993).

5. Rela Geffen Monson, "The Future of Conservative Judaism in the United States: A Rejoinder," *Conservative Judaism*, Vol. XXXVII, No. 2 (Winter 1983–1984): 10–15.

## CHAPTER 1

1. On the history of the Conservative Movement, see Mordecai Waxman, ed., *Tradition and Change: The Development of Conservative Judaism* (New York: Burning Bush Press, 1958); Moshe Davis, *The Emergence of Conservative Judaism* (Philadelphia: Jewish Publication Society, 1963); Neil Gillman, *Conservative Judaism: The New Century* (West Orange N. J.: Behrman House, 1993); Abraham Karp, "A Century of Conservative Judaism in the United States," in *American*

*Jewish Year Book* (Philadelphia and New York: Jewish Publication Society and American Jewish Committee, 1986), pp. 3–61.

2. *A Note on Terminology*: Throughout this book, we use the terms *party*, *faction*, and *camp*, in addition to the more conventional terms *movement, branch*, and *community*, to describe organized Conservative Judaism and its development. We have adopted this terminology from political science to add precision to our analysis.

The term *party* is perhaps the most easily understood as the institutionalized expression of a particular ideology or persuasion and the interests that surround it. For most of its history, within American religious life, the Conservative Movement could be viewed as one of two major parties, with the Reform Movement being the other, competing for the allegiance of American Jews.

A *faction* is a group within a party that seeks control of the party's ideology and institutions. Thus for many years the Reconstructionist Movement was a faction within Conservative Judaism, but more recently it has separated to become a party in its own right.

A *camp* embraces a group of parties sharing a common ideology, with each having its own separate adherents, institutions, and interests, as well as sharing certain institutions and interests. These parties may cooperate or compete with each other, or do both at different times. Thus American Orthodoxy from the start was organized into different groupings such as the one around Yeshiva University, which became the Rabbinical Council of America and the Union of American Orthodox Jewish Congregations; those around the traditional *yeshivot* (institutions of religious study) that soon found their way to Agudat Israel; Young Israel, which although founded by Mordecai Kaplan by the 1920s was a bastion of modern Orthodoxy; and, as they found their way to the United States, the various Hassidic groups. In our terminology, each of these groupings was and is a party in its own right, but all are part of a common Orthodox camp. At the same time, within Agudat Israel, each of the *yeshivot* with its followers constituted a faction. While there is much competition within the Orthodox camp, some of which generates real animus among the groupings, there is mutual recognition of their common Orthodoxy, which is what keeps them a single camp.

3. Moshe Davis has chronicled the early years in his book *The Emergence of Conservative Judaism, op. cit.*; Charles S. Liebman has disputed Davis' central thesis in "Orthodoxy in 19th Century America," *Tradition* 6 (Spring–Summer 1964): 132–140. For a thorough analysis of the "historical school" in Europe and the history of the Reform Movement, see Michael Meyer, *Responses to Modernity: A History of the Reform Movement in Judaism* (New York: Oxford University Press, 1988), and Seftin D. Temkin, "A Century of Reform Judaism in America," *American Jewish Year Book 1974* (Philadelphia and New York: American Jewish Committee and Jewish Publication Society of America, 1975), pp. 3–75.

4. On the "historical school" in Europe, see Meyer, *op. cit.*

5. Davis, *op. cit.*

6. Liebman, *op. cit.*

7. Rela Geffen Monson, "The Jewish Theological Seminary and Conservative Congregations: Limited Associates or Full Partners?" in *The Seminary at 100—Reflections on the Jewish Theological Seminary and the Conservative Movement*, eds. Nina Beth Cardin and David Wolf Silverman (New York: The Rabbinical Assembly and the Jewish Theological Seminary of America, 1987), pp. 63–72.

8. For an analysis of the impact of the "treifa banquet," see Meyer, *op. cit.*, and Gillman, *op. cit.*, pp. 25–26.

9. Seymour Fox, then assistant to the chancellor, to his class of junior staff members at Camp Ramah, Wisconsin, Summer 1952. The senior author of this study personally heard him offer this definition and quotation. Knowing of the discussion in the mid-1940s between Finkelstein and his childhood friend Solomon Goldman, then rabbi of Anshe Emet, the leading Conservative congregation in Chicago, witnessed by Albert Elazar, his father, then educational director of Anshe Emet, this rings entirely true. Goldman was then arguing for the changes that the Movement later adopted against Finkelstein's unbending traditionalism.

10. On the emergence of Orthodoxy and the premises on which it was founded, see Jeffrey S. Gurock, "Resisters and Accommodators: Varieties of Orthodox Rabbis in America, 1886–1983," *American Jewish Archives* 35 (1983), pp. 150–156; Samuel Heilman and Steven M. Cohen, *Cosmopolitans and Parochials: Modern Orthodox Jews in America* (Chicago: University of Chicago Press, 1989); William Helmreich, *The World of the Yeshiva: An Intimate Portrait of Orthodox Jewry* (New York: Free Press, 1982); Charles S. Liebman, "Orthodoxy in American Jewish Life," *American Jewish Year Book 1971* (New York and Philadelphia: American Jewish Committee and Jewish Publication Society, 1970).

11. On the Orthodox breakaway, see Jenna Weissman Joselit, *New York's Jewish Jews—The Orthodox Community in the Interwar Years* (Bloomington and Indianapolis: Indiana University Press, 1990).

12. On Solomon Schechter, see Gillman, *op. cit.*, ch. 3, "From School to Movement," pp. 32–47, and Norman Bentwich, *Solomon Schechter: A Biography* (Philadelphia: Jewish Publication Society of America, 1948).

13. On Cyrus Adler, see *I Have Considered the Days* (Philadelphia: Jewish Publication Society, 1941), and Ira Robinson, ed., *Cyrus Adler: Selected Letters*, 2 vols, Preface by Louis Finkelstein, and Introduction by Naomi W. Cohen (Philadelphia: Jewish Publication Society of America and Jewish Theological Seminary of America, 1985). On the role of the "Philadelphia Group" of Jewish influentials, of which Adler was a part, see *When Philadelphia Was the Capital of Jewish America*, ed. Murray Friedman (Cranberry, N.J.: Associated University Presses, 1993).

14. Eli Ginzberg, *Keeper of the Law: Louis Ginzberg* (Philadelphia: Jewish Publication Society of America, 1966), and Herbert Parzen, *Architects of Conservative Judaism* (New York: Jonathan David, 1964), ch. 5.

15. On the work of the Law Committee, see David Aronson, *The Jewish Way of Life* (New York: National Academy for Adult Jewish Studies, 1946). The early history of the Committee on Jewish Law and Practice appears in the 1927, 1929, and 1930–1932, *Proceedings of the Rabbinical Assembly*. The Committee's responsa on Sabbath observance are included in Mordecai Waxman, ed., *Tradition and Change: The Development of Conservative Judaism* (New York: Burning Bush Press, 1958). Responsa also appear in Seymour Siegel and Elliot Gertel, eds., *Conservative Judaism and Jewish Law*, Part Two (New York: Rabbinical Assembly, 1977). See also Isaac Klein, *Responsa and Halakhic Studies* (New York: Ktav, 1975) and Isaac Klein, *A Guide to Jewish Religious Practice* (New York: Moreshet Series of JTSA and Ktav, 1979).

16. On the controversy over the ordination of women, see Simon Greenberg, ed., *The Ordination of Women as Rabbis: Studies and Responsa*, (New York: Jewish Theological Seminary, 1988). On the status of women in the Conservative Movement and the growth of the Jewish Feminist Movement and its linkages to the Conservative Movement, see Sylvia B. Fishman, "The Impact of Feminism on American Jewish Life," in *American Jewish Year Book* (New York and Philadelphia: Jewish Publication Society and American Jewish Committee, 1989), pp. 3–62; Judith Hauptman, "Women and the Conservative Synagogue," pp. 159–181, and Rela Geffen Monson, "The Impact of the Jewish Women's Movement on the American Synagogue: 1972–1985," pp. 227–237, both in Susan Grossman and Rivka Haut, eds., *Daughters of the King—Women and the Synagogue* (Philadelphia: Jewish Publication Society, 1992). For a general overview of the first decade of the movement, see Anne Lapidus Lerner, "Who Hast Not Made Me a Man: The Movement for Equal Rights for Women in American Jewry," *American Jewish Year Book 77* (New York and Philadelphia: American Jewish Committee and Jewish Publication Society, 1970 1977).

17. On the religious revival of the postwar period, see Jack Wertheimer, *A People Divided—Judaism in Contemporary America*, Part 1 (Brandeis University Press & University Press of New England. 1997. Hanover, N.H.)

18. For a history of Reconstructionism, see Richard Libowitz, *Mordecai Kaplan and the Development of Reconstructionism* (New York: E. Mellen Press, 1983); Emanuel S. Goldsmith, Mel Scult, and Robert M. Seltzer, *The American Judaism of Mordecai M. Kaplan*, (New York: New York University Press, 1990); Mordecai M. Kaplan, *Judaism as a Civilization* (New York: Macmillan, 1934). See also Charles S. Liebman, "Reconstructionism in American Jewish Life," *American Jewish Year Book 1971* (New York and Philadelphia: American Jewish Committee and Jewish Publication Society, 1970), p. 3–99; Ira Eisenstein, *Reconstructing Judaism: An Autobiography* (New York: Reconstructionist Press, 1986).

19. On the *havurah* movement, see Jacob Neusner, *Contemporary Judaic Fellowship in Theory and Practice* (New York: Ktav, 1973); Bernard Reisman, *The Chavurah: A Contemporary Jewish Experience* (New York: Union of American Hebrew Congregations, 1977); Daniel J. Elazar and Rela Geffen Monson, "The Synagogue Havurah: An Experiment in Restoring Adult Jewish Fellowship to the Jewish Community," *Jewish Journal of Sociology* 21 (June 1979): 72–74; Riv-Ellen Prell, *Prayer and Community: The Havurah in American Judaism* (Detroit: Wayne State University Press, 1989); Gerald B. Bubis and Harry Wasserman, *Synagogue Havurot: A Comparative Study* (Philadelphia: Center for Jewish Community Studies, 1983).

20. On the history of the Union for Traditional (Conservative) Judaism (UTCJ) and the Federation of Traditional Orthodox Rabbis (FTOR), see Gillman, *op. cit.*, ch. 8, "The Ordination of Women," pp. 145–148 and Ronald Price, "Pluralism in the Conservative Movement," in *The Seminary at 100*, pp. 345–348. See also chapter 7 of Wertheimer, *op. cit.*, "The Right Secedes," pp. 154–156.

21. On the Union for Traditional [Conservative] Judaism, see David Novak. The responsa of the UTJ are published periodically in *Tomeikh kaHalakhah*. The group also has a quarterly review called *Hagahelet* ("the Ember"), its own Panel of Halakhic Inquiry, and its own seminary, the Institute of Traditional Judaism, in Teaneck, New Jersey.

22. On camps and parties in Jewish and Zionist history, see Daniel J. Elazar, *Israel: Building a New Society* (Bloomington: Indiana University Press, 1986), esp. ch. 4, "The Compound Structure of the Israeli Polity," pp. 68–72; *People and Polity: The Organizational Dynamics of World Jewry* (Detroit: Wayne State University Press, 1989), esp. ch. 5, "The Institutions of the Renewed Polity"; and Daniel J. Elazar and Stuart A. Cohen, *The Jewish Polity: Jewish Political Organization from Biblical Times to the Present* (Bloomington: Indiana University Press, 1985).

## CHAPTER 2

1. Marshall Sklare, *Conservative Judaism: An American Religious Movement*, rev. ed. (New York: Schocken, 1972).

2. On traditional *yeshivot*, see William Helmreich, *The World of the Yeshiva: An Intimate Portrait of Orthodox Jewry* (New York: Free Press, 1982).

3. For an excellent discussion of *wissenschaft des judentums*, see the early chapters of Michael Meyer, *Response to Modernity: A History of the Reform Movement in Judaism* (New York: Oxford University Press, 1988). For a briefer discussion, see Neil Gillman, *Conservative Judaism: The New Century*, "The Legacy of Frankel ch. 2." (West Orange, N.J.: Behrman House, 1993) *op. cit.*

4. Barry A. Kosmin et al., *Highlights of the National Jewish Population Survey* (New York: Council of Jewish Federations, 1991). The data on synagogue membership is recorded here relative to other Jewish organizations.

5. Sidney Goldstein, "Profile of American Jewry: Insights from the National Jewish Population Survey," *American Jewish Year Book*, Vol. 92 (New York and Philadelphia: American Jewish Committee and Jewish Publication Society, 1992), pp. 77–177, see esp. pp. 172–73. Of the core Jewish population in the NJPS (about 5.5 million), 33 percent reported that they were currently synagogue members, while 28 percent said that they belonged to one or more Jewish organizations. Of the Jews who considered themselves Jews by religion (about 4 million), 58 percent currently belonged to synagogues and 33 percent to one or more Jewish organizations.

6. Daniel J. Elazar and Stephen Goldstein, "The Legal Status of American Jewry," *American Jewish Year Book* (New York and Philadelphia: American Jewish Committee and Jewish Publication Society, 1972).

7. This model (pp. 8–22) was developed by Rela Mintz Geffen for "Planning for the Future of the Conservative Movement," a report by Daniel J. Elazar, Rela Geffen Monson, and Steven M. Cohen, submitted by the Jerusalem Center for Public Affairs, 1987.

8. Prominent among them were Lou Weiner, a leading Conservative layman in Chicago, who became the great backer of the camp, remaining active for nearly fifty years; Rabbi Ralph Simon of Rodfei Tzedek, who provided rabbinical leadership and support; and Albert Elazar, the educational director of Anshe Emet Synagogue, who proposed Ramah as the name for the camp and brought in the backing of Jewish educators in the region.

On the Ramah camps, see H. A. Alexander, "Ramah at Forty: Aspirations, Achievements, Challenges"; and Burton I. Cohen, "From Camper to National Director: A Personal View of the Seminary and Ramah," both in *The Seminary at 100: Reflections On the Jewish Theological Seminary and the Conservative Movement*, Nina Beth Cardin and David Wolf Silverman, eds. (Rabbinical Assembly and Jewish Theological Seminary, New York, 1987 pb) pp. 105–134; Sylvia Ettenberg and Geraldine Rosenfeld, eds., *The Ramah Experience: Continuity and Commitment* (New York: Jewish Theological Seminary of America, 1989); S. R. Schwartz, "Ramah—The Early Years, 1947–52," Masters thesis, the Jewish Theological Seminary of America, 1976.

Articles by Alexander Shapiro, Shuly Schwartz, Burton Cohen, Joseph Lukinsky, Arthur Elstein, and Louis Newman in *Studies in Jewish Education and Judaica in Honor of Louis Newman*, ed. Alexander M. Shapiro and Burton I. Cohen (New York: Ktav, 1984). There also is a symposium on Ramah in *Conservative Judaism*, Fall 1987. This symposium also highlights the connections between Ramah and the founding of the *Havurah* Movement For the most recent analysis of the history and impact of Ramah, see Sheldon A. Dorph, editor. *Forward from 50-Ramah Reflections at 50: Visions for a New Century.* National Ramah Commission. 1999.

9. On *havurot*, see citations in chapter, footnote 18, and also Robert Goldenberg, "The Seminary and 'Havurah Judaism': Some Thought," in *The Seminary at 100*, eds. Nina Beth Cardin and David Wolf Silverman (New York: Rabbinical Assembly, 1987), pp. 155–63.

10. On the development of the Solomon Schechter day schools, see Walter Ackerman, "The Day School in the Conservative Movement," *Conservative Judaism* (Winter 1961); Daniel J. Margolis and Eliot Salo Schoenberg, eds., *Curriculum, Community, Commitment: Views on the American Jewish Day School in Memory of Bennett I. Solomon* (West Orange, N.J.: Behrman House, 1993).

## CHAPTER 3

1. *Emet Ve-emunah—Statement of Principles of Conservative Judaism*—The Jewish Theological Seminary of America; the Rabbinical Assembly; the United Synagogue of America; the Women's League for Conservative Judaism; the Federation of Jewish Men's Clubs, 1988.

2. See Ismar Schorsch, *Thoughts from 3080: Selected Addresses and Writings* (New York: Jewish Theological Seminary of America, 1988).

3. On the Conservative Movement and *halakhah*, see the references in Footnote 15 in Chapter 1. In addition, see the overview in Elliot N. Dorff, *Conservative Judaism: Our Ancestors to Our Descendents* (New York: Youth Commission, United Synagogue of America, 1977); David Golinkin, "Halakha for Our Time: A Conservative Approach to Jewish Law" (New York: United Synagogue of America, 1991); Joel Roth, *Halakhic Process: A Systemic Analysis* (New York: Jewish Theological Seminary, 1986); Elliot N. Dorff and Arthur Rosett, *A Living Tree: The Roots and Growth of Jewish Law* (New York: Jewish Theological Seminary and State University of New York Press, 1988).

4. Nevertheless, recent surveys by Steven M. Cohen show that the Conservative laity rejects the Movement's official position opposing the recognition of Jewishness through patrilineal descent. This is true even of those who are synagogue members at this time, that is to say, not only those who vaguely identify with Conservative Judaism but those who actually are affiliated with Conservative congregations. Thus, if the Movement's leadership is serious about maintaining its position, it must undertake a major educational effort within the ranks of Movement members.

5. On the Conservative Movement and Zionism, see John Ruskay and David Szonyi, eds., *Deepening the Commitment: Zionism and the Conservative/ Masorti Movement* (New York: Jewish Theological Seminary, 1990). This volume

contains the proceedings of the September 1988 Movement-wide conference on Zionism and Zionist thought. For complete records of a mid-century debate on Zionism in the Movement, see the complete reprint of the debate from *The Torch*, (Winter 1960), on "Should the United Synagogue of America Join the World Zionist Organization?" "Yes" says Mordecai M. Kaplan; Nahum Goldman; "No" says Simon Greenberg; "No" says Abraham Joshua Heschel. Milton Berger, Joel S. Geffen, and M. David Hoffman, eds., *Roads to Jewish Survival* (New York: National Federation of Jewish Men's Clubs & Bloch Publishing Company, 1967), pp. 303–342.

6. Will Herberg, *Protestant, Catholic, Jew: An Essay in American Religious Sociology* (Garden City, N.Y.: Doubleday, 1955).

## CHAPTER 4

1. William Morris, ed., *American Heritage Dictionary of the English Language* (Boston and New York: American Heritage Publishing Company, Inc., & Houghton Mifflin Company, 1973).

2. Moshe Davis, *The Emergence of Conservative Judaism*, (Philadelphia: Jewish Publication Society, 1963).

3. Mordecai Waxman, "The Ideology of the Conservative Movement," in *Understanding American Judaism*, vol. 2, ed. Jacob Neusner, "Sectors of American Judaism" (New York: Ktav, 1975), p. 257.

4. This discussion is based on Rela Geffen Monson, "The Jewish Theological Seminary and Conservative Congregations: Limited Associates or Full Partners?" in *The Seminary at 100—Reflections on the Jewish Theological Seminary and the Conservative Movement*, eds. Nina Beth Cardin and David Wolf Silverman (New York: Rabbinical Assembly and Jewish Theological Seminary of America, 1987), pp. 63–72.

5. The Hassidic *rebbe* completely dominates his community, but he does so because of his presumably divine charisma (in the original sense of the term), rather than because of his superior rabbinical authority as a *posek*, or clerical authority, as a priest, even though he may play both roles.

6. The term *minister*, adopted by the Jews in Britain, despite its other objectionable qualities, is probably an accurate description of what the American congregational rabbi is. Until the 1840s, American congregations also recognized that their spiritual leaders were not rabbis in the traditional sense of *posekim* and, influenced by their Sephardic founders, they gave them the title of *hazzan*, which originally meant governor or manager of the synagogue, and is still used by Sephardim to describe what Americans refer to as the congregational rabbi.

7. Daniel J. Elazar and Stuart A. Cohen, *The Jewish Polity* (Bloomington: Indiana University, 1984); Stuart A. Cohen, *The Three Crowns: Structures of Communal Politics in Early Rabbinic Jewry* (Cambridge, England, and New York: Cambridge University Press, 1990).

8. David M. Ackerman, "A Not Too Distant Mirror—The Seminary Rabbinical School Curriculum," *Conservative Judaism*, Vol. 44, No. 4 (Summer 1992): 47–61.

9. A handful of Conservative congregations such as Beth El in Baltimore have indeed built their own *mikvaot*. See Daniel J. Elazar, *Community and Polity: The Organizational Dynamics of American Jewry*, revised and updated ed. (Philadelphia and Jerusalem: Jewish Publication Society, 5755/1995).

10. Daniel J. Elazar and Douglas St. Angelo, " 'Cosmopolitans' and 'Locals' in Contemporary Community Politics," *Proceedings of the Minnesota Academy of Science*, No. 2 (1964): xxxi; Robert K. Merton, *Social Theory and Social Structure* (Glencoe, Ill.: Free Press, 1949); Alvin Gouldner, "Cosmopolitans and Locals: Toward an Analysis of Latent Social Roles," *Administrative Science Quarterly*, Vol. 1, No. 2 (1957): 281–306, Vol. 2, No. 2 (1958): 444–480; Daniel J. Elazar, *Cities of the Prairie: The Metropolitan Frontier and American Politics* (New York: Basic Books, 1970).

11. Conservative Jews are more likely to be trapped by that syndrome, since they are more likely to want a very large synagogue and want it close to them, in contrast to Reform Jews, who are satisfied with large temples that do not have to be close by, or Orthodox Jews, who are not attracted to very large synagogues, but need small ones within walking distance, and do not move as much. In regard to decorum and other structural components of synagogue life, particularly in large congregations, see Rela Geffen Monson, "The User-Friendly Synagogue: Generating Primary Group Relationships in an Era of Impersonality" in *Conservative Judaism*, Vol. XXXVIII, No. 2 (Winter 1985–1986): 44–51. This issue contains a number of articles on the synagogue that were first presented at a conference earlier in the 1980s at the JTS on the Future of the Synagogue in America. Authors include: Neil Gillman, Robert Goldenberg, Donald Feldstein, Alan Silverstein, Lawrence A. Hoffman, Anne Lapidus Lerner, and Samuel Heilman.

12. Bernard Lazerwitz, J. Alan Winter, Arnold Dashefsky, and Ephraim Tabory, *Jewish Choices—American Jewish Denominationalism* (Albany: State University of New York Press, 1998), pp. 40–41.

13. Sherry Israel, *Community Report on the 1995 Demographic Study, Combined Jewish Philanthropies* (Boston: Combined Jewish Philanthropies, 1997), pp. 24–26.

14. Jack Wertheimer, ed., *Conservative Synagogues and Their Members, Highlights of the North American Survey of 1995–96* (New York: Jewish Theological Seminary of America, 1997), p. 35. A more detailed anaylsis of the data from

this project is not yet available. It included four studies: the 1995–1996 Conservative Congregational Survey; the 1995 Conservative Membership Survey; the 1995 Bar/Bat Mitzvah Survey; and a reanalysis of data from the 1990 National Jewish Population Survey.

15. Ismar Schorsch, "The Emerging Vision of Ramah," in *The Ramah Experience: Community and Commitment*, eds. Sylvia C. Ettenberg and Geraldine Rosenfield (New York: Jewish Theological Seminary and the National Ramah Commission,), pp. 184–195. 1989.pb.

## CHAPTER 5

1. The typology of concentric circles is fully developed in Daniel J. Elazar, *Community and Polity: The Organizational Dynamics of American Jewry*, revised and updated ed. (Philadelphia: Jewish Publication Society, 1995). See especially ch. 3, "The Community in Its Environment," pp. 90–115.

2. The 1990 NJPS indicated that some 250,000 former Jews have converted to another religion, usually a mainline Christian denomination.

3. Unfortunately, there are no systematic overall analyses of the 1970 study, though a number of books have been written based on the Community Studies of the 1980s. The data from the 1970 study appeared in a series of pamphlets entitled "Facts for Planning," issued in the mid-1970s by the Council of Jewish Federations. See Sidney Goldstein's article "Jews in the United States: Perspectives from Demography," *American Jewish Year Book 81* (New York and Philadelphia: American Jewish Committee and Jewish Publication Society, 1981), pp. 3–60.

4. Sidney Goldstein, "Profile of American Jewry: Insights from the 1990 National Jewish Population Survey," *American Jewish Year Book 1992* (New York and Philadelphia: American Jewish Committee and Jewish Publication Society, 1992), pp. 77–177; *Summary Report—Jewish Population Study of Greater Philadelphia 1996/97* (Ukeles Associates, Inc., 1998), p. 36; Sherry R. Israel, *Combined Jewish Philanthropies—Comprehensive Report on the 1995 Democraphic Study* (Boston: Combined Jewish Philanthropies, 1997), p. 46.

5. Sidney Goldstein, "Profile of American Jewry," *American Jewish Year Book*, Vol. 92 (1992), p. 131, and Appendix, Tables 19 and 21.

6. Jack Wertheimer, *A People Divided: Judaism in Contemporary America* (New York: Basic Books, 1993), especially ch. 6, "Orthodoxy—Triumphalism on the Right," pp. 114–136; M. Herbert Danzger, *Returning to Tradition: The Contemporary Revival of Orthodox Judaism* (New Haven, Conn.: Yale University Press, 1989). On women returnees to Judaism, see Lynn Davidman, *Tradition in*

*a Rootless World: Women in Orthodox Judaism* (Berkeley: University of California Press, 1991) and Debra Renee Kaufman, *Rachel's Daughters: Newly Orthodox Jewish Women* (New Brunswick, N.J.: Rutgers University Press, 1991). The latter two are particularly interesting, because a move into the Orthodox world is seen by outsiders as more restrictive and a move toward lower status for contemporary Jewish women than it is for Jewish men. Therefore, an analysis of the "pull" of Orthodoxy for women is seen as a particularly stringent test of its resurgence.

7. For studies of trends in the American Jewish family and of intermarriage today, see Steven Bayme and Gladys Rosen, eds., *The Jewish Family: Conflict and Continuity* (New York and Hoboken, N.J.: American Jewish Committee and Ktav, 1994); Gerald B. Bubis, *Saving the Jewish Family: Myths and Realities in the Diaspora, Strategies for the Future* (Lanham, Md.: Jerusalem Center for Public Affairs and University Press of America, 1987) (includes an extensive annotated bibliography); Natalie Friedman, *The Divorced Parent and the Jewish Community* (New York: The American Jewish Committee, 1985); Egon Mayer, *Love and Tradition: Marriage between Jews and Christians* (New York: Plenum, 1985); Egon Mayer, *Children of Intermarriage: A Study in Patterns of Identification and Family Life* (New York: American Jewish Committee, 1983); Egon Mayer and Amy Avgar, *Conversion among the Intermarried: Choosing to Become Jewish* (New York: American Jewish Committee, 1983); Peter Y. Medding, Gary A. Tobin, Sylvia Barack Fishman, and Mordechai Rimor, *Jewish Identity in Conversionary and Mixed Marriages*, Jewish Sociology Papers, published by the American Jewish Committee 1993, originally published in the *American Jewish Year Book, 1992*; Rela Geffen Monson, *Jewish Women on the Way Up—The Challenge of Family, Career and Community* (New York: American Jewish Committee, 1987); Susan Weidman Schneider, *Intermarriage—The Challenge of Living with Differences between Christians and Jews* (New York: Free Press, 1989); *Re-examining Intermarriage*: Trends, Textures & Strategies, Bruce A. Phillips. (The Wilstein Institute of Jewish Policy Studies and the American Jewish Committee Boston and New York, 1997); Rela Mintz Geffen and Egon Mayer, *The Ripple Effect: Interfaith Families Speak Out* (B'nai Brith Center for Jewish Identity and the Jewish Outreach Institute: Washington, D.C. 1997)

8. For an extensive discussion of the critical impact of migration for Jewish identity, see Sidney Goldstein and Alice Goldstein, *Jews on the Move—Implications for Jewish Identity* (Albany: State University of New York Press, 1996). See especially their discussion of denominational identification and Jewish identity in the context of migration on pp. 176–184.

9. Deborah Dash Moore, *To the Golden Cities: Pursuing the American Jewish Dream in Miami and L.A.* (New York: Free Press, 1994).

10. Ira M. Sheskin, ed., *Florida Jewish Demography*, Vols. 1–9 (1988–1996).

CHAPTER 6

1. There are many articles on the past, present, and future roles, training and goals, and relationships with congregants of and by Conservative rabbis in Nina Beth Cardin and David Wolf Silverman, eds., *The Seminary at 100* (New York: Jewish Theological Seminary and Rabbinical Assembly, 1987) by Elliot N. Dorff, Arthur Green, Aryeh Davidson and Jack Wertheimer, Bradley Shavit Artson, Debra Reed Blank, Samuel Weintraub, Barry W. Holtz, Gilbert S. Rosenthal, Jules Porter, and Alan Silverstein.

2. Daniel J. Elazar and Rela Geffen Monson, "The Evolving Roles of American Congregational Rabbis," *Modern Judaism*, Vol. 2, No. 1 (February 1982): 72–89; Charles Liebman, "The Training of American Rabbis," *American Jewish Year Book, 1968* (New York and Philadelphia: American Jewish Committee and Jewish Publication Society, 1970), pp. 3–112; Jacob Rader Marcus and Abraham Peck, with Jeffrey S. Gurock et al., *The American Rabbinate: A Century of Continuity and Change 1883–1983* (Hoboken, N.J.: Ktav, 1985).

CHAPTER 7

1. Figures taken from Sergio DellaPergola, "World Jewish Population, 1996," *American Jewish Year Book 1998* (New York: American Jewish Committee, 1998), Vol. 98, pp. 477–512.

Accurate population figures for the Jewish people are difficult, if not impossible, to ascertain. In several of the largest Jewish communities, there is no official census that counts all Jews, so sampling studies of varying degrees of accuracy have been undertaken and provide our sole sources of data. Beyond that, the definition of who is Jewish, both for censuses and studies, is normally a subjective one, which leads to further distortion.

For example, in the United States, where Jews have fought against any religious designations in federal or state censuses, students of Jewish demography have had to rely on various, albeit improving, methods. Moreover, the definition of who is a Jew in the United States is becoming increasingly fuzzy and ever more subjective. There is a contradiction between the national population studies, including the 1990 study, the best to date, and studies of individual Jewish communities that have almost invariably come out with larger totals than those projected on the basis of the national study.

Furthermore, in the former Soviet Union, the last Soviet census listed approximately 1.5 million Jews. Yet after the emigration of close to 1 million Jews, there are still reasonable claims made that 1.5 million Jews continue to live in the Commonwealth of Independent States. The problem is further complicated there because of the lack of an operative *halakhic* definition for the past two generations. Indeed, the definition that has been set forth for Russian Jewry is a three-part one: (1) those identified as Jews in their internal passports;

(2) those who everyone knows is Jewish but who have succeeded in having their passports marked with another nationality; and (3) those "who identify with the fate of the Jewish people" (definition supplied by Mikhael Chlenov, original head of the Soviet Jewish Va'ad).

Finally, as ease of aliya to Israel has become known throughout the Third World and as a small number of Israelis have tried to pursue those claiming to be Jews wherever they are, not-insubstantial pockets of "Jews" have emerged that were not known to be Jews before and are of doubtful Jewish origin by tradition-al standards of any kind. For example, 30,000 Jews have emigrated to Israel from Ethiopia. They were considered to include the entire Ethiopian Jewish popula-tion when they came. Now, however, perhaps another 30,000 have emerged to claim that they are Jewish or of Jewish ancestry (the Falash Mura) and demand to be transported to Israel. We can understand why they prefer the conditions in Israel to those in their native land, but that does not make them Jews.

Professional demographers, in the spirit of scientific caution, rely on the most accurate figures they can obtain and, it seems, they generally underesti-mate the total Jewish population if the subjective claims of individuals to be Jewish are included. Thus the perhaps 13 million Jews counted by the current demographic studies are, in Professor Elazar's estimation, at least 1 million less than the actual number of claimed Jews in the world.

2. Sidney Goldstein, "Profile of American Jewry: Insights from the 1990 National Jewish Population Survey," *American Jewish Year Book 1992* (New York and Philadelphia: American Jewish Committee and Jewish Publication Soci-ety), pp. 172–173.

3. Schmeltz and DellaPergola, *op. cit.*, pp. 469, 471.

4. Rabbi Narrowe retired in 1998.

5. Shlomit Levy, Hanna Levinsohn, and Elihu Katz, *Beliefs, Observances and Social Interaction among Israeli Jews* (Jerusalem: Louis Guttman Institute of Applied Social Research, 1993).

## Chapter 8

1. One example of a rabbi's efforts to increase levels of *Shabbat* observance of members in the Midwestern United States has recently been studied by Mor-ton Weinfeld of McGill University. Thus far it has been circulated as an unpub-lished article entitled "Enhancing Shabbat Observance: Judaic Inreach in a Sub-urban Congregation," 1996.

2. Elliot Dorff, *The Roots and Growth of Jewish Law* (Albany: State Universi-ty of New York Press, 1988); Robert Gordis, *Conservative Judaism* (New York: Behrman House, for the National Academy of Adult Jewish Theological Semi-nary of America, 1945); Robert Gordis, *Understanding Conservative Judaism*

(New York: Rabbinical Assembly, 1978); Abraham Joshua Heschel, *The Sabbath* (New York: Farrar, Straus, Giroux, 1951); Isaac Klein, *A Guide to Jewish Religious Practice* (New York: Jewish Theological Seminary of America, 1979); David Wolpe, *Our Useless Fears* (Boston: Houghton Mifflin, 1981).

3. Rela Geffen Monson, "Synagogue Life and Family Life," renamed "The 'User-Friendly' Synagogue: Generating Primary Group Relationships in an Era of Impersonality," *Conservative Judaism*. Volume 38 #2, Winter 1985–86. pp 44–51.

## CHAPTER 9

1. The designation "Traditional Egalitarian," sometimes shortened to "Trad-egal," seems to have caught on in popular and more formal settings. For instance, the revised By-Laws of Temple Emanu-El in Providence, R.I., a congregation of 1,000 households, which celebrated its fiftieth birthday in 1994, begin with a Mission Statement/Preamble that states, "We are a traditional, egalitarian Conservative synagogue. . . ." Emphasis on the term *Masorti*, which is the official name of the Movement outside of North America, should also be mainstreamed here. This would provide a clear traditional image and linkage with the Movement worldwide.

2. The edited works cited in Note 15 in Ch. 1 by Waxman, Siegel & Gertel, as well as the monographs listed in Note 3 in Ch. 3 by Dorff, Golinkin, and Dorff and Rosett, constitute a good beginning to this effort. The search for spirituality/self-help books, pioneered by Harold Kushner and more recently written by David Wolpe and Daniel Gordis, also meets part of this need. However, the latter are addressed to the broad Jewish community rather than to Conservative Jews, though their authors are clearly identified with the Movement.

3. This model has been followed in the cases of patrilineal descent and the deliberations on the admission of openly practicing homosexuals to rabbinical school and/or being placed in United Synagogue congregations by the Rabbinical Assembly Placement Service. In fact, since the mid-1990s, some deliberations of the Committee on Law and Standards have been held on the stage in the Feinberg Auditorium at the Seminary and have been open to students, faculty, or guests as observers. There are still some closed meetings, however, this format has made the Committee's deliberations much more accessible. Similarly the *Luah* (synagogue calendar) published annually by the USCJ and presenting the *Order of Prayers, Blessings and Torah Readings for Synagogue and Home Table* by Kenneth S. Goldrich is a positive model of a joint project of the United Synagogue of Conservative Judaism and the Rabbinical Assembly.

4. Some are even more restrictive, defining as a Conservative Jew only dues-paying members of a synagogue formally affiliated (that is, dues paying) with the United Synagogue of Conservative Judaism.

5. This is not to imply that Sephardim do not join Conservative congregations, as they are in Israel and the diaspora. Some do, in some cases, particularly in the diaspora, because they want to be religiously affiliated with a Judaism that is comfortable to their personal beliefs and practices, and Conservative congregations offer them the only possibilities, especially now that more and more Ashkenazi Orthodox congregations have reverted to an emphasis on Eastern European styles of prayer and Reform congregations offer nothing more Sephardic and offer even less Jewish tradition. In Israel, there is frequently an element of social climbing involved for those Sephardim who join Conservative congregations, seeing that as a way in which they can assimilate among Ashkenazim more effectively. There also are a few Sephardic congregations in the New York metropolitan area that have affiliated with the United Synagogue, but these exceptions should not lull the Movement's leaders into thinking that Conservative Judaism is now engaged in serious outreach to Sephardic Jews.

## Chapter 10

1. Sensitivity to this point was demonstrated in a complete evaluation and overhaul of the Rabbinical School curriculum in the early 1990s. Each student now participates in an ongoing small group, focusing on spiritual development, which meets regularly and continues throughout his or her years of study.

# Index